It's Only
Rock 'n' Roll

It's Only Rock 'n' Roll

My On-the-Road Adventures with the Rolling Stones

Chet Flippo

St. Martin's Press / New York

Library of Congress Catalog Card Number: 89-62598

ISBN 0-312-03851-8

First published in the United States as a Dolphin Book by Doubleday & Company, Inc., under the title *On the Road with the Rolling Stones: 20 Years of Lipstick, Handcuffs, and Chemicals.*

Cast of Major Characters:

Michael Philip (ˌmaɪkəl "Mick") Jagger, born July 26, 1943, in Dartford, Kent, England. Lead singer for the Rolling Stones. Best-known rock figure in the world and perhaps most enigmatic. As a conservative, social-climbing, money-conscious, leering rock idol, he is the perfect counterpoint to fellow Glimmer Twin Keith Richards and his sincere love for the music. "Mick's true personality comes out only onstage," former Stones tour manager Peter Rudge told me. My favorite exchange with Mick was back in 1980 when we were talking about a mutual friend who had almost died the day before when a famous person gave her heroin and told her it was cocaine. "What would you do, Chet, if I offered you heroin and told you it was coke?" Mick asked me seriously. "I would kill you, Mick, I promise—if I were still alive." He laughed grimly. "So would I. So would I."

Keith Richards (Keith Richard was his stage name early on), born December 18, 1943, Dartford, Kent, England. Lead guitarist and, as fellow Glimmer Twin with Mick, co-composer of most Stones songs. His menacing guitar chords, evoking a chilling image of urban apocalypse far beyond A Clockwork Orange, are a major reason why the Rolling Stones are what they are. There is no man on earth who knows more about or cares more about rock and roll. His disregard for society's conventions has given him a lengthy international arrest record and a deserved reputation as rock and roll's iron man. Years ago, before he cleaned up and got married, Keith and I were once drinking Rebel Yell sour mash whiskey late into the night in the Rockefeller Center office of Rolling Stones Records president Earl McGrath. Keith picked the office clean of anything he wanted ("This is my fucking record company") and offered me a large pile of glittering white powder on the tip of his hunting knife. I demurred. "Listen, Keith, man, remember, I'm not you. I can't do all that." It was the correct response. Keith was delighted. "Of course you're not me," he roared. "Nobody is!"

Charlie Watts, born Charles Robert Watts, June 2, 1941, Islington, England. The best drummer rock and roll has ever known and the one who still complains that jazz is all he ever cared about. When Boston Mayor Kevin White tried, via unsubtle press conferences, to force the Stones to play a free concert in Boston in 1981, Watts dismissed him by saying, "That's just political blackmail." There was no such concert.

Bill Wyman, born October 24, 1936, Lewisham, England (as Bill Perks). Stones stoic bass player and historian. Down-to-earth. I once asked him: "What happens if you believe your press?" "The people who believe that really get fucked up," he said emphatically. "As for being the greatest rock and roll band in the world, it's nice to be told it, you know. But if you take it seriously, you really have problems." I asked him about the whole sixties angry rock feeling of "hope I die before I get old." He laughed wryly. "It wasn't to me. It was, 'I hope I get a nice house together and a nice car before rock and roll dies.' That was my concept. Not to be incredibly rich, but just to make things a little more comfortable for my little family and then go do something else. And here we are."

Ron Wood, born June 1, 1947, London. The other Stones guitarist after Brian Jones died and Mick Taylor quit. Woody was born to be a Rolling Stone. Here's a random quote from an interview I did with him in 1980: "One person I'm getting into now is Jerry Lee Lewis. He's a fantastic guy. I wouldn't even mind getting into a fight with him."

Peter Rudge, impossibly dapper—and hopelessly volatile—Cambridge graduate, rock whiz kid manager of the Who and tour manager of the Stones. He ran a ship so tight that it seemed on the verge of exploding at any minute. The man could argue till the cows came home (and after they did, he'd start his lobster shift). The sky was his ceiling until a certain *hubris* (and the Stones' tradition of punishing those who aspire to be Stones) removed him from the arena. His sin? Speaking for the Stones. No one speaks for the Stones. Still a great guy. The strongest of the many casualties the Rolling Stones have cast aside over the past two decades.

Paul Wasserman. One of the last of the great Hollywood press agents with a genuine, elegant, show-business style. When did you last encounter a press agent who could tell his client Mick Jagger to get fucked and then go off to lunch with a malcontent of a writer such as yours truly? And still pay for lunch and charge it to Jagger? Why did Uncle Wasso get involved with a rock and roll band he never even bothered to listen to? They needed him (he is the top of the line and they wanted only the top of the line). And he was bored with clients who never got into trouble. Everyone needs a challenge now and then. Wasso also relished—secretly—the absolute craziness of a Stones tour.

Bill Carter. Native of Little Rock, Arkansas, Secret Service Agent under Presidents Kennedy and Johnson. Knew nothing about rock and roll, but knew instinctively how to take care of the Stones in certain areas. He found that he rather enjoyed the frenzy—and the perks—of big-time rock and roll. Now a big-time show-biz lawyer himself, Carter performs such chores as flying into Mexico to retrieve the body of the late Steve McQueen when said retrieval became a bit of a sticky international situation.

Contents

It's Only
Rock 'n' Roll

Introduction

This is why you should read this book about the Rolling Stones. First of all, this book contains no gratuitous references to sex, drugs, scandals or any sort, or other naughty bits commonly associated with rock and roll's most notorious band. No references to that sort of titillating fluff—unless it's essential to the plot. And this has quite a twisted plot. A lot of unexpected turns along the way.

Secondly, you should read this book about the Stones because they are the most important group to come out of rock and roll's first thirty years and because the reasons for that have never really been explained. You can read a lot of sizzling gossip about the Stones and much of it may very well be true, but it doesn't come close to defining why the Stones have occupied their curious spot atop the rock and roll hierarchy for two decades, despite their own best efforts to self-destruct.

Thirdly, what about the Beatles? you may well ask. And well you may. What about those four cuddly little Liverpudlians? Well, what about them? The Mop Tops hit a different note and aroused decidedly different emotions in the rock audience and the public-at-large. The Beatles also officially broke up in 1970. The Stones are still peddling their wares as the oldest living rock and roll relics out there on the hustings. They remain an ongoing adventure. One never knows what will happen when they open a door, as it were. My fascination with them comes from their impact: What happens when their presence hits real people and the real world? What results when two worlds collide?

The Beatles' influence was largely musical (even Leonard Bernstein applauded their sunny love songs as works of genius) and cosmetic (from where else did America get long hair for men?). The Stones' impact was far darker, visceral, more far-reaching and troubling.

And their touring was the real reason for that. Rock and roll tours were enormously influential in spreading new values and ideas to young people who might not otherwise reach out beyond their local vision. MTV now replaces touring. It hurls messages into living rooms that were long immune to rock and roll's message. But in the beginning, rock tours were a pioneering form, a new communications medium, a journey to a new-found land. Especially in the hinterlands, the South and Midwest, where rock stars were an exotic commodity and where rock music still had to be packaged sometimes in a plain brown wrapper. Worldly rock stars landing in the middle of Nothing Happening, U.S.A., had an enormous attraction for Nothing Happening's young people. The Old World tradition of the traveling troubadour took on a new meaning in the United States with the rock revolution. Generational conflicts divided families and communities. Traditionalists viewed invading rock and rollers as worthless carpetbaggers intent on exploitation and corruption. Young people welcomed diversion and new ideas and glamour and excitement and s-e-x and perhaps d-r-u-g-s. Violent ideological clashes were inevitable. Rock and roll tours probably did more to polarize this country in the sixties than anyone has realized. Tours were the Johnny Appleseed of the counterculture: Every town and city and hamlet, every nook and cranny eventually became accessible to the progressive movement that was flying under the banner and the appeal of rock and roll.

You must remember that the Beatles toured the United States only twice—and not extensively, at that. Their influence came from the media and from a carefully prepared media image. Clean, decent—albeit just cheeky enough and long-haired enough to stir up a fuss—balladeers that even your red-necked parents might eventually approve of. Totally unlike the Stones' perceived message—a real, physical, un-American invasion of Your Town, U.S.A., by a hairy, snarling mob of antisocial rebels who seemed to be intent on only one thing: corrupting your young people. A too real science fiction *Invasion of the Body Snatchers* come to life. That was the very real perception many alarmed citizens had of Stones tours. And those tours did affect young lives in ways that TV and phonograph records and radio cannot. And adult opposition to the mere presence of the Stones in Your Town united young people in an "us versus them" solidarity in ways that the Beatles' media saturation could never do. Even preparation for a rock show became for young fans an elaborate ritual involving ticket purchase, deciding what to wear and who to go with, and what drugs and alcohol to prep with and which to take to the show, and what to do afterward. The rock show became a new pillar around which teenage life existed. To say that these activities were new tribal rites is to restate the obvious. But this was a new social force.

The Rolling Stones' history has been told, ably, more than once, with lovingly recounted details of drugs and sex and sex and drugs and other assorted and entertaining tidbits of decadence. What I think has always been overlooked is the extraordinary impact that their touring persona has had. The Rolling Stones On the Road are a genuine other entity that takes on a striking reality of its own. Strangely, the popular perception of the Stones remains a sort of late-sixties marquee of marauding pirates and huns and vandals and dopers. And worse. Otherwise sane and reasonable people—authors, journalists, mayors, celebrities, television personalities— still seem to strain against and even burst the boundaries of good sense when confronted with the phenomenon of the Rolling Stones.

But the role of the Stones in the seventies and eighties has not been thoroughly examined. The Sixties Stones—they're still the ones written about and discussed and celebrated or cursed. Sure, the Sixties Stones were rebels, scruffs, bad boys pissing on garage walls and being arrested every other day. "Would you let your daughter marry one?" But that passed quickly and was not an image that was accurate. The Stones' image was created by their handlers out of whole cloth in the sixties and then staunchly maintained by their enemies, their supporters, and the press long after the Stones themselves became solid middle-to-upper-class burghers whose values mirrored those of any upwardly mobile nouveau riche stockbroker in Dallas who coveted comfort and flashy cars and nice threads and expensive women and quality drugs and posh restaurants and all of that package. It's no surprise that first-generation money always appreciates worldly pleasures and ostentatious displays of wealth.

What Mick and Keith most wanted, after they realized that they didn't really want to become middle-aged poverty-stricken sharecropping Negroes singing the blues in dirt-poor Mississippi was to become rich and comfortable Southern gentry. The Stones effectively became a United States rock and roll band in the Southern tradition. They were desperate to be American (Charlie Watts is fixated on the Civil War, Keith Richards will drink nothing but sour mash whiskey from the South, Mick Jagger developed a ridiculous Southern accent and then fell head over heels for a lovely Texas-bred honey). They wanted to be American, just like the earthy singers who were their heroes: Elvis and Buddy Holly and Jimmy Reed and Muddy Waters. They wanted, really, to be good ole boys. Earthy and raw. Guns and knives and smooth-drinking whiskey and the best-looking women on the hoof. Fast cars. And good dope, which the New South accepted and began to welcome and even overdid as it overdid everything in its enthusiasm to embrace new and fashionable things. If you had predicted twenty years ago that Southerners—rich and fashionable Southerners, at that—would rush out to embrace (foreign: German) Mercedes cars and (foreign: Colombian) expensive cocaine and (foreign: British) Rolling Stones music, you would have been called a foreign faggot or worse. No more. I know Dallas bankers and brokers who are "growing up with the Stones" and whose growing-up pains include elaborate pre-

Stones dope-and-alcohol parties and then the actual Stones concert and then the post-Stones-concert party. Have you ever seen a rich, 225-pound redneck ex-fullback high on the finest cocaine chugging Jose Cuervo Gold as he yells: "Stones rule!"? Some kind of cultural mix, that is. Rednecks came to finally fuel the Stones' myth of invincibility, of arrogant invincibility that should have been shattered by their initial fey image. Look at the movie *Gimme Shelter* of the 1969 Stones concert at Altamont Speedway and you are struck by the incredibly intense gazes that some Hell's Angels (who were, for no good reason, retained to be security for the show) train upon Jagger and the other Stones: We could take these Limey wimpos, say the Angels' expressions. That was effectively the end of whatever innocence rock and roll might have ever had. The Angels killed and maimed in the crowd; the Stones were helpless in the face of it. The Stones have never fought. They have hired fighters because they can't fight. They are, in effect, helpless prisoners of their myth. They are hopelessly comfortable middle-class and upwardly striving, even in their excesses. Even Keith Richards's sordid heroin addiction managed to evince a bit of sympathy. He just, as a Texas fan put it, "excessed a little". He had, it seemed, flirted with a dangerous extreme. A fashionable extreme. Formerly, it had been cocaine that had extended his Jack Daniel's-induced euphoria. He said that he felt obliged to try everything. This was one thing he might have omitted. Even when he was a heroin addict, though, he kept up the remarkable Rolling Stones Solid Front and the romantic image. The image of the decadent wastrel and James Deanish rebel-at-large. The Che Guevara jungle fighter guerrilla. The "Lock the doors, here come the huns" idea. All in the eye of the perceiver. Not necessarily hooked into the reality of the thing. Even though their largely unremarkable private lives managed to become grossly enlarged by the artificial fascination of gossip journalism. And even after Altamont and its terrible harvest of blood for the new rock generation, the Stones' luster lingered. Even though Altamont should have permanently defused the Stones as cocks of the walk. Emperor's clothes being transparent and all that. When the Hell's Angels proved that rock and roll's baddest bad boys (i.e., the Stones) were nothing but wimps in the face of real danger . . . well, so much for their implied menace and their assumed authority. What is strange is that the Stones' aura stuck to them through the massive upheaval from sixties to seventies, from flower power to street fighting and a real or imagined rock-based counterculture with a fragile dream of a hippie utopia that was knifed in the back at Altamont and clubbed into the concrete at the Democratic National Convention in Chicago. Oddly, the Stones flourished through all this. They physically grew up. But their image never did. Rock and roll's audience needed a set of sneering blackguards to foster the continuing illusion that rock and roll, born out of genuine teenaged rebellion in the fifties, still was a music of youthful hellfire. Even though it was manipulated by cigar-chewing executives in New York and Los Angeles, far removed from any garage bands in the Midwest or anywhere else. Even though it had become a multimillion-dollar business. And such businesses do not regularly tolerate genuine rebels. The Stones became part of corporate America very easily. They did not even have to be seduced. Street fighting men? More like playlike Che Guevaras wearing silly makeup and Halloween clothes and charging good money at the box office for this "revolution."

To their credit, they never said they were anything but musicians. A lot of addle-pated, air-brained "alternative journalists" carried the flag for rock musicians as forces of real social change and piled that onto the Stones' baggage. The Stones' image became graven in stone. The rock and roll public and, even more importantly, the world-at-large had a frozen picture of the Rolling Stones as sneering *Clockwork Orange*-ish leather-clad punks kicking over baby carriages and generally slouching about and ruining the neighborhood. For some people, that evoked the specter of General Sherman marching through Georgia and torching Atlanta. Or, more grimly and realistically, the scary vision of a demon-eyed Charles Manson and his filthy, hairy, mindless hordes picking up guns, knives, and clubs to murder responsible citizens and rape and drug dose their innocent children. And mainly of overturning the established social order. Rocking the boat. And probably corrupting the young people by encouraging them to grow their hair long, listen to loud and subversive rock music, sass their elders (and therefore their betters), smoke marijuana, oppose the Vietnam War (and *ipso facto* all Established Authority), maybe have weird sex, wear tight blue jeans, and otherwise strive as teenagers always do to not be carbon copies of their parents.

"Blame it on the Stones," Kris Kristofferson used to sing. Kristoffer-son, a Rhodes scholar and Vietnam helicopter pilot turned Nashville song-writer, wrote that song about the Stones and meant it. Anything wrong? "Blame it on the Stones," Kris said and he was dead on. Hell yes, blame it on the Stones. Got to have a scapegoat when things turn sour with the family and the job and the economy out there in West Widget. When little Johnny is flunking everything and his bedroom smells like a Jamaican marijuana plantation. When little Susie is running around with obvious hoodlums and is clearly headed for total ruin and then Mommy discovers Susie's birth control pills. Who caused all this societal upheaval and mess and tumult and headache and unnecessary fuss? Certainly not society as we know it. Alien forces must have been at work. "Blame it on the Stones," Kris sang. The Stones, of course, loved it. It was the sort of publicity money cannot buy. That the Stones were increasingly the results of, rather than the causes of, certain social changes never occurred to many observers. The battle was on. And the distinction between Stones (real) and Stones (image) was forever blurred. To everyone's gratification. The Stones finally had an important role and function: to be the *Stones*, huns and atheistic devil-worshiping, daughter-raping, pill-popping, coke-snorting, dope-smoking, kitten-hating, lawless, unwashed, rude, crude, and socially unacceptable, worthless, left-wing Limey trash. And maybe faggots, to boot.

NO SHOES, NO SHIRT, NO SERVICE was a sign that popped up on café and restaurant doors across the South and Southwest and Midwest and West and East and Southeast and Northeast and Northwest and other places as a public rebuttal of that whole rock and roll image. Never mind that Mick Jagger wore costly hand-stitched Capezios (shoes, that is) that cost more than some of the pickup trucks in Texas that boasted bumper stickers telling him to love or leave America. And never mind that Keith Richards was sporting genuine snakeskin boots that most Jaycees in the South daydreamed they could wear and get away with wearing, which they couldn't. So, as much as the Stones relished their defined role, so too did their spirited opposition. Grateful indeed was the opposition to have such an easy target: scruffy, filthy, godless, foreign, anarchistic, short, snotty Brit twits who, furthermore, enjoyed being attacked. Bad influences they were, these foul-mouthed Limey knockabouts with their tight pants and their suggestive songs. Nothing at all positive in their message, no sir! Just naysaying and tearing down and criticizing and sneering and defying rightful authority and celebrating rebellion and perhaps drug use and certainly sloth and indolence and disrespect and not wanting to get up early in the morning any more. All in all, totally un-American.

What a windfall these strange Stones were for their critics and opponents. Right-wing preachers and politicians and other zealots welcomed them as long-lost enemies. If the Stones did not exist, their enemies would have had to have invented them; such a perfect target are they. There is a rumor that has been repeated so many times in government circles that it cannot be totally discounted to the effect that the CIA and the FBI both actually helped the Rolling Stones during difficult times in their career, with governmental pressure applied here and there and abroad as well. It stands to reason that such a rumor exists. The Stones are a political presence and they like nothing more than dueling with the enemy, especially when the enemy might not exist were it not for the Stones' existence. What we have here is a perfect symbiosis: each side needing and increasingly appreciating the other side. Rolling Stones as Huns/Dark Forces being battled by the crusaders and defenders of law and order and curfews and decency. So who wins? Both sides do, of course. It's a healthy exercise in democracy.

Stones tours may not quite be what the Founding Fathers had in mind when freedom of expression was extended to one and all, but they're certainly vigorous tests of the limits of American tolerance. After the first couple of times that I boarded the Stones juggernaut, almost everyone I knew put the same sort of breathless and perverse and insistent question to me: What is it *really* like out there? What is life really like in that rarefied atmosphere where the Stones travel? I sort of got the impression after a while that everyone thought I was secretly taking part in some fabulously decadent rituals where pleasures unknown to mortal man were being revealed to me. Everyone was so eager to believe in the myths that I found it hard to let them down. I found that a "no comment" and a wink made people much happier than being told the truth. They wouldn't have believed the truth anyway. Stanley Booth grappled with this weighty issue in his Stones book *Dance with the Devil* and I like his conclusion: "I didn't know it yet, and it would have seemed insane, knowing as I did what I had been doing, but it was possible to suspect a man on the road with the Rolling Stones of having a real good time. And not without justice."

I may add that, after all my careful research, I have yet to find a single instance of any person being forced at gunpoint to go on a Rolling Stones tour. Being on the road with the Stones is an existence quite unlike any other. If you take a bit of a traveling circus and a dark hint of a carnival geek sideshow and some of the blatant hype and horn blowing of a political campaign and a whiff of the musky lures of the flesh peddlers and some of the mindless frenzy of a bikers' run and the giddy hysteria of young and rich and coked-up socialites determined to be hip at any cost and the pied piper effect on a tattered teenaged Stones army too young and perhaps too cough-syruped out to perceive of the Stones as anything but middle-aged roués and then you throw in some local pols who are strictly from the blow-dry generation and are eager-beaver to glad-hand it with Mick and then you stir in some tough cops from the old school who wouldn't mind putting the bracelets on these mincing foreign fairy rock stars—and you put all that together over a couple of decades and, brother, you have got yourself one hell of a rock show. Over those years, the Stones, in effect, became a sort of traveling government-in-exile with an international constituency, a loyal following that kept the treasury full and unquestioningly supported the regime. Generations of these supporters have kept the regime afloat: ever since the first real Rolling Stones show on July 12, 1962, at London's Marquee Club. Up to the night of the long knives Hell's Angels dance at the Altamont Speedway in Livermore, California, on December 6, 1969. Up to the Stones of the eighties, who last played at Leeds in England in July 1982 and who may never quit. They've run through seven American Presidents (Kennedy, Johnson, Nixon, Ford, Carter, Reagan, and Bush) and through Vietnam and Watergate and Charlie Manson and Patty Hearst and Son of Sam and Moonwalks and Michael Jackson and Iran and worse and they still are their own best news. If they're not getting busted, then they're a staple of the gossip page: romancing or dating or divorcing or just still being a presence. Sometimes people forget that the Stones' footnote in history is for music. Such is their effect on social chroniclers that the Stones' mere presence anywhere can make news.

A comprehensive Stones' history has not been written and may never be, as myths grow and facts slip away. Non-Stones write about them but—make no mistake about it—through a glass darkly. Now and then there's an epiphany, but it's mosquito-sized. The Stones will guard their secrets. Mick Jagger is overdue with his version of what happened—Keith is waiting to read Mick's stone tablets before starting his book. Bill Wyman has kept thorough scrapbooks since day one and has the best documentation of the group and he's thinking about doing his book.

What follows here is a highly personal look at the phenomenon of the Rolling Stones. And what it's like for nonroyalty to be in that exalted presence. After all, what can a poor boy do except write about a rock and roll band?

1 Getting Ready Again

In early 1973, the State Department of the United States of America made a ruling, in tandem with the United States Immigration and Naturalization Service, to never again issue entry visas to the members of the Rolling Stones. The Rolling Stones were banned forever from the U.S. of A. That has never been made public and certainly was not being bandied about during those roilsome days of 1972 when the Nixon White House —beset by real and imagined enemies from every side—was also working very energetically to get ex-Beatle John Lennon deported from the States (and trying to keep that a secret as well).

Why were these particular rock and rollers so high up on Nixon's Enemies List? We now know that Lennon was targeted because Nixon had an urgent, night-sweat fear and certainty that Lennon might try to disrupt the 1972 Republican National Convention (and thus spoil King Richard's coronation). But why were the Stones singled out for exclusion from the world's greatest democratic society? The ban started in late February 1973 when Stones lead singer Mick Jagger was flying back to London from Australia and was denied permission to touch down on United States soil. His last previous contact with the contiguous forty-eight states had been on January 18, when the Stones had performed a benefit concert in Los Angeles for victims of the earthquake in Nicaragua. After Mick was flagged away from U.S. airports, the Stones were informed that their filed plans for another tour of the United States were unthinkable. The band members themselves never really knew why they seemed to have such persistent problems every time they landed in the U.S. of A. and didn't know why they were banned. As a result of the ban, they feared that their careers were over. This is why they were banned: The State Department and the INS decided—whether there was influence from higher up will likely never be determined—that the Rolling Stones were unacceptable American visitors for three reasons. The first was the band's history of arrests for drug violations. Which was, certainly, a lengthy one. No one ever accused the Rolling Stones of posing as the Osmonds. The second reason was that the Stones had apparently fomented considerable civil disorder in the lower forty-eight states during their 1972 "S.T.P." (for "Stones Touring Party") tour. There was some trouble on that tour— a couple of bombings, some fighting in the streets—but certainly there were no tour-related deaths; unlike 1969's bloody Altamont Speedway concert, during which Hell's Angels (hired as security guards by the Stones, in a transaction deemed dubious at best, for $500 worth of beer) brutally killed one young man and stomped many other suddenly disillusioned members of what was then considered to be the "Woodstock Nation." The high point of 1972's oddly skewed tour, for Stones watchers, must have been the famous airport punch-out and bust and subsequent forgiveness. (Basically, the Stones were enroute to a Boston show; were diverted to Warwick, Rhode Island, due to fog; punched a newspaper photographer at the airport there and got arrested and jailed; were delivered from chains and bondage by Boston Mayor Kevin White because his city was about to go up in flames from other urban unrest and he desperately needed the Stones to appear onstage in Boston and thereby cool down a certain part of his constituency that night.)

The third reason for the ban of the Rolling Stones was disrespect. The United States Government had observed and taken note of the fact that one Mick Jagger, lead singer for the above-mentioned rock group known as the Rolling Stones, had worn—onstage, in public—an Uncle Sam suit. Spit on the flag if you will, but none of these horsefeathers with Uncle Sam. Huh? Yes! The White House had been greatly offended that a mincing Limey troublemaker had donned the red, white, and blue (Great Britain may have had those colors first, but this still spelled desecration). So out with him. This was obviously a disruptive element. J. Edgar Hoover had warned Nixon against such wild cards. What can possibly be so evil and subversive about pint-sized Brit rock and rollers that a real government will mount a full-scaled offensive to deal with them? Why was Richard Nixon afraid of rock and roll?

Because he was smart, that's why. He knew full well that the values behind the culture that nurtured rock and roll subverted everything that he stood for. He was smart to be afraid of rock and roll because it is a fearsome force that has yet to flex its real muscles. But Nixon was stupid in trying to outlaw rock and roll. Or deport it, as he attempted with John Lennon. Or stop it at the gates, as he tried with the Stones. Poor Nixon. Back when he was bullying ordinary lawmakers and regular citizens, he had no idea that there were aborning political and musical tidal waves that would knock him and his ilk ass over tea kettle.

Even so, shed no tears. In the early seventies, Nixon and his fellow idealogues rode roughshod over any opposition of any sort from anywhere.

They kicked ass left and right. Rock and roll was bruised and battered but unbowed. It got wearily up off the canvas and came back fighting.

Welcome, 1975. Nixon was gone, but his tendrils still ran deep as the Stones geared up to tour the States. The State Department was gradually lulled beyond Nixon paranoia by an old pro, as the Stones deftly outmaneuvered the government. The Stones hired a guy by the name of Bill Carter, a dyed-in-the-wool Arkansan from Little Rock, who just happened to have been a Secret Service agent under Presidents Kennedy and Johnson and then went home to open his legal practice. He had liked the fast life outside of the quiet hills of Arkansas and started representing such musical talents as Tanya Tucker. He was a sharp, tough-talking Southern lawyer with extensive Washington contacts. From his Secret Service days, he knew half the police chiefs in the country and if ever a group needed help in dealing with the police, it was the Stones. The Stones also liked the "Don't tread on me" attitude he developed after seeing the inner workings of government. He was not a Stones fan, but he had a certain love for the type of music that reflected his spirit of independence. The Rolling Stones zeroed in on him in a New York minute. Soul brothers, kindred spirits, whatever you want to call it, the Stones were the spiritual equal of an Arkansas "Freebird." Freedom was the central issue and everyone knew that; who cares if a stone Hank Williams redneck from Arkansas links up with these anarchistic Limeys with arrest records longer than their reputations? Results are all that count in the legal world. And from all accounts, Bill Carter went to work for the Stones in such a miraculous fashion that no one noticed that he was doing so (which is, of course, the first hallmark of a great lawyer). He found that, on paper at least, the government's main objection to admitting the Stones was that the band could not guarantee the safety of concertgoers who bought tickets to their concerts? Who could, after all? Looked like a paper tiger. So Carter drew up and submitted comprehensive security plans for a mass gathering (based on Secret Service plans for a presidential visit) which became gospel for rock concerts. He put Jagger in a coat and tie and had him visit the State Department and charm all the bilious lifers who were sharpening their rock and roll axes. He got entry visas for them. Quietly. Very quietly. And, as the Stones carefully plotted a 1975 United States tour (which Mick Jagger was careful to herald from the first as the "Rolling Stones Tour of the Americas '75"—including many South American dates which never seemed serious and which, in fact, did not happen), the U.S. State Department did not seem to really notice it if Limeys named Jagger or Richards chanced to place their applications to enter the United States via the Immigration and Naturalization Service office in Memphis, which office was a long ways away from the bustling INS centers in L.A. and N.Y., where red flags were already waving for so-called Rolling Stones. Memphis was a tranquil zone, a free territory for musicians of any stripe: "Ollie, ollie, oxen free" and all the other variants of that childhood game still applied in Memphis. The South—still "Dixie" to some Stones fans— was the Stones' promised land. "Glory, glory" and welcome, Rolling Stones, to the modern U.S.A. Welcome to Gloryland!

And welcome, U.S.A., to the Stones again, I reflected as I lazed on a soft chaise lounge poolside at the Royal Orleans Hotel in New Orleans on a balmy May afternoon in 1975. Could there possibly be anything more pleasant, I wondered, as I sipped from a tumbler of Rebel Yell sour mash whiskey, the aroma of which rivaled and indeed almost overwhelmed the heady fragrance of the magnolia trees encircling this impossibly elegant little hotel. I idly watched as a riverboat, the *John Penn*, glided lazily by on the serene waters of the wide Mississippi River. I smiled as the *John Penn*'s steam calliope merrily broke into the strains of "Dixie." The Stones always wanted to be a Southern blues band, I knew, and this is the sort of scene they are desperately always trying to be part of. They insisted on starting this tour in the South, mainly, I think, so they can stay at the Royal Orleans, which is in the French Quarter, but not so much in the French Quarter that the Stones can't have their luxury, if you know what I mean. Being funky on Bourbon Street is one thing, but waking up with Al Hirt's horn blasting away in your very eardrum is a totally other thing. The Stones do, after all, like to have their funk served up with a certain decorum and silver and linen and a red rose on the room service tray. And a good bottle of wine, if you don't mind. And a lovely rooftop pool, with nice views of the Quarter and the river, even though the Stones, to judge from their appearances, do not appear to have glimpsed sunlight, much less been immersed in chlorinated water outdoors, for some years. Still, it's there. That's what matters.

Nothing could possibly be more pleasant than this, I decided. Lying by the pool in the French Quarter is a great way to prep for observing the start of the Stones' big tour and what seems to be their bid to reclaim their status as the king bees, an honorarium that seems to have slipped away from them in these curious seventies. Fans and critics regard them a bit as quaint holdovers from the sixties, even as—a harsh word—"irrelevant." As if anything in rock and roll were relevant. Compared to what?

I continued my poolside mental meanderings on the significance of the Rolling Stones' reentry into Western culture and simultaneously pondered another dip in the pool and another drink and maybe making dinner reservations at Antoine's or somewhere. I was suddenly and roughly shaken out of my golden reveries by a colleague, Robert Hilburn of the Los Angeles *Times*. He rushed up to me to say—in so many words—"Gird up your loins and get it together soonest because TV is eating our lunch." I, of course, knew exactly what he meant and the chill of that threat sent me hurtling to my room to dress and get ready for action. What it was, was this: The Stones were staying here at the Royal Orleans, easing into their first North American shows up at Louisiana State University in Baton Rouge. And rehearsing a bit, especially with ex-Face Ron Wood filling in for departed Stone guitarist Mick Taylor. And was the band breaking up or not? And with all the rumors about what guitarist Keith Richards was doing, or not doing, or ingesting or not or whatever, global journalistic competition was as fearsome as piranha fish fighting over the last morsel. Reporters from England as well as from across the United States were filling up the hotel, but so far all press had been barred from the rehearsals or from any Stones contact. Hence all the leisurely pool time. But Hilburn had discovered real trouble. He had been nosing around —actually working—while I was checking out the pool ("pool reporter," that's the origin of the term) and heard that the worst had happened: that Geraldo Rivera was on the scene and getting access while we print boffos were generally being given little leper's bells to wear and being asked to sweep up after the elephants go by in the parade and that sort of thing. I knew the Stones were a bit nervous about the press, for many reasons. For one, a very revealing book *(S.T.P.: A Journey Through America with the Rolling Stones)* had been written by Robert Greenfield, who had covered their last tour for *Rolling Stone* magazine, which was what I was now doing, and that they had vowed to never again allow that kind of access to anybody. Secondly, the documentary film that they had commissioned Robert Frank to do of their 1972 tour—a film called *Cocksucker Blues*— was deemed forever unreleasable once the Stones got a look at it (the title gives you some clue). And, given the Stones' legal status in this country, any press could hurt them badly. They needed money. Thus, they had to work and the United States was their major market. If Keith, for example, who was a devoted drug consumer, should go to jail or lose his visa, there wouldn't be much left of the band. Still and all, if you're going to climb into that public arena, the public is going to want to read about you. Which is where my job comes in. What I don't especially like is having my job made difficult or impossible because TV coverage gets higher priority. That's fine; we all know that one minute coast-to-coast on the tube equals all print coverage. What we resented, there on a lovely afternoon in New Orleans, was the notion—that seemed to have been advanced by one certain TV reporter—that all press should be barred except for TV. Except for one particular TV person. So Hilburn and New York

Times writer John Rockwell—likewise alerted by Hilburn's last-minute ride—and yours truly leaped into a fast rent-a-Cutlass and sped off for Baton Rouge where apparently the Stones were rehearsing without telling us gentlemen of the print and where apparently Geraldo of the tube was calling the shots. We shall see about this, we decided, and we hauled ass up the road.

Geraldo was, as we feared, oiling his TV way around the rehearsals at LSU's Assembly Center.

The place was surprisingly placid for a Rolling Stones event. The seven semitrailer trucks that hauled in the one hundred tons or so of equipment for the show were lined up orderly in a parking lot under shade trees. No groupies or fans of any stripe near the stage doors. An officer named Cole from the LSU police force let us in. The first person we ran into was a tall, bearded man wearing jungle khakis. In Baton Rouge. He held up his palm for us to stop. This was Paul Wasserman, the press agent for the Stones (as well as for the likes of Bob Dylan, Neil Diamond, Paul Simon, and Linda Ronstadt. With such clients, his job is not to get press; it's to keep the press away). He scowled: "What are you doing here? No press allowed! You knew that!"

"Wasso," I said, "Geraldo is here, so we are going to be here too." Rockwell and Hilburn voiced agreement.

"Okay," Wasserman smiled. "C'mon in."

We went out into the cavernous 16,000-seat hall to inspect the much-vaunted Stones' lotus petal stage. It looked okay, but it was empty.

"Where's the band, Wasso?"

A resigned sigh. "C'mon."

Before we left, Mick Jagger appeared onstage to, as it turned out, road test a giant balloon of a phallus that is one of the special effects. A sickly white wraith, it first slowly uncoiled from stage front and then, whipped by an air jet, popped out to an astonishing eighteen feet or so. A giant wriggling phallus. Jagger straddled it, letting it billow around his legs. Then he punched it. Then he let it seem to bugger him. He laughed as it collapsed. Jagger disappeared. The phallus, postcoitus, slithered back into its sheath.

Back in a gray-tiled hospitality room in the tunnels of this basketball arena, the Rolling Stones sat around and waited for Ron Wood to show up for rehearsal. He was already three hours late. And he was not even a full-fledged Stone. Just penciled in, so far.

Stones drummer Charlie Watts, decked out in a purple jacket and white duck trousers, sipped coffee at a table with a silver candelabra on it. He was sporting almost a skinhead haircut. "I cut it off because I was growing bald," he said. Stones bassist Bill Wyman sat down at the table and talked about the rehearsal. "We're doing some things we've never done onstage before, like songs from the last album and some things that haven't been released. So we've rehearsed about forty songs. A hell of a lot of numbers. We usually rehearsed twenty or twenty-five before and then ended up doing about fifteen onstage." He was bored, as was everyone else. Rock and rollers spend 92 percent of their time waiting for something to happen. Over in a corner, apart from the musicians' klatches, Stones wife Bianca Jagger chatted idly with Ben E. King, Earl McGrath, and Atlantic Records head Ahmet Ertegun.

Wyman talked desultorily about *Metamorphosis*, the compilation record album of previously unreleased Stones' sessions that former Stones manager Allen Klein had just released. "It has nothing to do with us."

"It's just a lot of junk, really," Watts chimed in, nodding and looking monkish over his coffee mug.

Wyman continued, "We wanted to have it done historically, so that it would have at least had a value to collectors."

"We spent months going over material," Watts almost spat.

Wyman: "And we provided an album which he turned down. I selected about eighteen titles, laid it all out historically, with details."

Watts: "We gave him our album and he said no." He grimaced.

Wyman: "And he said no. I wouldn't even want our own album out now in addition to his because there's really no point—"

Watts interrupted him: "We'll bring ours out sometime."

We sipped coffee for a while. Keith Richards, astonishingly sporting a sunburn, stopped to say hello. After a while he volunteered that "I have a ringing in my ears for an hour after a show. I went to a doctor a couple of years ago to have my ears checked." We talked for a while about how our ears felt after a long, multidecibel rock show. No definitive conclusions were reached.

Keith wandered off to an upright piano and sat down and started picking out Charlie Rich tunes—"Lonely Weekends" and others—and Officer Cole walked over to listen, appreciatively.

"The stage," Charlie Watts was saying. "The stage. It's twice as big as it looks. You should go up later and look at it. It's the biggest stage we've ever had."

Wyman chimed in: "And we have a PA [public address] facing back, so there's no bounce echo."

"We had a lot of ideas," Watts said, "our floor was covered with drawings. But I'm glad we kept the circle [stage design]. Money has a lot to do with it, if you're talking about gimmicks. We had this idea of something going off in the air during a number and it was thirty grand, man, ten grand a night to put it in! In the end, it was $200,000 to have an effect. So we got the basic stage together and it is marvelous, as you'll see."

Wyman: "We've always tried to make the show better than the usual rock and roll show and it's a large expense."

Watts: "But it's worthwhile."

We pondered that a while and sipped coffee. Journeyman keyboardist Billy Preston, who had been added to this tour, walked in. He spotted "press" and said, "Uh oh, they got tapes rolling" and he kept on walking.

Said Wyman, "We're starting in Baton Rouge because it's always nice to start in a quieter place. You can get yourself together straightaway. It's a bit more relaxing and you can concentrate on the show. I had to get used to the stage. It slopes up about five feet and I got terribly tired the first hour on it just from having to lean back to compensate for that angle."

We got some more coffee. This is the apex of rock and roll—the be-all and end-all. People would kill to take my place.

Over in the corner, Mick and Billy Preston put on a cassette tape of some cuts they had recorded in Munich a couple of months back. Mick was glowering. He was not pleased to discover that reporters had gotten into the rehearsal. Mick turned up the volume of the recorder, effectively drowning out Keith's piano.

"This cut," Wyman said, "is Mick and Billy singing lead. It's very jazzy. We just have a few rough recordings of the next album so far. The working title for this song is 'Vagina.' Why? Because someone called it 'Cunt' in the studio and we couldn't write that." He laughed congenially. He says he's called the "Silent Stone" only because "No one ever asks me anything."

Watts was not as eager to pass the time in genial conversation. For no good reason, I asked Watts how it was to record with Southern guitarist Wayne Perkins when the Stones were auditioning him as a possible replacement for Mick Taylor. Watts bristled and all but leaped across the table to snap at me: "Why do you want to know that? Why are you asking such a question?" My answer—pure musical curiosity—mollified him, but it was Wyman who spoke up: "Wayne is very good. He's penciled in as a potential future choice."

Watts: We wanted a horn [player] for this tour, but couldn't find anybody. David Newman would've been good, but we couldn't get to him."

Mick and Billy continued to play songs loudly, ignoring everyone else in the room. Wyman volunteered that the next song was "called 'Melody.' It's very nice."

Tour percussionist Ollie Brown (whom the Stones met when he was playing with Stevie Wonder in 1972) spoke up: "That sounds like blues."

Wyman, who is approaching middle age and who is white, laughed as he said to Ollie Brown, who is twenty years old and black, "Ollie, that's twenties blues. Come on, Ollie, do I have to play your roots for you?"

At about 11:30 P.M., Ron Wood, his usual rooster hairdo aflop, wandered in with a crooked grin and rasped, "I thought I'd wander up." Tour manager Peter Rudge told him wishfully, "We've got Mick Taylor coming."

Out to the hall for rehearsal. For some reason, Stravinsky's *Firebird* was playing through the public address system. Geraldo Rivera appeared from the wings. The band members straggled onto the stage to *Firebird*, followed by *Bolero*, played at ear-splitting levels to a nonexistent audience. Keith tried to kick into "Little Queenie." Finally, after no one could hear anything, Ollie Brown bellowed, "Turn off the music!" Exit *Bolero*.

Jagger grabbed a tambourine and popped a can of Budweiser and pranced out to the points of the six petals of the lotus stage with Billy Preston. At stage front, Geraldo posed in front of a ColorTrans light for his TV crew.

From that viewpoint, the stage looked disappointing: just another stage. "Go upstairs," Charlie Watts told me on his way to that stage. "You really can't see the star effect from the floor because the line of amps cuts it in two. But it's marvelous. It's the best stage we've ever had." I went upstairs and had a look and discovered that he was right on. From up above, the stage was a delicate, shimmering dish with six gently curving star points leafing out from the center: like a perfectly formed artichoke when you get to its heart. It was seventy-one feet across and had such a rake that the back was five feet higher than the front, which is why Bill Wyman was complaining of a sore back from having to perform on a downhill slope.

Jagger was mincing backward out to the tips of the stars to see how far he could go before falling. As the only audience—apart from Geraldo —Hilburn and Rockwell and I studied Mick closely, even bringing out binoculars like weird anthropologists or something. Through the binocs, though, you could notice such things as: the fact that Jagger is absolutely impassive as he sings. Heavy-lidded and indifferent to what is going on around him. Professional, but that's all. These guys up here are his sidemen and that's it, Jack, his expression clearly says. So this is how a Stones' rehearsal goes. A lot of very muddy jamming for a while. For a few minutes, Billy Preston, the new kid and obviously a Jagger favorite, tried to dominate the sound with his bright and meaningless and squeaky-clean organ licks until he was quietly and definitively put in his place forever by the soft-spoken master drummer Charlie Watts who—without ever saying a word or even looking at anyone—suddenly, with his beat, crushed Billy Preston's little ice cream melodies into puddles with the granite-solid backbeat that is his and rock and roll's signature. He sent out a message that said, loud and clear: You can tie ribbons or balloons on this music if you like, but, brother, you ain't ever gonna change it. So why bother? Preston got the message and turned into a Sammy Davis Jr.-like foil for Mick on the tour.

Meanwhile, Keith and Ron Wood were trying to figure out guitar parts and that ain't easy. They worked through "Honky Tonk Women," the slashing guitar lead-in of which is a Stones signature itself. If you got no menacing-sounding guitars, then you got no Stones. It's that simple and Keith was coaching Wood again and again to get the sound that would be the sound of a "gin-soaked barroom queen in Memphis." It's clearly not easy being Keith Richards and less easy teaching someone else how to be Keith Richards.

2 Geraldo
and Baton Rouge

"BATON ROUGE, La., June 1—The Rolling Stones today will begin a three-month jet-caravan tour of both North and South America here with a 3:00 P.M. and 9:00 P.M. concert on campus at the Louisiana State University. The tour, the most extensive they have undertaken in nearly a decade, will have them crisscross the United States and Canada and perform for the first time in Mexico, Venezuela, and Brazil. Present capacity figures for the tour will see the Stones appearing before 1.5 million people in fifty-eight concerts; forty-two will be given in the United States and Canada and sixteen in Mexico and South America." —Press release from Paul Wasserman.

On this night in Baton Rouge, the Stones would be lucky if they could play fifty-eight minutes, the hell with fifty-eight concerts. They're fifteen hours away from their first show in North America in three years and they sound like a garage band that skipped learning "Louie Louie." A ragged-sounding band, I mean to say. Chords and dischords rattle around in the hall like fluttering pigeons in the rafters. Ron Wood—musically—is chasing Keith Richards with no hope of ever catching him. Billy Preston's organ inserts, as it were, and percussionist Ollie Brown's random fills were still wild sounds with no reason to come from a Rolling Stones stage. Even so, the rhythm section—Wyman and Watts—remained an unflappable, unshakable steady force. They shall endure. After a bit, after much coaching by Keith, Wood started falling into line. Preston and Brown remained marginal and even a bit irritating. Jagger remained impassive. He and Preston practiced trading off falsetto vocals. Keith teaches Wood the guitar break in "You Can't Always Get What You Want." Mick sets down his beer, sweeps away from his mike stand and prances up to the tip of the star, wheels around and starts shaking his ass prettily at the audience— which still consists of the ever-present Geraldo, Hilburn, Rockwell, and yours truly. A cynic might call that performance a bit perverse. But no one has ever accused the Stones of practicing false gentility.

ROLLING STONE CHET FLITTO [sic] DLR 78 EAST 56 ST NYK
10016: THE ROLLING STONES INVITE YOU TO A PRESS AN-
NOUNCEMENT AT 11:30 A.M., THURSDAY, MAY 1ST, AT THE
ROOM ADJOINING FEATHERS IN THE FIFTH AVENUE HOTEL AT 24
FIFTH AVENUE AND NINTH STREET. TV CREWS SHOULD BRING
PORTABLE EQUIPMENT ONLY. PAUL WASSERMAN 751–2060.

—Telegram from Paul Wasserman regarding the press conference announcing the "Tour of the Americas '75."

Some press conference that was. I got down to the venerable Fifth
Avenue Hotel, practically in the shadow of the Washington Square Memorial Arch, early and found perhaps a hundred or so of my colleagues
milling around, tramping through the geraniums, and generally making
the hotel staff nervous. And looking for the open bar—which is the only
draw that will lure the press out before noon. Wasserman, a large, bulky
man whose somber mien and quiet intensity cloak a ribald sense of humor
(and often get him described in the press as either a rabbi or a Stones
bodyguard), solemnly ushered the media rabble inside. TV crews raced to
set up their cameras at a microphone-laden table that seemed to be set up
for a large press conference. Burly TV technicians knocked each other
down and elbowed aside the peasant print journalists in the rush. Minutes
passed. More minutes passed. TV crews started yelling obscenities: TV
waits for no man. Where are the (bleeping) Stones?

Wasserman finally clomped heavily to the mike stand and ponder-
ously introduced—to loud boos—"a man who needs no introduction." It
turned out that a good introduction would have helped him and might
have cut down on the volume of the ensuing boos. He introduced "Professor" Irwin Corey, a wild-haired comedian of dubious credential, who is
known as a master of double-speak. As in gobbledygook: ordinary-sounding
words that make absolutely no sense at all when strung together into
ersatz sentences. Perfect for the Stones. Corey delivered a few nonsensical
paragraphs to a media crowd that appeared to have been poleaxed: glazed
eyes everywhere you looked. Then, hark! A heavy bass note from far away
out on Fifth Avenue rumbled into the Fifth Avenue Hotel. Heads started
to turn. Then came the beat of a drum! A heavy backbeat! The sound
seemed to be drawing nearer. Something was obviously happening outside.
One or two media rabbits raced outside to scout the action and then
sprinted back inside, red-faced and out of breath, to announce: "It's the
Stones!" A heavy media stampede fortunately resulted in no fatalities and
only minor injuries. Out on Fifth Avenue, a flatbed truck pulled up to the
hotel. On the flatbed truck were the Rolling Stones, with a portable gener-
ator and sound system. They were playing the hell out of "Brown Sugar."

Media bedlam ensued. Then the Stones jumped off the truck into waiting cars and raced the hell away. Gotcha! say the Stones to the media. It's the sort of perverse maneuver they lie awake at nights trying to think of and improve upon. Perfect example of Stones sensibility.

Back in Baton Rouge, a month after the Fifth Avenue trailer show, I hauled out my handy-dandy portable Nikon binoculars to check out the stage action. Not much action for a rehearsal of what's supposed to be the World's Greatest Rock and Roll Band. Wyman stood off by himself, dapper and sipping a beer and smoking a cigarette, a true Stone Alone. Ollie Brown, overawed by this sudden rush of stardom for a young musician, didn't know what to do and looked about nervously a great deal, his huge Afro haloed by spotlights. Ditto for Billy Preston. Mick and Wood were trading a joke, one told obviously by Mick, since Wood was laughing insanely the way a new employee might when the boss cracks a good one. Keith, in his droopy, faded jeans and black T-shirt and silver bracelets and massive turquoise belt buckle and silver skull ring, was supremely indifferent to what went on around him. He concentrated on his blond Fender Telecaster guitar and his bottle of Rebel Yell. Nestled back in the thicket of his drum kit, Charlie Watts was equally imperious, twirling his drumsticks and looking up at the rafters and waiting for action.

By 2:30 or so in the morning, it started to sound like a hell of a good rock and roll band on "Tumbling Dice"; Wood and Keith meshing on guitar and Mick finally starting to really sing. Hilburn and Rockwell and I, sprawled on folding chairs in the front row and throwing down coffee to stay awake, had started to leave at about 2:00. Then, as the bone-rattling licks of "It's Only Rock and Roll (But I Like It)" washed over us, as the Stones' only audience that night (Sleep tight, Geraldo) in that hall, we— without speaking—realized in a flash how foolish it would be to not stay the course. The Stones knew, of course, that we were not tape-recording the rehearsal. Wish now that I would have. For better or for worse, what we were hearing was the emerging sound of the modern Stones, postsixties, post-Mick Taylor, and long ago post-Brian Jones (who?). This was the hard, slashing, take-no-prisoners Rolling Stones that Mick and Keith sometimes argued about but ultimately agreed upon as their musical forum. Everyone and everything else rapidly became secondary to Mick and Keith and their rock and roll vision. Charlie and Bill had become resigned to the fact that they were salaried employees. Woody (supposedly only on loan from Rod Stewart but, of course, wooed away forever in typical Stones style) felt it an honor to stand in Keith's very shadow. And Billy Preston and Ollie Brown learned pretty damn quick that they were just hired hands. By six o'clock on that gentle Louisiana morning, when the rehearsal finally wound down, we heard nothing from that stage but Mick and Keith. For better or for worse, they were finally wedded forever as far as rock and roll and the Rolling Stones were concerned.

Six hours later, the sun shines bright in Baton Rouge as the press corps, after two hours' sleep in New Orleans, cruises back into town, down LSU's green-lawned Fraternity Row, where brawny frat boys—ignorant of or disdainful of the Stones?—while away a pleasant Sunday afternoon playing touch football and drinking beer. At the hall, there is a total absence of bedlam. Two hundred tickets remain on sale for the matinee show, at $8.50 a pop. There are no ticket scalpers. The only lines are at the women's rest rooms. Even the cops, bored to distraction, seem eager to admit the tiny press corps backstage without even the usual quibbling over credentials. Opening out of town, as Wyman said, certainly has its points.

Backstage, absolutely nothing was happening. Charlie Watts was the only Stone in the so-called "hospitality room" and he was verbally jousting with a novelist that the New York *Times Magazine* had sent down to apparently do a "think" piece on the Stones. "You will notice," the novelist said to Watts in an unwittingly foolish bid to gain Stones Access, "that I am not taking any notes." He smiled smugly, expecting a return conspiratorial smile from Watts: Nobody here but us good buddies, right? Watts is not amused by what he—perhaps rightly, after all these years—views as an amateur journalist. The novelist, flustered, asks a garbled question about the "money figures" on the tour and that just about seals his fate. Watts is always happy to dissect an inept interviewer and, brother, does he have fresh meat today.

Out in the hall, the place was like church, compared to your usual frenzied Stones bash-up. Everyone nice and orderly and not yet totally wired or frenzied or screwed up. Still early, though.

Three o'clock comes and goes. Announced starting time, but nothing happens. A few screams of "Where's the Rolling Stones?" but nothing else. Finally, at 3:50, the Meters, a superlative New Orleans group, gain the stage. They play for a distracted Stones audience till 4:35, do an unasked-for encore, and disappear down the backstage chute to raucous calls for the Stones. Roadies come out and remove the blue sheeting that covered and protected the precious Stones stage during the Meters' set. Backstage, Ahmet Ertegun and Bianca and Ben E. King get to the hospitality room. Out front, the crowd exercises great patience. At five, there's thirty seconds of foot-stomping, which inexplicably stops, as if on signal. Out in the crowd, I find a general bliss-out. Hey, the Stones happen when they happen, you know? Only one young crazy grabbed me to let me know that, hey, "I'm goin' crazy. This crowd is bummin' me out. I went around all day wishin' everybody a happy Rollin' Stones Day. Don't seem like so much now. The Meters bum me out, man. What a bad choice." He was the exception. The rule exploded with cheers at 5:20 when the house lights went down and the first keening notes of Aaron Copland's *Fanfare for the Common Man* flooded the hall and the crowd surged forward and strobe lights winked like angry flying insects around the hall. A surging Super Trouper spotlight pinioned Jagger as he lay on his back at the tip of the star point out front. Keith ground into the down and dirty opening chords of "Honky Tonk Women" and we were off to the races.

There's terrible feedback, though, as Mick minces around in his baseball uniform and leather jacket and his heavily overdone eye shadow. Keith joins him at stage front to sing harmony—or something like it. Keith is wearing a white jacket and snug red pants festooned with gold stars. He looks as if he doesn't need makeup to look bizarre or sinister. Mick dramatically ends "Honky Tonk Women" by kneeling and curling his arms around a knee and bowing his head. Nice applause, but nothing approaching the Richter scale. This well-bred or at least affluent college crowd is not terribly enchanted by the sight of Mick Jagger in heavy makeup and a silly outfit prancing all over the place. The next song, "All Down the Line," redeems the Stones, led as it is by Keith's savage metallic attack. He's apparently regained his control of the band.

Almost to counter that, Mick starts his court jester routine. In a ridiculous mock-Southern accent, he announces that "We ain't never been here before in our lives. Sounds like a good place, though." Moderate cheers and at least no booing, even though he begins a dangerous slowdown by pouting, "Get my rocks off" after "Rocks Off" and then stops everything to announce haughtily, "We gonna sing in a minute. I'm gonna talk to Billy." Preston, that is, and Mick and Billy conferred for a while, to everyone else's dissatisfaction. Finally, Mick launched into "Ain't Too Proud to Beg," which had sounded better at the rehearsal only a few hours before, and started trying to mend his fences by reaching down into the crowd and kissing and feeling the girls in the front row. Someone in the crowd tossed an Uncle Sam stovepipe hat up to him and he pretended to put it on, turned and held up three fingers to Keith as a signal to bring around the final chorus of "Ain't" three more times, and rolled on the stage in a mock James Brown finale. Mick sprang back up to start "Star Star" (better known as "Starfucker") and as he did so, the trap door in front of him that houses the giant dick and the inflatable dragon and other special effects slowly opened and a human hand reached out, snaked around and finally located the stovepipe hat, grabbed it and then hauled it away forever.

A moment later, the same trap door rises to release the gradually hardening large white phallus. It slowly billows forth, to much front row laughter (Mick didn't count on this reaction) as Mick spits out the words "starfucker, star, star, star, yes you are." He starts to play with the huge condom and then, inexplicably, it detumesces and disappears back through its little door. The rest of the show is equally up-and-down. A titanium-hard version of "Gimme Shelter" trails into Preston singing "You Got to Move." Then it's the first public performance of "Luxury" and then Mick announces, as he picks up and straps on Woody's silver Gibson Les Paul guitar, "We're gonna slow down and see how we're gonna get on it." He demonstrates his new zeal for the guitar, if not his acumen, in "Fingerprint File," wrapping it up by lying flat on the stage and whispering, "You know, these days it's all secrecy and no privacy. Good night, sleep tight." You had to be there.

And then—people have forgotten this—Mick as much as turned over the stage to his good pal Billy Preston. "Hey, Billy, you want to do a number? What do you want to do?" (This is verbatim, guaranteed.) "Like to do one from my new album," Billy beamed as he lurched into "That's Life." Stones watchers noted that Ollie Brown took over Charlie Watts's usual seat at the drums. Mick and Billy pranced around and failed to drum up any enthusiasm. Which encouraged them to let Billy do another Billy song, "Outta Space." After it trickled out, Watts jumped back to his usual place and ran through his drums angrily, an ominous sound. And he started the rumblings of "Brown Sugar," a sound like thunder and lightning rolling in from the Gulf of Mexico. It was then that the college crowd, a hard act to please, finally leaped out of its seats and embraced the new Rolling Stones: Better than an IV. Bill Wyman even started tapping his right foot. What was supposed to be the last number, "Jumping Jack Flash," sounds like a 747 crashing at JFK: heavy metal blowing up everywhere. Mick rolls on the stage as Keith's Fender howls the shriek of Apocalypse Now! After speeding through "Rip This Joint," the band finally—after almost two hours—hits its groove and "Street Fighting Man" is a textbook lesson in how to rock and roll. Now that these collegians have warmed to the Stones so much that they're going apeshit here at LSU's Assembly Center, stomping enough to raise Huey Long from the dead, how is Mick gonna work an encore that will empty the joint so that it will be refilled half an hour hence by ticket holders for the second show and what if the first-show fans decide to stay the hell there? Mick leaps out of sudden darkness into a hot red spotlight and caresses his way through a steamy version of "Midnight Rambler." He's howling and kneeling on the stage as he fingers his silver-studded belt and starts lashing out with it. Not bad for a Baton Rouge encore.

Mick, knowing full well that he has just regained the heavyweight championship belt, dances in delight as he croons, "Good night!" Keith grins broadly, holding his Telecaster skyward, the crack of his ass showing as his red pants droop. The hall looks like a bonfire as matches and lighters are ignited to call for another encore, but it's too late. Got another show coming up in just a minute.

Backstage, there were exuberant whoops and hollers. With twenty-three songs performed, the show was clocked in at two hours and five minutes, supposedly the longest Stones show ever (of course, given the nature of the record keepers, it's hard to be certain about such things). Mick's makeup man ran into me and screamed that he had put "two tons of powder" on Mick's face. It looked like it.

Outside, Baton Rouge had suddenly been Stoned: as in when angelic-faced teenaged girls who had not even been born when these Stone yahoos first raised a ruckus start acting moon-eyed over these old farts and when the scalpers suddenly wake up and raise their ticket prices by a sudden few dollars and when those incredibly beautiful women (the ones in the stiletto heels and the black net stockings and the slit skirts and the push up bras . . . enough, already) appear out of nowhere and announce that they are guests of the Rolling Stones. Well, why not? What is rock and roll for if not for fun?

Security suddenly became tight. John Rockwell, who needed to file his article for the New York *Times* immediately, was thrown out of backstage and spent his afternoon sitting out on the lawn, writing and fuming and then filing his *Times* piece on a pay phone at the corner.

Back in the hospitality room, Ahmet Ertegun was playing Ping-Pong with Bill Wyman. Charlie Watts was still jousting with the novelist. Ben E. King and Bianca were there, not saying anything. Mick, still sporting his—extremely—heavy eye makeup, was talking to five or six of the pop press writers. Geraldo Rivera, in crisp, creased white trousers and blue crew sweater, circled Mick, as Geraldo's TV crew panted behind him. A dude—no other term will fit—wearing maroon velvet trousers and a white satin shirt took over Keith's backstage operations.

Geraldo came up behind Mick and just kind of hovered there, beaming with a protective "Don't mess with me" smile. Charlie Watts, fresh from his latest bout with a damn writer, came striding in with the fumes rising off him visible to all but the insensitive. Geraldo fucked up. He thrust his hand hard up against Charlie's chest and stopped him. You don't do that. I could have told Geraldo that, but why not let him learn what life is all about on his own? Eh? He gets paid enough, after all. Geraldo knows no boundaries. After he intercepted Charlie, he instructed him—and it was no question—"Have you got a couple of minutes for TV." He was ready to start filming and all when Charlie said, "Fuck no."

What a surprise. Geraldo's mouth tightened noticeably. What fun in the hospitality room. Geraldo finally secures Mick for his TV interview. They're seated on a threadbare couch staring uncomfortably at a TV lens. Around them swirl what amounts to what happens to the Rolling Stones when they're between a matinee and evening performance. Which they have never done before. Which Geraldo Rivera does not seem to know. The first thing he did wrong was to sing out to the entire room: "Ladies and gentlemen, could we have quiet, please? I am doing an interview." What a challenge. Mick's eyes perceptibly turn to granite. He gives Geraldo exactly two minutes of question-and-answer and it's the usual Mick mirrors and smoke sort of razzle-dazzle that the city slickers get. Geraldo laughs very heartily—too heartily—after each answer. A hollow laugh. When the TV lights go off, Mick gives Geraldo a piercing gaze and turns on his heel and walks away. Good-bye. There is no farewell quite as final and as stinging as the one from a superstar whom one has courted in vain.

You want to know what Mick last said to Geraldo? This is what he said: "You've got gloss makeup on your lids and I don't."

3 San Antonio

I was having dinner later with Wasserman in the hotel. I noticed that he kept looking across the room, almost as if he were a security guard on the alert. Later I found out that he actually had been one. What he had been scrutinizing behind me was the ABC-TV table. Geraldo and friends. The captain told me later that the ABC party had walked the check and Wasserman—ever vigilant—noticed that. So he signed Geraldo's name to our dinner check. (Happy expense account, Geraldo.)

Geraldo later appeared on a New Orleans TV news show. "Mick wasn't available," purred the announcer, "but here's a close friend of his, Geraldo Rivera." Geraldo preened a bit on-screen and said seriously, "Mick told me the show went very well and he's going on to St. Louis from here." Well. Mick and the band were actually going to San Antonio from "here," but, what the hey, why let the facts get in the way?

Wasserman mentioned that the governor's office had called the Stones' floating headquarters and said that the governor's three daughters very much wanted to meet Mick Jagger and what about it? "Dunno about that," Wasserman told the gov's office. "Well," said the gov's office, "just tell us where Mick's having dinner tonight and we'll get out the chopper and they can go and watch him eat."

Wasserman, a high-powered L.A. press agent with top stars as clients, had not really needed the Rolling Stones account, but couldn't resist the attraction when they called him up just before this tour. "The litmus test was this," he said. "Mick and Charlie had designed the stage and the screaming eagle tour logo. When I met Mick, he had three eagle drawings laid out in front of him. He said, 'This is your first job. One of these drawings is mine, one is Charlie's, and one is the artist's. Which one is the best?'"

Wasserman laughed at the memory and continued, "I told Mick that I'd never really gone in for eagles. Maybe that's why he hired me."

This was back at the Royal Orleans Hotel in New Orleans after the second Baton Rouge show. The concert went well, the band members having gotten over their extreme nervousness before the first show. Now they had their confidence back, they were standing taller, they were once again the one and only bleeping Rolling Stones, so watch out, Jack! The second audience was more attuned too, a hyped-up crowd cruising into the hall with unfocused eyes and Levi's pockets stuffed with chemicals and little bottles of hooch. A raucous time was had. By all. Bianca Jagger had brought a wardrobe bag with her and changed outfits before the second show. Mick, bowing to intense pressure, met briefly with the pack of British journalists slavering, unsuccessfully, to get Stones Access. Mick was curt. He said he believed in "social revolution." He was asked if the Stones had performed "Sympathy for the Devil" since "then" ("then" being the disastrous Altamont concert of 1969 when demonic powers of darkness seemed to accompany that anthem to the unknown void). "Oh yeah," Mick said casually, "we've done it hundreds of times." Total bullshit, of course. The Stones had done it fourteen times on their 1970 European tour, but had been careful to drop it from their 1971 British tour and their 1972 dates in the United States. No one dared to call him down on that; Mick being the exalted Mick, after all.

My first meeting with Mick was very casual. We were waiting for the elevator in the Royal Orleans and he actually struck up a conversation, as people will do when they get nervous waiting for an elevator or something. Room service was his opening gambit. It turned out that neither of us was totally pleased with the quality or the speed or dispatch of the room service and we had a very spirited and quite agreeable discussion on what the hotels of the world should be doing as regards their room service. "I'm thinking of getting a hot plate," Mick concluded as our car reached the lobby, "so I don't have to wait an hour and a half for my eggs." I told him he was exactly right and we shook hands on the matter. What a heartwarming way to meet a first-magnitude quasar of the rock universe. Just a regular guy.

Meredith Wilson should have been there. The sun was beaming down, the American flag was blowing proudly in the wind, and a high school mariachi band dressed in fire-engine red saluted the Rolling Stones as their chartered Boeing 707 Starship touched down at the San Antonio, Texas, airport. The 707, which had last seen service on Elton John's tour, still had some of his artifacts: cheap, peeling Mylar mirrors, unraveling upholstery, fading stars on the fuselage. The Stones' one attempt to upgrade the airplane did not entirely work. They had slapped a screaming eagle on the tail, but it looked more like a smudge unless you were maybe two feet away from it. After the horrors of Stones' plane flights depicted in the film *Cocksucker Blues* (very explicit drugs and sex and a total atmosphere of decadence that might even have shocked Lenny Bruce), the Stones had—wisely, from their point of view—forever banned any press from traveling with them. So I got to go out to the airport to watch them land and then I could climb aboard and check out the plane. Not really worth getting up early for. The Stones descended from the plane to great cheers from about two hundred teenagers assembled behind the enthusiastic and almost-in-tune mariachi band. Jagger went over to the screaming kids and pressed the flesh, campaigning just like a Southern diplomat, as Chuck Berry once observed. At the hotel, the graceful Hilton Palacio Del Rio (so-named because it's planted right on San Antonio's downtown river walk), Mick stopped to pose for pictures as Instamatics winked away in the hotel lobby. Maybe two dozen kids milled around, eyed lazily by cops from the three patrol cars parked outside. As the day wore on, more and more curious fans started drifting in, until the cops had to set up a command post and the hotel had to station guards by the elevators to keep anyone who did not have a hotel key from using them. I didn't know that until Bob Hilburn, who hadn't been able to get a room at the Hilton and was quartered in a hotel several blocks away, called me from the lobby after he had been turned back by the guards. No Stones Access. A very serious liability for a writer on the Stones tour. So I gave Bob my spare room key. When I went down to meet him in the lobby, I almost staggered from the hot, steamy aroma of raw lust and hot sex that hit me like a cheap whore. The lobby was literally crawling with flesh. Even a blind man could have figured that scene out. Chicks. Chicks everywhere. Aside to politically and socially correct critics. No other word will describe these females but "chicks." These are not bimbos, even. These are budding teenies. They call themselves "chicks." They are astonishing and awesome in appearance. Pert, first of all. Everything is pert, from the perfectly uptilted nose to the high cheekbones and the casually tossed back golden mane of hair to the impossibly impertinent skyward thrust of the cherry nipples on the Rocket 88 tits straining against the very fabric of their flimsy Stones T-shirts and the incredibly tight—How do they do it? Sit wearing them for hours in the tub?—blue jeans that are near epiphany. And suede loincloths and halters. And straining leather. And silk scarves here and nothing there. Whew. That was the first—and only—time I have ever been in the midst of a fetid orgy just aching to happen. I had to go take a cold shower and lie down for a while. How do the Stones cope with this sort of temptation? They apparently don't take cold showers.

San Antonio was gearing up big for the Stones. The hall, the convention center, was just a short stroll away from the Hilton, so fans and ticket scalpers and rip-off artists and dope dealers and chicks and crazies and

Stones freaks and leftover sixties hippies and just plain interested citizens swirled around the Hilton. It was as if the circus had come to town. And maybe it had.

"ZODIAC [Zodiac News Service], Sept. 11, 1973. The tour manager of the Rolling Stones admits that he is terrified that Mick Jagger, or another member of the company, will be assassinated during a concert. Manager Peter Rudge said that security during the Stones' current concert tour of Europe has been tighter than ever. During the Stones' show in Vienna, Rudge said: 'You know the more exciting a show is and the more emotions Jagger expresses, the more trouble we have with freaks. We take every precaution we can, but then I am sure the Kennedys did, too.' Rudge added: 'Alice Cooper has said it won't be long before the first pop star is assassinated onstage and, unfortunately, I agree with him.' In a lighter vein, three Russian 'spies' were said to have viewed the Stones' Vienna appearance. German promoter Joachim Lieben reports that three representatives of Moscow's Ministry of Culture returned to the Soviet Union immediately after the Stones' performance. The three will apparently recommend whether Jagger and company should be granted entry visas to the U.S.S.R. for a tour there."

From the looks of things, San Antonio was more hostile to the Rolling Stones than was the Soviet Union. San Antonio is a peculiar town with a hazy identity: Its economy is generated by the big military bases there, but its population is largely Hispanic. It is a very conservative town and it was San Antonio that Australian "killer bee" newspaper publisher Rupert Murdoch first chose as his foothold in the New World. He was dead-on perfect. He bought the San Antonio *News* and transformed it into a role model of a breathless rip-off scandal sheet that promised more than it delivered. The Murdoch forces were more than ready for the Stones invasion. The newspaper had already called the city's vice squad to complain that a foreign rock band was going to unveil a gigantic obscenity onstage here in our hometown ("a big dick," they said) and what was the city therefore going to do about that? Well! The city was pissed off, that's what. No big dicks allowed here in our hometown—if you don't mind. Cops were alerted: Bust the Limey fags! As the aromatic groupies filled the Hilton's lobby, a scant block away, cops got ready to arrest and handcuff and jail the Rolling Stones if they unleashed their "obscene" biggus dickus in public view. All kinds of turmoil went on. The head of the San Antonio Police Department's Vice Squad, James Despres, called Sergeant Harold Hoff in his office and told him to get over there soonest to the Hilton and talk to the Stones' lawyer—if the Stones even had a lawyer. Despres knew that he did not especially need a splashy, front-page story in the *News* about how he had arrested a giant, inflated rubber and those responsible for it. There is publicity and then again there is publicity—if you know what I mean. Despres certainly did. He later said, "It was a mutual agreement that it would be best for everyone concerned that they not use that thing. They didn't.". That is gentle understatement for the fierce fighting that went on between the Stones and the San Antonio police. You must remember that the Stones are a floating island politically, with an annual budget probably—hell, undoubtedly—much larger than the city of San Antonio's and a feisty organization with well-paid lawyers of which there are none better in the world. San Antonio put up a hell of a fight, though, and the city's firm promise to arrest the Stones if they erected their biggus dickus onstage backed the Stones down. No phallus onstage in San Antone. Rupert Murdoch's San Antonio *News* pressed the city to ban the "obscenity" and the city did.

On June 3, after the first San Antonio show, I met with Stones lawyer Bill Carter and he was some kind of angry. "I went to see the judge," he said, "and even he told me that that newspaper story was not entirely accurate. Tonight at the show, two plainclothes narcotics officers showed up and made a scene at the door because they didn't have any identification. One officer pushed his way in. They said that there were so many complaints from city councilmen that they felt obligated to come down and make some busts. Then three detectives sent by the mayor showed up and said they wanted to examine the Stones' show. They said that the mayor and the city council had received several hundred phone calls about the show being obscene or pornographic. I really can't believe that there's that much difference between Baton Rouge, Louisiana, and San Antonio, Texas."

Carter smiled wryly. We were smack in the middle of the Hilton lobby, now converted into a veritable flesh palace, with fresh arrivals of dressed- and undressed-to-the-nines female Stones fans. He sipped his drink and continued: "I asked the police what their intentions were—after I warned them that the kids might well have burned that damn building down if the Stones got arrested onstage. They said they weren't there to create a scene, but if they thought that the show was pornographic they would seek a warrant and charges would be filed. They said they already thought that the show was pornographic. So I went off to speak to Mick and the Stones about this. They laughed about it. Mick said, 'Well, we're in San Antone, we're guests of San Antone and if they're gonna take this that seriously, then I won't do it [hoist the phallus onstage].' But I told the cops: 'We could beat your ass on this case if you file charges.' As an attorney, I know that this is not pornographic. But it would have hassled us and used up our resources. They put the Rolling Stones on trial because kids are smoking marijuana at rock concerts all over the world."

Carter was really getting wound up: He obviously believed in his new charges, the Rolling Stones. He got up to fetch us fresh drinks and I idly studied the never-ending parade through the Hilton lobby. Oops! Here come the two biker chicks from Houston I ran into at the show and—too late! They recognize me and stop to chat. Tiger and Claire, their names were, and they were barely wearing tight black leather bikinis and a lot of shiny metal and studs and some things I didn't want to know about. They were happy, though. At the show, they had sort of caught my eye, inasmuch as they were the only seminude leather chicks leaning almost on the stage and heaving a massively studded leather belt onto the stage, almost hitting Mick. They assured me that they had thrown the belt just to give it to Mick, not to hit him with it. They said that they had put their card inside the belt and that the card read: "L&L to Mick from Tiger and Claire, Slave. It was hot, ha ha." I didn't pursue the matter. They did so for me. Tiger—or was it Claire?—said, "This is kinda sex and violence. Mick really crawls around onstage. Look at when he does 'Midnight Rambler' and plays harmonica with no hands. That's a very S&M slave thing. Obviously, Mick is very into it." Well, we had a merry little talk for a while, till it developed that they kind of wanted to get Stones Access and could I provide it? I said that, despite my Stones backstage pass, I was actually an undercover officer and Tiger and Claire exchanged glances and started to uneasily ease away, leather creaking and metal and chains clanking, as Carter came back with our drinks. "What the hell was all that?" he asked. "That's your new fan club," I said. "They can't have Mick, so I gave them your room number."

He just laughed. Not bad for an ex-government agent now defending a public enemy. "I'll tell you what I have most noticed," he said. "The constant attitude is 'Blame it on the Stones.' Goddamn it, if the audience died of natural causes, they'd find a way to blame it on the Stones. In Milwaukee, the county commissioners voted to bar the Stones. Our guy there petitioned for a re-vote. I went up there to represent the Stones and pleaded the case. They had a police lieutenant testify that a girl was raped in San Francisco, gang-raped, and the cause was the Rolling Stones. This was eleven and a half blocks from their concert. They've been blamed because of things that go back for years. Maybe their image was bad and maybe they wanted their image to be bad, but they have been condemned for things that they are not! Mick Jagger is not the devil."

He laughed sarcastically. We sipped at our drinks for a while and eyed the lobby fashion show. "Well, Carter," I finally said, "I guess this is nothing like the Secret Service, eh?" He just smiled and said: "You never traveled with Jack Kennedy." I fell silent. That put me in my place, all right, and the Stones in their place, too. Never traveled with JFK.

"So, Bill, what happened tonight?" I finally said. He pulled at his bourbon and replied, "Well, there were a few problems tonight. First of all, the band doesn't control the security that the promoter provides for the concert. Rudge asked me to go in and check it and if what they have isn't enough, then to get more. Tonight San Antonio had twelve off-duty cops for ten thousand people! That's the last time we'll allow that sort of thing. We want young guys the fans don't resent. Local police often resent what's going on anyway. But the cops here, the off-duty cops, were armed and that shocked us. That won't happen again. There were cops with dogs outside the hall, going after the ticket scalpers. I really expect trouble only in Milwaukee or New York City. L.A. will be okay, we'll be at the Forum out in Inglewood. But in Milwaukee, the Stones and Pink Floyd are the only groups they're allowing in there this year. Some damn retired cop up there has announced that he's gonna be out there taking pictures of kids pissing on lawns and smoking dope. The kids'll take his camera away. I told that detective here that we'd beat his ass on this case, but we decided to compromise to avoid a hassle. It's a matter of being rebellious or giving in a little. In Arkansas, the legislature tried to outlaw rock and roll in the whole damned state. So I'm the straight man on the tour. Groups like this need someone who can deal with the local authorities. I don't agree with them always, but, hell, it is their town."

After a final toast, Carter was off to sleep, so he could spring up energized in the morn to fend off foes of the Stones.

I wandered through the lobby. When he had said, "It is their town," that struck a chord in me. This was almost my town. I had moved only eight months earlier from Austin, Texas, to New York City. And Austin and San Antonio are so close (in Texas freeway terms, under an hour apart) that I saw many old friends. Some reacted strangely, seeing me for the first time on the Other Side, backstage, with Stones Access. I discovered quickly who the *arrivistas* were, the social climbers eager to leapfrog off my back to what they thought was the exalted circle of rock royalty. And I found out who the people were who were genuinely glad to see me cross that physically miniscule but professionally enormous barrier between non-Access and Stones Access. And I quickly learned the limits of what that Stones Access meant. In San Antone, I saw a friend from years past, who was apparently drunk or stoned, trying to get backstage. Cops grabbed him and he foolishly fought back and they clubbed him down into the concrete. As I ran to his aid, I was brought up short by one of the Stones' big and burly bodyguards. "Don't even try it," he told me quietly, as he held me back. "There ain't nothing you can do. You'll just get it, too." True enough. But sad.

Life up on the eighteenth floor at the Hilton was a merry round, it seemed. I could have sold my room key for: a) a pound of finest uncut cocaine fresh from Colombia; b) as many Thai sticks as I wanted air-freighted in overnight from Hawaii; c) fifteen-year-old girls or sixteen-year-old girls; d) anything. But sleep. The Hilton lobby was crammed with every teenaged girl in the world and each and every one of them had exhausted the resources of her makeup larder and was spangling and spar-kling and off-the-shouldered and slit-skirted and glossy-lipped and heavy-lidded and high-cheeked and reeking of essence of "Yes, I am available." Remember, you can't get on that elevator to the Stones' floor—number eighteen—without a room key for eighteen. So the auction action around the elevators was furious indeed. I had to—unfortunately—fight my way through the flesh pile to get up to my room—"Sorry, ladies, I'm a cop"— but there was still merriment aplenty on eighteen. Lots of dim lights, thick smoke, and loud music.

And people wandering up and down the hallways. I meet Keith Rich-ards and Ron Wood and they invite me in for a quick visit. In Keith's room, distinguished only by the fact that he has draped his usual Mediter-ranean scarves across all the lamps to give a San Antonio Hilton room a certain Tangier atmosphere—aided by the aroma of foreign fragrances—I do my best not to endear myself to the lead guitarist of the Rolling Stones by accidentally kicking his beautiful National Steel guitar, on the floor there. It rings beautifully. I apologize profusely. He just laughs, Keith does, and pours us all oversized shots of Rebel Yell. We scatter across the beds and chairs. "How was it tonight?" I venture after we all light ciga-rettes and knock back a little Rebel Yell.

Ron Wood leans up on an elbow and says, "Against all odds, it was coming on tonight, much better than Baton Rouge. Because now I'm becoming better acquainted with the show. Keith was really aggressive, too."

Keith, in his dry, pointed voice (he sounds more like William Buck-ley, Jr., than any other rock star and I'll stake ten dollars on that), says, "At the end of 'Jumping Jack Flash' tonight, my cords went out; every-thing was cracking up tonight. I blew an amp right at the beginning. Those things can throw you and also tend to throw the people who are working with you, the roadies and so on."

Ron Wood reached for the bottle and said, "Yeah, they end up kick-ing everything over."

I asked, "Isn't this the first time you're doing two-hour shows?"

Keith borrowed a Dunhill from me and lit up and answered: "We're doing some newer songs and if we want to still give them a few of the older favorites and still get our chops in on the new ones, then it's necessary to give longer shows so we don't do the same show every time, just so we can put a few new songs in."

"Are these," I asked, "songs from the Munich sessions?"

Keith said, "We will probably be doing those as we do some live recordings later on; we'll be doing some of them."

Wood: "In L.A. and New York, especially."

Keith: "We've got something special lined up there."

Me: "These two-hour shows tire you out, now that you're 'old men'?"

Keith reaches for the bottle and says, "No, it hasn't seemed to and I'm really surprised. Baton Rouge was two two-hour shows the same day."

"Yeah," Wood said, "and I've never done that before and that just went by and we thought that—"

Keith cut in on him: "And since everybody was keeping up and since we take that little break with Billy's [Preston] thing, it surprises us. Everyone's saying, 'Let's cut this down' or 'Try this' and even today we were supposed to leave out 'It's Only Rock & Roll' and—"

Wood says, in astonishment, "That's right, we left that out!"

"Why did you change that song order?" I asked.

"Well," Keith said, "we decided that 'Midnight Rambler' wasn't really a good ending. You can never tell what will work onstage. 'Honky Tonk Women' was like that for a long time. You can never tell how long it takes to get something from the record to live playing. Sometimes we fiddle around, like with 'Wild Horses.' We must've fiddled around with that for four or five years before putting it into a show."

We talk for a while about how Keith and Ron work out who plays what, lead or rhythm.

I ask, "Have you two worked out leads and rhythms?"

Keith says, "No, I just keep playing my bits and Ron works in." [Go figure, says Keith's expression.]

Ron: "It's terrible, see, to get a plan as two guitarists. Maybe it would work great and maybe it would take us too far away from the band. I've never done much with the band except one silly morning when we stayed up. I mean, I play rhythm when he plays lead and the same for Keith!"

"Yeah," Keith says in the early morning San Antonio light, "rhythm and lead are blurred because it gets past that. Someone strumming away in the background and someone else doing all the playing, it's past that. We're just playing with each other and just clicking in together."

"So," I say, "the Stones are a guitar band again?"

"Really," Keith says affirmatively, with a palpable sigh of relief.

"We've been planning it like that," Ron Wood tells me, none too convincingly.

I ask Keith to compare Ron Wood with Mick Taylor or Brian Jones. Keith backed and filled for a moment. "There isn't any way, really. They're so totally different. Brian was different from Mick Taylor and Ronnie's so different from Mick it's impossible to compare. I mean, you can't . . ."

Wood: "I feel a lot in common with both of them. I mean, sometimes when I'm playing a number, I'll just say, 'Yeh, this is a Mick Taylor line,' which is so necessary sometimes, otherwise, I'll just play one of me own. And other times I have to play what Brian played." Ron gets uncomfortable and Keith seems to take over for him.

"Yes," Keith says, "he has to decide how much he's gonna use of what our people have played and how much of himself."

"It's quite a good experience," Wood says, "because I never really know until we're actually onstage. Because we can't get that same fever pitch, right, when we're just messing about."

"Well," I ask, "what if you had to play 'It's All Over Now' right now?"

"I would play Brian's part without even thinking about it," Wood said.

"Well," I ask, "what about horns? Especially since you could use horns on some numbers for a bit of extra push."

Keith was concerned about that. First, he located a bottle of Jose Cuervo Gold tequila for us to share. "I've found experimenting with horns —I really enjoyed working with them, especially after listening to all these tunes live. I think, seriously, to keep a band together with a horn section you basically have to be a brass person. Because if you're just sort of tacking them onto a band that's already formed—unless you keep on it, someone has to lead these people, keep them together, and if you're not really a brass person, if you're a guitarist like me? Well, I don't think of the brass. I think they're gonna keep themselves together and then when I listen to them halfway through a song, I realize there isn't anyone looking after them, there isn't any discipline. Now, I'm not a brass person. I can't tell them what to do and there isn't any leader amongst them and so they just carry on in their own sweet way until somebody realizes there's something wrong. That's what I've found. We found that we really couldn't discipline brass. So we thought we'd use percussion."

Keith busied himself pouring fresh drinks for all. We talked for a while about things that undoubtedly would not interest you, things such as song selection and order, the desirability of older songs over newer ones, Mick Jagger's guitar playing, the relative qualities of Rebel Yell and Jack Daniel's, trivia such as that.

"How do you," I asked Keith, "write songs with Mick?"

He answered seriously: "There's no procedure, really, or formulas. It can work in a wide variety of ways."

Wood added, "I've seen songs that I'd thought were a Jagger/Richards thing that Keith had completely written—and the other way around."

"Exactly," Keith said smoothly. "Some songs are completely written by one person. With others, the music is written by me and maybe the words to the chorus, which would also include the title of the song. And Mick would write the verses to fit in with the general thing I've got already. Other songs are really two completely different songs stuck together. You've got something that I wrote and something he wrote which are completely different, but you put them together and it's whole. And you've written half a song each."

Till Keith hushed him up, Wood started talking about how "It's Only Rock and Roll (But I Like It)" had been presented to Keith in the form of a very rough demo tape recorded by Wood, Jagger, and David Bowie.

More drinks and more small talk.

"How well can you guys hear each other onstage?" I asked.

"We were just wondering about that tonight," Keith said. "If everything's working well, the general idea is that you should be able to hear what you want to hear onstage. That's what you work for. You usually find that everyone wants to hear something different. Charlie wants to hear me, I don't care what I hear as long as I hear something, Mick needs to hear drums and me and himself, Preston wants to hear me and Mick and drums and himself. And the bass just wants to hear the drums. Basically, I just hear myself because those amps are very directional. If you move just six inches to one side, then I can hear the drums."

"I had to stand right in front of Charlie tonight to hear him," Wood said.

"If we can hear the drums," Keith said, "hear the rhythm, that's it. If you're sure of what you want to play on this number and you know what other people will play because you've heard it in rehearsal, then as long as you can hear—you know what you need to hear from that song in order to be able to play it properly. It doesn't matter too much what other people are doing as long as you know what they are supposed to be doing. I don't think you're compromising anything by not hearing it all, although that would be nice. The halls are a problem. We always end up playing in something that was built for something else. Football's got a huge audience and they've got big stadiums. Ballet has a huge audience and they've got places. Why haven't they got a bleedin' rock and roll convention center? Basically, I guess, because nobody can make up their minds about what's the ideal place to play rock and roll."

"Is there," I asked, "such a place?"

"Oh yeah!" Keith sounded excited for once. "It holds about five hundred people. Basically, that's what these concerts are about: how successfully you can translate the band playing in a little room and put that on, on a large scale. A few years ago, when we first used to come into America, what you heard was what we were because we were in total control of the sound. You went into a hall and sang; the singer sang through boxes on the wall. Now you're in the hands of these PA [public address] tyrants, these dictators of the mixing board and these cats will give you a sound that approximates a takeoff to the moon. These are the people who will give you a cassette of 'Honky Tonk Women' without any guitar on it. So if we're no longer in control of our sound, totally relying on this guy who we've just met and is mixing our sound—" He stopped to compose himself and stifle his anger at people who have controlled—for better or for worse—the Stones' pipeline.

"Is there?" I asked, "a way to beat that?"

Keith said grimly, "The only way is to beat him first. Once you've done that, then you've got the system beat."

More drinks are poured. "Did Giorgio Saint Angelo really design all you guys' outfits, like the program says?" I asked.

Keith just harrumphed. "I never heard of this guy."

I tried to get back onto music. "Why have you dropped certain songs from the set, like 'Dance Little Sister'?"

Keith was relieved to talk about music again. "That was a purely technical reason. It's in a key that means another guitar change and that's one of the things that slows the show down. What we're trying to avoid is getting into the same rut that most bands get into, which we usually get into by starting a tour off and after the first ten days or so whittling it down to the numbers that you know you're playing best and then playing it safe from there on. Whittling it down until you've got a really streamlined piece of show business and you know exactly what's gonna happen for the next two months. We're trying to avoid that, even if it means that a few of the shows are sloppier."

More talk about how to pace a show and a tour. Outside this room, in the frenzied Hilton hallways and down in the out-of-control hotel lobby, there were untold numbers of Stones fanatics who would literally give anything to penetrate this Stones sanctuary. Keith was saying, in his dry, dispassionate voice, that "The reason it's such a long show is that we want to keep doing a few new songs each night."

I asked Ron Wood, "What did you think when you were asked to join the Stones?"

Keith just laughed and said, "It was 'Will he or won't he?' "

"Right," Wood said. "The only way to do it was to give it no thought. I obviously took into consideration the rest of the boys and how they would feel. I couldn't just take off suddenly. I had a word with each of them [Rod Stewart's band, the Faces, to which Wood was supposedly wedded] individually. Once that was over, bang! I just came!"

For some reason, since it was very late in the night—or very early in the morning, depending on your orientation—there was a lapse or something for a while there in Keith's suite. You might say that we lost the picture there briefly. And the sound, as well.

After a bit, Keith was talking again, for some reason, about the Stones' South American tour. "That may be delayed," he said. "One of the reasons for this tour, apart from not playing the usual places, was to try to get rock and roll off the same old beaten track and take it to—"

"To Caracas and all that thing—" Ron Wood interrupted him.

"We do get requests all the time," Keith said, "from promoters and everybody. But nobody actually goes there and does it. To do even a ten-gig tour in South America would take months. Just to move the equipment and set up the stage. Plus, the Latin temperament. Every time some guy picks up a hammer, it's siesta time already."

Keith was pacing back and forth and obviously wearying of being questioned. I threw one final question at him: "Will you do a solo album?"

He laughed and sat down for a final drink. "I'm not interested in that right now. I don't really see that I could do anything on my own that would add anything. I mean, anything that I want to do, I can do with the band I've got."

After many drunken handshakes and exchanges of phone numbers and expressions of mutual regard, I finally took my leave of Keith Richards and Ron Wood.

Out in the hallway, a man wearing a white terry bathrobe and an extremely dour expression brushed against me as I walked to my room. It was Mick Jagger.

An excerpt from the Rolling Stones tour newsletter for Thursday, June 5, 1975: "Memo from Alice Cooper and Dave Libert: 'We want to thank you for your hospitality and we also consider it a great honor that you have chosen to feature an exact replica of Freddie Sessler's pecker as part of the show. We sincerely hope you have an opportunity to visit our show and observe our new star-shaped stage, for which Peter Rudge sold us the blueprints at a very reasonable rate. Thanks again. Alice Cooper.' "

4 Kansas City

Mick Jagger was totally depressed when I ran into him in Kansas City in the gloomy bowels of the Sheraton-Royal Hotel, hard by Arrowhead Stadium, where the Rolling Stones were due in a few hours to entertain a sold-out crowd. It was maybe five in the morning and the Stones' rehearsals, down here in the Sheraton's netherworld, kept breaking down. They sounded like crap and they knew it and, what was worse, they didn't know what to do about it. Everybody in the band was all screwed up, for one reason or another, and here it was, only the third city of their big comeback tour of 1975. I had a tentative appointment to interview Mick at 4:00 A.M., maybe—as with any traveling rock and roll band (and especially so with the Stones), there are no hard and fast realities and I never knew from one day to the next whether the damn band would even stay together, much less be lucid enough to provide good copy. Mick had said he wanted to talk, though. He finally came out through the big double doors of the banquet hall where the Stones were trying to rehearse—hell, he was almost driven out of the hall by the massive, metallic wall of noise coming from Keith's and Woody's guitars (dive bombers out of control; bursts of flak all around)—and apologized to me for the press ban on the rehearsal. Things were tough all around, he said. "It'll get better," he said, with a wry smile, as he sat down heavily on a Naugahyde carousel of a couch in the grim hallway. He rubbed his eyes; he looked incredibly tired. We traded small talk for a bit about the tour. It was obvious, though, that he was not up for a full-blown interview and he and I both knew it. Taking a large chance, I said, "This ain't working. Why don't you call me when things are a little looser? I'm in the hotel." By then, for some arcane reason, Mick was down on his hands and knees on the institutional green carpet and facing the doors of the rehearsal/banquet hall. "Sure," he said. After a bit of studying the rehearsal/banquet hall, he said, "Man, the fans don't even want to hear what we did on our last album. Why would they want to hear what we haven't even put out yet?"

Mick Jagger's stage outfits on this "Tour of the Americas '75," you will be happy to hear, were designed by Giorgio Saint Angelo. His red sleeveless jumpsuit, trimmed in black, with a reversible yellow and black jacket and a red and black battle jacket cost $1,100. The white Lycra bodysuit with the green stretch pants and the white kimono cost $1,100. Another $1,100 for a satin jacket, green sweat jacket, green pants, and red wrap vest. Also $1,100 for this outfit: black pants, red and black body shirt, red and black kimono coat. And $1,100 for this one: blue safari jacket and pants; sleeveless, reversible red and green vest. And $1,100 more for the white overalls, shirt jacket, and kimono over jacket. And $1,100 for the black cotton tie pants, leather vest, black leather belt, and black cotton shirt. And $1,944 for an embroidered lavender stretch top with rhinestones and gold metal and black velvet stretch pants. Two thousand dollars for an embroidered and hand-painted red and white top with red pants. Two thousand dollars for navy and burgundy and silver Lycra pants and top. Eleven hundred dollars for beige and gray muslin shirt and pants and red hip cummerbund. Eleven hundred for red pants and a "sheer" green chiffon shirt and a black leather vest. Two hundred and fifty for a Lycra jumpsuit with ribbon trimmings. Plus the likes of two trimmed T-shirts at seventy-five bucks per. And Mick was depressed. Maybe he was depressed over his wardrobe. Maybe all he needed was to go out shopping.

Before the Stones left San Antonio for Kansas City, they stopped to pay tribute to the proud Americans who had died at the Alamo and to see the Alamo and mainly to pose for pictures in front of the Alamo. I made the mistake of going with them. It turned out that the reason for the Alamo stop was the fact that the London *Daily Mirror* had paid the Stones four thousand pounds for an exclusive picture session at the Alamo. The *Daily Mirror* photographer had brought big cartons of props, from which the bored Stones began plucking things. Keith Richards grabbed Confederate flags and started to stuff them into the crotch of his jeans. Ron Wood did the same with the Texas flags. The *Daily Mirror* guy, ecstatic with the stuff he was getting, yelled at para-Stones musicians Billy Preston and Ollie Brown to get the hell out of the picture; he just wanted the real bleeping Rolling Stones. What he didn't count upon was that, once bassist Bill Wyman heard that, he decided to leave, too, after the first pictures. It was not a pretty scene: Ugly Brits abroad, rich rock stars being paid to cavort in front of an American shrine that they obviously didn't know anything about. I said to Tour Commander Peter Rudge, "You just set back Anglo-American relations by a hundred years." He just laughed: The Stones had their photo opportunity and that was all that mattered. *Time* magazine, in fact, ran a picture as the lead item of its

"People" page in the June 23, 1975, issue. The accompanying text, as is *Time*'s wont, was glib and cute and insubstantial and meaningless: "Although they will play to 1.5 million fans during their three-month tour of the Americas, Mick Jagger and the Rolling Stones are only tourists in some places. After two performances at the San Antonio Convention Center, the British rock megastars decided to pose for pictures at a famous Texas landmark. As they gathered together near a wooden door, it suddenly opened and a woman in her sixties emerged. 'Would you mind not leaning against the door?' she snapped. 'You're blocking our way to the Alamo.' Jagger and company stepped aside and regrouped for their photo, then headed for their next concert in Kansas City. 'I don't know what it is or where it is,' joked Jagger of the Alamo later, 'but we'll never play it again.' " Very slick of *Time*. The only problem is that it is also wrong. That incident didn't happen. I was curious about it, since I had been at the Alamo at the time and I knew that no one from *Time* magazine had been there. I later looked up the *Time* correspondent's file on which the item had been based. It had been sent to *Time* in New York City from a Boston-based *Time* correspondent eight days after the Stones had posed at the Alamo. The correspondent's file was even more vague and lacking in detail than was *Time*'s "People" page entry. It read, in part: "Before they hopped on a plane to meet their next engagement in Kansas City, they wanted to see the Alamo. It was a quick stop—just a few minutes to snoop around and pose for a couple of pictures. As they were posing against a wooden door outside one of the Alamo buildings, the door opened and a woman in her sixties, oblivious to whom she was speaking, said, 'Would you mind not leaning against the door? You're blocking our way to the Alamo.' Mick's reaction to the Alamo when he was asked was somewhat obscure. 'Oh, I don't know what it is or where it was, but we'll never play it again. The sound was awful. It wasn't even on the iternary [sic] and I hate daytime shows anyway.' "

Where did all this "somewhat obscure" information come from? From Somewhat Obscure Information Central, as far as I can tell. This was not a big deal, but—not to make too fine a point of it—I can certainly appreciate some of the Stones' acute paranoia regarding the press.

When Karen Durbin asked me into her hotel room one night after a Stones concert, I heard that several of the Stones staff women chortled: They were sure that "something" was going on there that confirmed all their darkest suspicions. I began to suspect that she represented something of a threat. A few days before, a "highly placed" Stones staff woman had even drawn me aside to advise me to chart a course away from this Durbin woman. "All she has is a cupcake body," I was told in no uncertain terms.

Well. After a few days on the tour, all I could tell was that Karen Durbin was smarter than most of the Stones women, more knowledgeable musically, and more aware of what this tour actually meant. She was also better-looking, too, on top of that and in addition to That.

Durbin was covering the tour for *The Village Voice* and was, as far as I knew, the first woman writer to really hit a Stones tour in a gut bucket, locker room sort of way. Or any rock and roll tour in something other than a fan magazine hum job or a "Gee whiz, look at these freaks" approach for a "real" publication. As a realist, in other words.

So she asked me into her room to talk and to have a glass of wine. I had already told her that I was happily married, was on this tour strictly to work, and had no interest in cupcake rumors. She was happy to hear that. Durbin is a stone feminist; I am a fierce independent. Our common ground was that we both loved the Rolling Stones' music and what it evoked in our lives. She was catching flak from fellow feminists for not condemning the Stones across the board as totally worthless cocks of the walk.

"There is more to the music than that," she said, "and it's sometimes hard to articulate it."

"Remember," I said, "when Bianca tore into Mick for wasting his life with this worthless rock shit? And he retaliated by writing 'It's Only Rock and Roll (But I Like It)'?"

(This was, of course, before Mick slagged Bianca as "the easiest lay on the White House lawn" after her much-publicized "meeting" with President Gerald Ford's son, Jack.)

She agreed: "It's only rock and roll."

She joked that many feminists' fantasies were that either they didn't go to bed with Mick and then regretted it or that they did go to bed with Mick and then really regretted it. She said that she herself had problems reconciling her love for the Stones' music with her feminism. And with the sexuality the Stones conjured up.

"Chet," Durbin said to me in the early morning hours, very earnestly, in her hotel room (which I suspect was watched closely by Stones women), "Chet, I think that Keith would get you into a room and then . . . and then . . . and then do things to you." The way she almost whispered the word "things" rendered me speechless.

(Note: Karen Durbin went back to New York, worked without sleep to meet her *Village Voice* deadline, and wrote a very good article. As a reward, then-*Voice* editor Clay Felker sent her a huge bouquet of roses. Instead of a pat on the head.)

Life on the road: What do you do in the predawn hours in the gray tunnels of a hotel in Kansas City when Mick Jagger's just blown an interview with you that you must have to meet your deadline (and thus keep your job)? And you think maybe you'll nail Jagger sometime the next day (hell, check the clock; later today, you mean), but who knows, especially given the competition? Six in the morning; everything closed down as tight as Mick's lips. You don't dare leave the hotel, ever, because—sure as hell, if you do—you'll miss The Call. That's the one phone call that will plug you right into the middle of things and means that you either have a story or you have a desk to clean out when you get back to the office. So you trudge back to the Room, the Willy Loman Memorial Module, that seems to follow you around the country, like part of some Bed 'n' Barf Motel chain, where looming dust balls and vaguely sinister stains are franchised along with the greasy bedspread and the Sano strip on the toilet seat. You doze fitfully and wait for The Call, knock wood and hope it comes (if there is any real wood in this module).

And maybe fan through your pages of notes, hoping to find an overlooked morsel. But what do you do with something as opaque as this, for example: "SA hotel. Keith & Ron departure for Reed's Red Derby delayed when 2 weird guys show up. Door closes. They emerge. Ron sez see ya later. Keith turns to me & sez wanta come along?" Or how about this gem: "From some angles, Mick is beginning to strongly resemble Carol Burnett." What? Did I actually write that? If so, why? Under what circumstances? In what condition? Was Carol Burnett actually there, for purposes of comparison? Was I actually hoping for Mary Tyler Moore, instead? Is Rudge or Wasserman sneaking into my room and writing this gibberish in my notebooks?

It is matters such as this that keep you miserably awake at dawn in Kansas City, while waiting for TV programming to resume (in those precable days). And searching through your bags for a bit of a leftover Nestlé's Crunch or even some airline peanuts—anything, please—to stifle the hunger pangs while you wait for room service to kick-start its fitful way back to life and start thawing those rubber scrambled eggs with cardboard toast.

Ah, here's another note, a forgotten item scrawled on a matchbook cover from Antoine's, in New Orleans, just a few days earlier. It reads: "Mick is in a totally foul humor after Bianca tells Geraldo [Rivera, on the program 'Good Night America'] that Mick does not think a lot of women." Well, what about this? Maybe Mick was mad because he thought Bianca meant that he does not think about a whole lot of women. Or about all women, maybe. Or perhaps Bianca meant to say, before she was likely cut off by that wordy Geraldo, "Mick does not think a lot of women can play middle linebacker for the Dallas Cowboys." Maybe she was saying, "Mick does not think a lot of women should be shoveling cow manure down in the K.C. stockyards." Or she might have said, "Mick does not think, a lot of women experts are willing to testify under oath." Or Bianca, that sly fox, might have said, "Mick does not, think a lot of women who should know." She could have said, "Mick does, not think, a lot of women gratefully say who belong to the Satisfied Stones Veterans." So who's to say? Not me because we'll never know about this one. Because, as you wrestle with dawn there in the Sheraton in Kansas City, the Stones newsletter for the day is whisked underneath your door. A brusque, half-page, photo-copied memo, it tells everyone on the tour where to go and when for that day. It also includes a short item that says much about Bianca and Mick. It was just a one-liner that said, "Farewell to Mrs. Benz. See you in New York." That needs some translation: All the Stones register under assumed names in hotels. So far, on this tour, Mick and Bianca had been "Mr. and Mrs. Benz" (no "Mercedes" as a first name, as far as I know). Bianca, after being virtually invisible on the tour (she did do Mick's makeup in San Antonio), had flown the coop for Manhattan, where she was the star.

So you drift in and out of sleep, careful to not drift so far in that your senses are not attuned to the sound of a ringing phone—especially not so far in that you dream that the phone rings and you dream that you answer it and you dream that you carry on what seems to be a sparkling, brilliant, bright, quotable, and eminently printable interview with The Star. And everything's rosy until you wake up twelve hours later and discover that the tour has left you behind. And you dreamed it all. I know poor wretches that has happened to.

There it is, finally. The phone ringing with a reassuring firmness to its tone. No wrong number, this. It is, in fact, Mr. Benz, calling with a cheerful invitation to drop by his room soonest. It is 1:00 P.M.

I went to his room. It was just like my module, down to the same imitation lithograph of a duck in flight, except that his module was the sitting room of a suite, so it had no bed in it. Jagger was padding around in a blue and white polka-dot bathrobe, just exuding charm and warmth. Quite unlike our almost nonsensical encounter a few hours earlier and a few hotel floors away. He flashed the dazzling, designed-to-win-over-anybody Jagger smile, with the diamond in the incisor catching a ray of sunlight and beaming it right back, as he busied himself pouring coffee for both of us. I was surprised to see the beginnings of crow's-feet around his eyes, especially since he and I are the same age and I certainly was not seeing any such effects of adulthood—at least not in my mirror. We sat down at a table by the window and drank our coffee and talked about everything and nothing for a while. Jagger's reputation as a charmer and disarmer is well earned, I found. If ever there was a public figure who can give you a quick read and then tell you—in the most charming way—exactly what you want to hear, Mick Jagger is the guy. (Up to a point, more about which later.) You murmur something to him about his isolation as a superstar and you immediately get perfectly formed paragraphs on the loneliness of the long-distance lead singer. Delivered to you in such a tone of utter sincerity and confidence that you are absolutely certain that Mick has never, ever, before bared his soul to anyone as he has to you just now. Never mind that you never wonder why Mr. Rolling Stone would suddenly tell all to some jerkola reporter he hardly knew. It's because you're so special, you feel, basking in the superheat of his glowing presence.

"Yes," he sighed, "when the fans start closing in, you just hide away." What a revelation. "It affects your private life, yeah, so that you sometimes get a bit paranoid and you don't feel like having to face anything. Sometimes it gets to be a bit much. I just try to disappear into the wallpaper." Just breathtaking. I nodded sagely and reached for my china cup of room service coffee and listened to the world's most famous rock star virtually try to dictate a room service interview. The stage? Oh yeah, let me tell you about the design, et cetera. Why does it seem as if we won't play South America after all? Well, that's a good question and it has to do with logistics and geography and so let me tell you all about it. And let me tell you about the twenty-foot back elevator we were originally going to put in the stage. Finally, just as he seemed about to bore even himself to sleep, room service finally arrived with Mick's breakfast. As the waiter uncovered Mick's lukewarm eggs and soggy toast, Mick got up and looked out the window, his hands clasped behind him.

"It's really flat here and green," he finally said. "I thought I'd go out for a walk later before the show."

He sat down and started on the eggs and I suddenly caught a sidelong glance, in which I—rightly or wrongly—read messages of simultaneous disdain and dare. He seemed to be saying: If you treat me like a superstar, then I'll react like one, so what about it?

The proverbial light bulb winked on above my head. So that was the game! All right! Cut the crap!

"So, Mick," I said, "when you let the San Antone cops lock up your cock this week, what did that do to the rebellious tradition of the Stones? Wasn't that compromising your history?"

He pushed back his plate and smiled, obviously relieved that I had figured out what his game was. "Well, yeah," he said, pouring us both more coffee. "Cream? Sugar? Yeah, I just thought that, practically, in the long run it'd be better if we didn't use it because if we did and then we got arrested, we wouldn't be able to use the fucking thing at all any more. They [police] would be waiting for us everywhere. This way, they won't know about it. I mean, it'll be of minimal proportions. The cock has now reached minimal proportions." He winked and continued, "Rather than if we'd said, 'Oh fuck 'em,' you know. I thought of doing that. Of course I did. But you know what they can be like, especially in Texas, and I didn't fancy spending the night in some jail somewhere or hassling or paying out money. You always have to pay out $15,000 or so, you know, in legal fees. It's more trouble. Anyway, we haven't decided to use it every night."

"Will that," I asked, "hurt you with the staunch Stones fans who identify with the street fighting man image?"

"Ah," he said after a pause, "yeah, we've always had trouble with the police, even where they try to come onstage and stop the show. You just have to realize where you are and whether it's really worth it. I wanted to use the thing again and I knew what would happen if we got arrested for using it: We couldn't use it again. It's not so much a compromise, it's just being a bit more farsighted, rather than going in and banging your head against a brick wall. That would be a drag. You know these towns like Cleveland and Milwaukee."

"Why do you think some people are so afraid of the Stones' image?"

"That's just . . . that's just"—he gestured angrily—"just people who don't know you, so how can they get that opinion of you? Oh, I guess just by reading about you and listening to the records. So they get their image of you that way."

"Do you think that people still hold on to the 'Prince of Darkness' image and the whole 'Sympathy for the Devil' thing?"

"Oh yeah." He grinned his crinkly grin. "We may put that song back into the show. That will be part of one's makeup again. I mean, that was an unintentional role."

"Did you see," I asked, "that biker girl throw the belt to you or at you in San Antonio?"

"Yeah, ah, yeah."

"Did that make you apprehensive, that close proximity to the stage and that worked-up audience?"

Mick answered quickly, almost too quickly: "No. It's all right."

"Are you ever afraid onstage?"

"No," he said, looking away. "No, you shouldn't ever be afraid of it, but it is pretty scary sometimes." He fell silent, then stood up: "Want some more coffee?" That case was obviously closed. We talked about the general state of rock and roll (no better or worse than ever) and the future (who knows?) and this and that.

"How," I asked, "do you deal with aging as a rock star doing teenage songs. Pete Townshend of the Who talked incessantly of that and how he was going to have to stop doing teenage songs."

Mick just laughed. "But I never was a teenager. I don't remember doing any teenage songs, either. But I know what Pete means. But, then, he's got 'My Generation' to cope with. We don't have anything like that. We stopped doing 'Satisfaction' quite a long while ago."

"Well," I said, "is it easier for a Dylan to just get up and be a troubadour forever?"

"Maybe I can do that," Mick said. "It's not difficult to go onstage and just sing. As long as you can hold people. You don't have to dress up, really. It's not necessary."

"Do you think Elvis proved that?"

"Proved what?" Mick asked sharply. "I saw him on the TV last night. I thought it was awful. I'd never seen Elvis before. But, I mean, it was just the crowd, where he was, and all that. I'd never seen him and I don't know. He's still going on. He's an example. But a lot of people think he's stupid, you know."

"Could that be why he doesn't give interviews and you do?"

Mick laughed. "Yeah. You'd say, 'Hey, Elvis, how come at the age of' —however old he is, he's quite old—'how come you still want to dress up in a silly suit and get onstage? At the fuckin' International Schlock Hotel in Las Vegas?' 'Wal,' drawled Elvis, 'it's the money and the fame.' " Mick dropped his mock-Elvis drawl and sat up straight. "Damn straight! That's what the guy does. He'd be lost if he couldn't do that. I think the same goes for most performers. I mean, why is Frank Sinatra still performing? Maybe he needs the money, I don't know. He can't need it that badly. But I would like to do without money as you get older. Leave the follies of our youth behind." He laughed.

"Can you get by on what you were making ten years ago?"

"Oh no! It probably costs me far more. I spend more on travel than I used to, since I don't live so much in one place any more. I'm not as domesticated as I used to be. By domesticated I mean, what I mean is, living in a house with a woman and all that, permanently settled in one place. That's domestication."

"Even between tours?"

Mick laughed. "I just keep going."

"So no dog and a fireplace for you?"

"I don't give a shit for that . . . How do you open this window? I fixed it last night so I could open it." After a brief struggle, the window succumbed and Mick continued. "I was talking to someone the other day about that it's not necessary any more, though it used to be, till very recently, to have Someone and a hearth and home. But that seems to get less important."

"What is important to you? Your work?"

Mick only giggled.

"Well, then, is a bar of candy important to you?"

Another giggle, then: "I don't think anything is really important to me, you know? Not really. I mean, not overwhelmingly."

"Possessions, cars?"

"Not really, no."

"Adulation of the masses?"

He seemed to grow serious. "That's a difficult thing, you know, because . . . because I've been living like this for so long that if I stop doing it, it's bound to affect me, you know."

"What does it feel like to have twenty thousand people directing all their energy at you? Overwhelming?"

"Yeah! It is. That must be why most of those people never give up performing. Because they just can't go on without that sort of rush."

"Is that, do you think, the most intense sort of feeling?"

"I suppose," Mick said. "It's a bit like having an orgasm. Sometimes an orgasm is better than being onstage; sometimes being onstage is better than an orgasm."

"Could you imagine that stage feeling still happening to at, say, age fifty?"

"Sure! Age is immaterial. It's weird. You can't get that same feeling from movies."

"Did you ever go see yourself in your movies?"

"No," he said, seeming to act modest. "I just didn't go. Kind of nervous about it, I guess."

"Will acting be the next thing for you, then?"

"Well, yeah, I'd like to try some more. I don't know how I'd get with it. You need a lot of push, you know, to get the right parts. You've got to want to be a movie star, you know. I'm not sure if I've got that relentless, ruthless ambition any more. To want to be a star. Because, I mean, it's hard, it's ruthless. I don't know if I want to do that."

He sounded as if he meant every word.

5 75 On and On

Surprisingly, the Kansas City show that sun-drenched afternoon in Arrow-head Stadium may well have been the musical high point of the 1975 tour. All the bickering and the musical arguments had been resolved at the all-night, boisterous rehearsal back at the Sheraton and the Stones came out roaring. The sound was crisp and clean and sharp and, from the moment—just at purple-tinged twilight—that Keith hit the first ominous notes of "Honky Tonk Women," the Stones had 53,231 friends dancing in the aisles. Backstage was relaxed: nothing but smiles and tubs of cold beer everywhere. After the storm trooper atmosphere in San Antonio, what a relief it was to see friendly, businesslike cops doing their jobs without wanting to hit someone on the head. Or wanting to lock up the whole band for singing "Starfucker" (a/k/a "Star Star"). Jagger kicked out the jams and delivered the goods, dancing like a dervish and bellowing like a bull. Under a sparkling sky, at 10:00 P.M., the Stones finished off song number twenty-three—a long show for them—and, with the notes of "Jumping Jack Flash" still ringing in the air, audience screams for yet another encore were drowned out by the rumble and flash of a fireworks exhibition overhead. A nice touch that Mick and Commander Rudge had decided to add. What an All-American afternoon. No fights, no trouble, no discernible "civil disorder." I lingered a while to watch the fireworks and then walked back to the Sheraton with a group of Kansas City teen-agers who wanted to share their one remaining joint, their few remaining beers, and their bubbling-over enthusiasm for what they had just wit-nessed. Hey, I don't mean to say that these were scrubbed-cheeked Young Republicans, but some worked for a living and some were still in school and they liked their goddamned Rolling Stones and if they wanted to smoke a joint and drink a beer, why should they get clubbed over the skull for it? I can tell you that I had absolutely no fear that they might throw me down by the side of the interstate there and cut my liver out and then pray to Satan while tinny Rolling Stones' "satanic anthems" struggled out of a $29.95 Sears cassette tape player. While municipal police departments around the country were gearing up to counter the menace of a Stones' invasion, these Kansas City teenagers reminded me of what those police departments most feared: kids having fun. That's all rock and roll was really about, really: Blow off some steam, dance, have a good time. That's what the K.C. police wisely recognized and the police knew that those 53,231 (a record for a music event at Arrowhead) Stones fans in the stadium would likely not be a problem if they were handled decently and not pushed to the wall. There were no major problems. Although trouble lay in wait down the road (Milwaukee, a perennial Stones' problem spot, was next and the city council there had approved by a margin of only one vote a Stones' appearance), K.C. was an emerald oasis of sanity, by look tour standards. Back at the Sheraton, a few dozen fans milled around the lobby good-naturedly, exhibiting the sort of mild euphoria that a high school football win induces.

Upstairs, I found the Stones in a suite, savoring their victory. There was a buffet table of cold cuts and potato salad and cold beer and wine and of course plenty of Jack Daniel's sour mash for Keith. There was also a palpable sense of genuine relief on everyone's part. It was exactly like a locker room after a football team finally does what it's capable of doing. Mick was like a man rejuvenated and he smiled a lot. Keith, relieved that Woody could finally carry his share of the load, grabbed a fifth of Black Jack and went off to do whatever it was he was doing behind closed doors. Woody was beaming with confidence and hugging everybody and trying to "buy" them a drink. Watts and Wyman, relieved that there was finally a guitar team out there to play in front of their unflappable, unshakable, incomparable rhythm, relaxed a bit and shot the shit with reporters. Wasserman and Rudge did not try to put the arm on reporters. Everything was very mild, I mean to say. Much calmer than the average traveling salesmen's cocktail session. No orgies. No drugs out in the open. Sort of—actually—boring after a bit. Life at the top of the rock and roll heap. Things are never what they seem.

So, I reflected on my way to tonight's Willy Loman Memorial Module (a pastrami sandwich and two bottles of Heineken firmly in hand, ripped off from the Stones), are these the lawless pirates and degenerates who are trying to subvert America's youth and undermine the U.S. of A., as I read in some papers? Or are these some journeymen musicians who are, thanks to their naïveté, almost broke and fighting for their survival as a band? And now victims of their own hype from the sixties—the bad boys of rock and roll was the image, the scruffy punks who kicked over baby carriages and were arrested for urinating in public and should probably be thrashed by any decent two-fisted man. Their reputation survived only too well: Cops dearly wanted to be known as the cops who finally busted the law-flaunting Rolling Stones. It was as if there was a bounty on their heads. Police departments knew that Mick's and Keith's visas were on waivers because of their history of drug arrests and the cops were just eagerly sniffing the air in anticipation of a historic bust. It would be the final payday of the whole sixties radical business; chickens finally coming home to roost for these arrogant, long-haired, short, doped-up, rich foreigners who only want to get high school football players onto hard drugs and then gang-fuck all the high school cheerleaders. Some cops were serious about all this stuff.

Later on the tour, the Stones heard that the Louisville, Kentucky, radio stations reported that the Louisville cops were boasting that they were going to bust the Stones when they played the coliseum there on August 4. Stones attorney Bill Carter went ahead to Louisville and discovered that, indeed, the Louisville police fully intended to bust the Stones and their Starship 707 the very minute it landed on Kentucky soil. So he and Rudge drew up a plan, the first step of which was to ensure that the Stones' plane would be totally clean, as in drug-free. And he devised two scenarios for the landing, since he had heard the main police goal was to bust and impound the airplane. He had a bus waiting on the runway, so that the Starship could land, disperse its famous passengers, and then immediately take off again. His alternative was a bus that was sort of hidden on a side ramp. The Starship landed and taxied up to the ramp, sort of blocking the police cars that sought immediate access to that ramp. The human cargo deplaned to the bus and then the plane taxied away. The cops elected to follow the bus to the coliseum. When the Stones finally gained their dressing room, forty narcotics agents gathered outside the door, ready for a massive bust. Massive Stones bodyguard Bob Bender and lawyer Carter stopped them from going into the dressing room: "Not without a warrant." There was a hostile standoff. Carter went and called the District Attorney's office—Secret Service experience does come in handy—and finally located the DA and told him, "Come out here right now. I'm ashamed of this police harassment. Come here and I'll take you into the Stones' dressing room and if there's anything illegal, you can bust 'em all if you want to." The DA hastened to the scene, posed for pictures with the Stones, and told the furious cops to get the hell out.

The Memphis vice squad had vowed to bust the Stones if they performed "Starfucker" (a/k/a "Star Star") on July 4, 1975, in Memorial Stadium. Our nation's birthday. Mick, tired of police threats, got his back up and told a raging, screaming Peter Rudge that he was gonna by God sing it and then see what happened when the rubble cleared. By God, Memphis cops in full riot regalia approached the stage. Attorney Carter told the commanding sergeant, "If you bust the Stones, these kids'll burn down this stadium and your city along with it. And the Stones will litigate you forever. These aren't some broke hippies. They will sue." Besides, he said, at least one Memphis radio station had been airing "Star Star." The commanding sergeant actually went to a phone to check that. It was so. So much for possible public obscenity charges. The helmeted cops backed away. Who knows what might have happened if they'd waded in with clubs swinging? Ain't it grand to see the power—or the positive power, that is—of rock and roll?

Fordyce was another matter entirely. Fordyce, to this day, is mainly an inside joke with Stones' insiders. For legal reasons, which should not surprise you. What sort of happened is that, after the Stones' above-mentioned Memphis show, Keith decided that he had to finally witness the South firsthand. The South that he had always fantasized about, ever since he discovered blues records and sat in England listening to scratchy 78s by Howlin' Wolf and Muddy Waters and Robert Johnson. If ever there was an authentic White British Negro, it is Keith. Blues is the only color he can see. He is ripe to see the South and he's confident that he can get down and be right with anybody he comes up against, black or white or red of neck or whatever. The odd thing is that he's right. The problem is that Keith has never really learned how to drive, at least well enough to escape state troopers in the South. Another problem is that Ron Wood, who knows about as much about the South as he does about Antarctica, decided to go with him, to absorb the soul and flavor of the South, along with a lot of Rebel Yell and Jack Daniel's and who knows what else. Keith announced his plan at the Memphis airport, as the Starship was about to sky off to Dallas for the next show there, on July 6, at the Cotton Bowl. Peter Rudge went crazy when Keith told him and Rudge's tantrum only reinforced Keith's desire to experience the real South. So he and Woody got a limo and security man Jim Callaghan was assigned to drive it and keep them out of trouble. Now, I have driven through Arkansas many times and I never ran across Fordyce and Keith is still not sure how he got there. It's way the hell off the interstate and it's deep in what might be charitably called "extremely conservative" territory, i.e., no white Negroes of any race are encouraged to even drive through the place. Boasts a population of over 4,000. Keith and Woody decided to stop there and get a burger, a real Southern burger. Kids at the burger joint, naturally, call their friends and say, "Hey, the Stones are here. No, man, *really.*" So a crowd of maybe seventy-five gathers at this drive-in. The cop on duty hears about it and eases his cruiser up, just off the highway, just below the drive-in's entrance. When Callaghan pulls the limo onto the asphalt of the highway from the loose gravel of the drive-in's lot, the wheels of the limo spin and burn rubber before grabbing the road. Here comes the siren.

Cop car pulls them over. Cop later says that he smelled dope and that there were enormous clouds of smoke rolling out of the car, which cop said was sufficient reason to stop and search the car.

NEWS BULLETINS: From the New York *Times* of July 7, 1975: "FORDYCE, Ark., July 6 (AP)—The British rock guitarist Keith Richards of the Rolling Stones was free on $162 bond today after being charged with reckless driving and illegal possession of a knife, police officials said." From the New York *Post* of July 7, 1975: "Driving in a rented car to perform at the Cotton Bowl in Dallas, Keith Richards and Ron Wood of the Rolling Stones and two companions were stopped by police in Fordyce, Ark., Saturday night. Held for seven hours on charges of reckless driving and carrying a concealed dagger, lead guitarist Richards was released on $162.75 bail. Guitarist Wood, newest member of the Stones, and James Callaghan, a security guard, were not charged. But a California man named Fred Sessler, who had hitched a ride, was charged with possession of cocaine and released on $5,000 bail. The other touring Stones—vocalist Mick Jagger, drummer Charlie Watts and bass guitarist Bill Wyman—flew without incident from Memphis to Dallas, where the group entertained some 50,000 fans last night."

About this guy Fred Sessler: Remarkable, isn't it, how he is mentioned in a June 5 Stones newsletter in San Antonio and then miraculously turns up hitching a ride with Keith and Ron a month later, on July 5, on a back road in Arkansas? And this Fred Sessler was charged with possession of cocaine? Well, I don't see any pattern here. Do you?

There was one arrhythmic incident, if you will: Keith and Ron and Jim and "hitchhiker" Fred were busted at about 3:00 in the afternoon in Fordyce, which is really, to be charitable, way back in the sticks. At 5:30 that afternoon, an NBC-TV crew from Dallas hit Fordyce. Who told them? By 5:30 P.M., young people began gathering at the tiny one-story jail where Keith and Ron and Jim and the hitchhiker were held. State police were called in when the crowd started to reach unmanageable proportions: The news was on the radio and kids everywhere with nothing better to do headed for Fordyce, where the action was. The state police put up roadblocks when the crowd outside the jail seemed to eclipse the population of Fordyce: more than 4,000, that is. It started to look like the mob scenes in the *Frankenstein* movie when the townspeople decided to take matters into their own hands. It got pretty tense.

Attorney Carter had been having lunch in West Memphis when he got the beeper news that his clients had been thrown under the jail down in south Arkansas. He chartered a plane and got there after the TV crew did. How *did* those TV people get tipped off? Carter called Mike Crowley of the Stones' staff and had him charter a plane into Fordyce and had him carry the Rolling Stones' little black bag with $50,000 in cash in it, in case the bail was excessive. It was imperative to get Keith out of south Arkansas and out of jail, after all. Carter called his law partner Kathy Woods in Little Rock, Arkansas, and had her charter a Kingair round-trip to Fordyce —with no questions asked—and to keep it on the runway in Fordyce with the engines running for as long as was necessary. Things in Fordyce's courtroom became very heated—there was at least one fistfight between city officials over how best to administer justice to these captive Rolling Stones and one official sent out for a bottle of spirits before the spirits stores closed and the Stones were not at all sure that they would ever leave Fordyce. Testimony indicated that a crowbar was used to break into the trunk of the Stones' limo and thus produce the alleged cocaine. No warrant or reasonable search there, it seemed. Still, it was Fordyce, Arkansas, and the rules went with the territory. No guarantees of anything. It was a good thing that Peter Rudge wasn't able to get there and throw one of his proper British tantrums and get everyone locked away for a good long spell.

After Carter argued illegal search and seizure and especially after the crowd outside became a force to really be concerned with, everyone was set loose. Keith posted his bail of $162.75 (charges against him were later dropped). No one provided details on how Fred "the hitchhiker" Sessler made his $5,000 bail. It was certainly a miracle of random chance, how often this man Sessler's path continued to cross that of the Stones.

Because of the crowds, the state police had to escort the Stones to the airstrip. Fred Sessler, the "hitchhiker," held a whiskey bottle out the car window as a victory symbol. On the Kingair, Kathy Woods had bottles of Jack Daniel's Black Label waiting for Keith and Ron as the plane gunned its way airborne out of the darkness. Keith had finally discovered the real South. Keith's knife is still hanging on a plaque in the courtroom in Fordyce, Arkansas, along with a picture of the judge posing with Woody and Keith. And wearing the biggest smile a Southern judge ever exhibited.

The Stones survived their two big challenges: The cops were unable to get them and they proved they were still the biggest draw on the road. And were still, after all these years, front-page news in every town they hit. The Stones continue to enjoy a bizarre relationship with the press. More so than with any other rock and roll band, they inflame passions all across the political spectrum, ever since their calculated "Would you let your daughter marry a Rolling Stone?" campaign back at the beginning. The Stones, in many ways, were a reporter's dream: always good for copy of some kind, an excellent hook on which to hang outrage, certain to stir some kind of reader reaction. Even in 1975, when half the press coverage

concentrated on the burning question of the Stones' ages and whether or
not this would be the last tour and perhaps should it be the last tour, the
conservative *Wall Street Journal* had a man on the tour preparing a front-
pager concerned solely with the business and logistics of mounting such an
undertaking. Meanwhile, the New York *Times* and Los Angeles *Times*
seemed to be running voluminous daily reports studying the tour in micro-
scopic detail. *The Christian Science Monitor* dropped in on the show in
Boston and was not amused by what it saw: "The Stones don't just play
music, they promote debauchery. Their '72 tour was reportedly the scene
of enormous quantities of drugs and liquor. There was mild applause and
laughter in Boston when a road hand brought Keith Richards's bottle of
whiskey onstage. Jagger and the Stones have to take responsibility for the
kids that emulate their stage personalities, even if, perhaps, the Stones are
not that way in everyday life."

Really, though, city editors, young reporters, and lazy columnists
should pay the Stones for the mileage they've gotten out of them over the
years. Back in San Antonio, Australian press lord Rupert Murdoch's San
Antonio *News* had literally frothed at the mouth at the prospect of obscenities performed—live! in person!—onstage and dope smoking in the
audience and had rushed to a municipal court judge to urge a vice raid on
the Stones. What kind of great copy would that have been, if all had
worked according to schedule! Mick and the Stones clapped into irons
onstage, police dogs charging the howling mobs, flames in the streets, a
city out of control. Fortunately, Murdoch's newspaper does not run San
Antonio and cooler heads prevailed.

Then Murdoch's *National Star* got into the act. The *Star* is a particularly ripe supermarket tabloid full of astrology, mild gossip about celebrities, bizarre ailments and obscure miracles, and UFO news. The *Star's*
chief columnist, a notorious blood-and-guts Australian writer named Steve
Dunleavy, wrote a column on the Stones that fairly reeked of gunpowder
and singed flesh. The Stones were, he wrote, no better than international
pirates stealing the souls of American youth and their cash as well. Mick
was very pleased when I showed it to him; proud, he said, and relieved
that the Stones could still elicit such outrage.

That goes all the way back to the beginning, to the carefully orches-
trated Stones image of filthy, long-haired, amoral huns bent only on rape
and plunder. It was all nonsense, of course, but it sold back there in 1964
and the Stones were stuck with it, for better or for worse, even as they
became millionaires with nice art collections. Back in October 1965, at
the band's first press conference in the United States, you could see the
long knives of the media being sharpened. Pete Hamill of the New York
Post caught the Fear of the Stones epidemic very badly and it showed in

his column (which was titled "The Enemy Camp"): "There is something elegantly sinister about the Rolling Stones. They sit before you at a press conference like five unfolding switchblades, their faces set in rehearsed snarls, their hair studiously unkempt and matted, their clothes part of some private conceit, and the way they walk and the way they talk and the songs they sing all become part of some long mean reach for the jugular. We are the enemy, of course, you and I, because these are children and only children can sustain hatred of such pure fury." Perfect! Mick could not have written it better himself.

Then, again, over the years, you have devoted Stones fans in the press corps. Carl Bernstein (pre-Watergate) wrote what amounted to a long love letter to the Stones in the Washington *Post* in January 1969. In his review of the album *Beggar's Banquet*, Bernstein practically ran out of adjectives. He praised the Stones for having "always been outcasts," unlike the lovable, cuddly Beatles, and because the Stones "are ready to man the barricades" and he added, "Musically, the Stones have developed into the perfect rock 'n' roll band . . ." Carl Bernstein, rock critic.

And, just to run around the journalistic spectrum a bit, consider a few excerpts: A weighty *Time* magazine essay in 1972—by dint of likening the Stones to the "coarse" satyr Marsyas who challenged the (Beatle-like) god Apollo to a musical contest—concluded that the Stones' success meant that instinct had triumphed over reason: "Marsyas, the unrepressed goatman, has won; the Rolling Stones are one of his incarnations. Unlike the Beatles—the very prototype of nice English working-class lads accepted everywhere, winning M.B.E.s from the Queen—the Stones from the start based their appeal partly on their reputation as delinquents."

Ralph Graves, *Life* magazine's managing editor, went to see the Stones at the Garden because "I'm a spectacle buff" and kind of liked the show, but the audience reaction unnerved him. "I am not one of those who think the Rolling Stones are a threat to the Republic," he wrote in an "Editors' Note" in *Life*, "but the sight of 20,000 people doing exactly the same thing in unison is discouraging."

Things got deadly once Serious People decided to take the Stones seriously. James Chace, the managing editor of *Foreign Affairs*, than which there is no more earnest quarterly publication, actually observed on a TV rock awards show that Mick Jagger was the "Marlene Dietrich of our time." In an obvious fury, the New York *Times* television critic (a man named John Leonard, who for some reason signed his "TV View" columns in the *Times* as "Cyclops") leaped to the defense of Western civilization: "It is not Mr. Chace's opinion, but it is mine, that the principal difference between the two is that once upon a time Marlene Dietrich had talent. The Stones are not a particularly good band; Jagger is a mediocre vocalist; and all the hopping about onstage is no threat to Tina Turner and on occasion is quite spavined . . . Maybe women were raped and men were murdered at Altamont not because of the frenzy but because of the ennui." Well, all right! Claws back into the sheaths, eh? The heavyweights, sort of, were finally noticing all this Stones business. Everyone, at heart, is a rock critic, after all.

Even *Saturday Review* magazine—remember *Saturday Review?*—had a solemn rock critic, Ellen Sander, who in 1969 wrote: "Violence? The Stones typify it; they don't imply it. A Stones concert is a raging assault, a fiery menace of music and freneticism choreographed by the devil's disciples. The Stones confront their audiences; they don't mess around. Jagger, on vocals and various rhythm instruments, dances like a dervish, moves like a matador, teases, threatens, and taunts his crowd into submission; half the show is in the fight they give him . . . Misunderstood, misused, and, in many ways, classic misfits even in their own milieu, the Stones are the original outlaw bluesmen. It's easy to understand why they are so well loved by their fans, so passionately resented by their detractors. In the establishment 'pop' has become, the Stones are the only real rebels left." Maybe she really believed all that. In the Vietnam years, cheering as the Stones sang "Street Fighting Man" was the only sort of release many earnest liberals had, after all. Those were different times, different mores. Same Stones, though.

Women's Wear Daily geared up in 1969 with a rock critic for the Stones, Martin Gottfried. Martin got quite wound up. Here are selected excerpts from his critique of the Garden show: "The Beatles rejected rebellion ('Revolution'), the Stones took part in it ('Street Fighting Man'). The Beatles were on the side of the angels, the Stones on the side of the devil. The Beatles were for peace, the Stones for war. The Beatles were classy, the Stones crude . . . It isn't like Paul and John and George and Ringo. The Stones are Jagger and Jagger has made himself into the prince of evil. So it seemed kind of evil at the Garden—at least, not nice, the way it is at most rock concerts. Usually, everyone feels good vibrations from good groups. The Stones don't give off good vibrations. Intense, all right, but not 'good' . . . Jagger is there. He is singing 'Sympathy for the Devil.' He is very skinny. He is wearing very tight black bells with silver buttons up the sides. A tight black, long-sleeved polo shirt with a silver Omega on the chest (symbol for what?). A long red silk scarf. He keeps flouncing his long hair. He is dancing all over the stage. My God, Mick Jagger looks like a queen—a limp-wristed faggot. There has been a lot of talk about ambisexuality being groovy. In *Hair,* one of the heroes is in love with Mick Jagger. Jagger knocked up Marianne Faithfull, the singer. He looks very, very gay . . . The Stones come on dirty. Not just sexy. Dirty

. . . And Jagger prancing, mincing, bumping across the stage. One way of looking at it, he is a creep . . . Another way, he is beyond containment, beyond any convention, beyond morality—a desperately free spirit." Martin may have been all over the map with his review, but consider seriously his description of Jagger as "a desperately free spirit." He may have hit much closer to the bone than he knows. Think about it. Mick has.

For one more stop on the Stones' press merry-go-round, let us look at a 1969 San Francisco Chronicle column by Ralph J. Gleason. Ralph was the dean of serious jazz and popular music critics and the first one to recognize the worth of rock and roll. He was also the man who, with founding editor Jann Wenner, started Rolling Stone magazine. And, in the hazy sixties aura of hippie stoned radical paranoia, Ralph was virtually the only "adult" music critic that everyone in music—jazz, rock, fusion, whatever—took seriously. (When Ralph died in 1975, I had just flown in to San Francisco from the Stones tour and was sitting up all night, writing away, in Rolling Stone's old offices on Third Street, next door to where Jack London once lived. I was up on the cozy, red-bricked fourth floor, at 4:00 in the A.M., pleasantly ensconced in associate editor David Felton's office and banging away on his old Royal manual typewriter. Sitting in the dental chair he had hauled into the office because it was comfortable and also because it was utilitarian in case any nitrous oxide should make itself available. [Just strap yourself in and hold on for the ride.] I was sipping a little of Keith's "smooth" Rebel Yell and just writing the hell out of a Stones tour story. Jann came in to the office. He couldn't sleep; still grieved over Ralph's death. We repaired to Jann's corner office overlooking the parking lot in back and drank a lot of toasts to Ralph and actually debated at great length whether the Stones should be the cover of the next issue of RS or whether the cover should be Ralph. All of us owed a great deal to Ralph, the Stones especially, Jann particularly, and me, just because Ralph was maybe the only influential "adult" journalist in the late sixties who busted his ass to open doors for young writers who were basically told elsewhere to "get a haircut, buy some wing tips, and then bend over and grab the soap." He had done the same for rock and roll bands and the Stones should actually have put him on a retainer for what he had done to erase the stigma attached to what then passed for a counterculture. Anyway, Mick and Keith wound up as the next cover of Rolling Stone instead of Ralph J. Gleason, because Jann and I decided, drunk at dawn, that "that's the way Ralph would have wanted it.")

So back to R.J.G.'s 16 November 1969 column in the San Francisco Chronicle (this is but twenty days before the disastrous Stones Altamont show). Ralph wrote: "The Rolling Stones' show last Sunday night deserves some comment . . . Not only did it have interesting sociological implications but there are some musical second thoughts . . . Jagger and company were obviously ill at ease for the show . . . Jagger kept copping out through the first part of his show about the sound and getting it on and getting themselves together. Methinks the lady (if you will excuse the expression) doth protest too much. Midway through the Stones set, his managers and the tour people became upset because 'Mick wasn't getting the response from the people.' He wasn't because it was relatively dull [this was in the Oakland coliseum]. So the people who came with the show, from his manager's office and the agency, went through the hall and told the ushers to let the people down into the aisles. A huge man, looking like Theodore Bikel, went along the seats and told everybody to go down and crowd the stage. I saw him do it. There was an onstage fight between Bill Graham and one of Jagger's management, which ended with Graham throwing the cat offstage. What Jagger and his management want, really, is controlled riot. Apparently Mick is so insecure that he cannot believe people dig him unless he is threatened by a mob at the lip of the stage. It is really a shame. The withdrawal of the ushers and guards, over Graham's objections, was quite obvious. I witnessed that too and it created a situation which was quite dangerous. A three-year-old child had to be lifted from the crowd onto the stage for safety (let's bypass for the moment what kind of a responsible adult got her in that situation in the first place). I simply do not think that the Stones (and I am beginning to suspect, the Beatles) really know what the hell this country and their own audience here is all about. It would be highly educational for them to spend some time here—not just in Hollywood but in the country itself. This is not 1965. Their music is loved and appreciated by millions in 1969 and the audience need not go through rituals playing out a symbolic, childish 'rush-the-guards' game to show its appreciation. Jagger is a very talented man, not a boy, and his audience is as adult—if not more adult—than he is. Telling them a flat-out lie that the forty-five-minute delay was caused by lack of transportation from the airport when, in fact, the group was backstage all the while in the dressing room says what the whole thing about prices has said: They fundamentally despise the audience. On the question of ticket prices, let me note two things. (1) According to the contract, all ticket prices must be approved by the artist; and (2) according to the contract, there could not be any student discount. What CAN a poor boy do?"

Would any member of the jury like a better indictment? And this was in 1969. Do you remember 1969 and what so-called rock music was supposed to sound the hell like and what it was supposed to stand the hell for way the hell back in 1969? Think about it. How did the sixties perform such a Velveeta-like meld into the quasi-eighties with no one noticing? How, in fact, did the Rolling Stones (Public Enemies No. 1, if you believed their hype) stick around and still roil up trouble in these bland years? Maybe it was because there was no competition. And never would be. The job slot tabbed THE ROLLING STONES was forever filled, despite Mick's and Keith's best efforts to capsize their fragile craft and sink out of sight.

6 Canadian Adventures

Thursday, February 24, 1977

So here we have the World's Greatest Rock and Roll Band (no one anywhere seems to know where that sobriquet came from, least of all the members of the band, who perhaps might know) loping along toward middle age. And not necessarily gracefully. "Middle age" for rock and roll band members is any age past twenty-five. Most of the Stones in early 1977 claimed to be creeping up on thirty-five (though they didn't say from which side). Critics had been calling them dinosaurs for years and, indeed, some young fans who showed up on the "Tour of the Americas '75" said that they had bought tickets just to see "what rock and roll used to be like." That 1975 tour had kicked up a bit of a fuss, what with the revival of the old "Stones versus the Established Authorities" business. That tour had also, though the band never released exact figures, generated about $27 million in tour receipts, which supposedly translated into a net profit for the band of about $3 million. Some radicals, eh? Some real street fighting men, right?

Some great way to gently nod off into middle age, and go buy charming three-hundred-year-old estates near London, and make wise investments and then sit clipping coupons by the fire and composing pungent letters to the editor of the London *Times*. Right? Not these boys. Maybe they had nothing new to say, but they might have a different way to not say it. Like doing it with mirrors and smoke. They spent 1976 touring Europe to get the dollars. Their United States album release in 1976, *Black and Blue*, got more attention and publicity for its publicity campaign than for its music. The music was good and it really marked the emergence of the Jagger/Richards writing team from songs of the totally self-indulgent sixties counterculture and from their own self-imposed male-macho-whatchamacallit view of the world. They started writing about real feelings, about real emotions, rather than about attitudes. That a song such as "Fool to Cry" was actually a tender and sentimental little song about a father-daughter relationship, though, remained secondary to the matter of the Stones' image. Which, in the case of *Black and Blue,* became a women's issue. The publicity campaign for the album (a brainchild of the Stones, naturally) featured a beautiful young lady, scantily clad in a disheveled silk teddy, with her wrists bound above her head, as if she were hanging from a rope. Her creamy flesh was dotted with black and blue bruises. She is looking dreamily at the viewer and is saying, "I'm black and blue from the Rolling Stones."

Well, sir, when a giant billboard featuring that went up on the Sunset Strip in Hollywood, a lot of people got offended. A bunch of women who liked rock and roll but didn't like the message that this ad was pushing got together and formed an organization (Women Against Violence Against Women) to try to get record companies and rock and roll bands to tone down their generally misogynist ways. Not a great deal was accomplished. The Stones were pleased that, at their advanced age, they could still stir up some outrage.

The album still didn't sell well, maybe 600,000 copies by one industry estimate. Not bad for the old days, but these weren't the old days any more. Fleetwood Mac had sold four million copies of their album *Fleetwood Mac* the year before; even such lightweight groups as the Eagles were leaving the Stones in their dust. There was great pressure—both from within and without—for the Stones to live up to their reputation. And their publicity. Additionally, the Stones' record deal with Atlantic Records was about to expire (Stones records, although on the Rolling Stones Records label, were manufactured, distributed, and promoted by Atlantic). The Stones were being courted by other companies, such as CBS and MCA, who hoped to pick up the contract. Obviously, the Stones wanted a bidding war so they could drive their price up and sign for a huge bundle of cash so they could keep on living the good life. To keep those record companies interested, the Stones needed a hot piece of product for their next record.

What they had in mind was a live double album from the last two years of touring. The tapes from the U.S. tour of 1975 were spotty and erratic, but they had a hot (consistently hot, which has always been a Stones problem) show from June 1976 in Paris. That was enough material for three sides of a four-sided double album. For the rest, the band decided to pull a surprise show in a small club or bar somewhere, where the sound would be good, the audience excitement would be feverish, and where everything would be on a small enough scale as to not get out of hand. And in someplace out of the way, so it would not turn into a freakish, full-blown, Stones-crazy Media Event. And someplace close enough to New York City for the band to carry on negotiations with the major record companies for a new contract.

Mick Jagger, who was by then effectively running the band himself (primarily because Keith Richards had become addicted to heroin), decided on Toronto. It was a cosmopolitan city with a big Stones following; it was a quick flight away from New York; and it was a city civilized enough to afford the Stones some privacy. It looked pretty easy and comfortable: Fly in to Toronto, rehearse for a few days, dine well, play a couple of nights at a small club, sign a great new contract, and then get the hell out.

How tough could that be? Well, that's reckoning without the wild card marked *hubris*. The Stones had long been accustomed to the reality of one set of laws for the rest of the world and a whole other set of laws that existed only for the Rolling Stones. That can make a person get careless.

In January 1977, Keith went to trial in Aylesbury, England, on charges of possession of cocaine and LSD. The latter charge was dropped and he was fined 750 pounds for the former. That left him free to travel to Canada for the club dates there. On February 24, he and his common-law wife, German-born actress Anita Pallenberg, and their son Marlon closed up Redlands, their country estate, and flew British Airways from London to Toronto. Keith was apparently not holding any drugs when they landed, but he had failed to vet Anita's luggage. And Anita had twenty-eight pieces of luggage. Maybe that's what prompted the search. Maybe it was the fact that Anita acts and dresses rather flamboyantly—gold boots and dresses that resemble taffeta bedspreads. At any rate, the Richards party drew considerable attention from customs officers at the airport.

This is an excerpt from the secret report filed to the Royal Canadian Mounted Police (RCMP) by RCMP Constable A. J. Hachinski of the RCMP's "Drug Enforcement Section, T.I.A. [Toronto International Airport] Unit, Special Investigations Branch":

"On Thursday, February 24, 1977, I was on duty at the Toronto International Airport Drug Section. At approximately 7:25 P.M., arrived at Terminal #2. Upon arrival I was advised by Canada Customs they had in custody a lady with a small quantity of hashish and other drug-related paraphernalia, namely spoon [and] hypodermic needle. The lady identified herself as Anita PALLENBERG, common-law wife of Rolling Stones guitarist Keith RICHARDS. She was subsequently arrested and taken to the office of Terminal #1 and charged with Possession of Hashish (10 grams), and released on a appearance notice.

"The spoon and hypodermic needle was taken to the Dominion Analyst and the hypodermic needle was found to contain traces of heroin. Subsequently a warrant was obtained for the arrest of Anita PALLENBERG and a warrant to search her residence was obtained.

"Charges against Anita PALLENBERG:

—Possession of Hashish. Section 3(1) N.C.A.
—Possession of Heroin. Section 3(1) N.C.A."

While Constable Hachinski took Anita to nearby Brampton (which has legal jurisdiction over the airport) to be booked and released, Stones logistics director Alan Dunn drove Keith and seven-year-old Marlon to the Harbour Castle Hilton, a massive concrete slab of a hotel perched on the shore of Toronto Harbour. Keith registered under the name "Redlands" in suites 3223, 3224, and 3225. Some of those rooms were just blinds or "floaters" (as they are called in the rock and roll world) and they can be very useful indeed to rock stars. After all, when you have no real name and you have many rooms, then you are not really there.

Now, so far, all we have here is yet another Stones-related arrest, which is not too unusual. No cause for dire alarm on anyone's part. The Stones would pay the fine and that would be that. Ever since the days when Mick and Keith had actually been jailed in England and discovered the unpleasantness of the experience, they had realized the wisdom of retaining high-priced legal talent, lawyers capable of full-scale attacks on any government, organization, or individual threatening the existence of the Rolling Stones. Mad dogs on a leash, as it were. In recent years, the Stones had reaped the benefits of their legal mad dogs—after all their close scrapes and their jailings and near-jailings and their arrests and all the threats of arrest and the lawsuits and the assault charges and all the other bags and baggage that come with the territory if you dare to be a Rolling Stone.

But how far can you test the boundaries of that territory? Many enemies lay in wait out there, beyond the safe glow of the campfire. Enemies hoping for a test.

Came now a major testing time. Unbeknownst to Keith as he slumbered all day in Suite 3224 of the Harbour Castle after all-night rehearsals at the Cine-a-Vision studio, he was about to test the mettle of the mighty Royal Canadian Mounted Police. Or maybe vice versa.

Sunday, February 27, 1977

On this day, the Royal Canadian Mounted Police gained a permanent and prominent place in rock and roll history. (See Appendix II.)

The following is an excerpt from the secret police report of RCMP Constable A. J. Hachinski: "Accompanied by four members of the RCMP

(Peter HADLEY, Bill SEWARD, Bernie BARBE, and Beverly PURCELLS), I attended at the temporary residence of Anita PALLENBERG at the Harbour Castle Hotel and after approximately two hours of attempting to locate her room, a search warrant was executed at room 3223–24–25, which was registered under the name of K. REDBLAND [sic] and is an alias used by Keith RICHARDS.

"The following exhibits were seized.

—One passport in the name of Keith RICHARDS

—Minister's Permit to enter Canada

—Hypodermic needle cover

—Plastic bag with traces of white powder

—Plastic bag with traces of white powder [sic]

—Three red-coloured pills

—Harbour Castle sugar bag containing 2 grams of resin material (believed to be Hashish)

—Gold foil paper with traces of white powder

—Plastic bag containing 5 grams of Cocaine

—Razor blade with white traces of white powder

—Switchblade knife with traces of white powder

—Hypodermic needle with liquid in the base

—Brass lighter with traces of white powder

—Silver bowl with traces of white powder

—Teaspoon with traces of white powder

—Purple pouch with traces of white powder

—Plastic bag containing 22 grams of Heroin

"These exhibits were turned over to Constable SEWARD, RCMP who acted as exhibit officer. RICHARDS admitted ownership of the exhibits and was arrested on the charge of 'Possession for the Purpose of Trafficking.' Mr. RICHARDS was released later the same evening after a mini-bail hearing before a Justice of the Peace in the presence of Mr. Clay POWELL, who was Mr. RICHARDS' Attorney at the time.

"Charges against Mr. Keith RICHARDS:

—Possession of Heroin for the Purpose of Trafficking. Section 4(2) N.C.A.

—Possession of Cocaine. Section 3(1) N.C.A."

That RCMP document excerpt is as remarkable for what it does not say as for what it indeed does spell out. Almost everything in it has never been made public, never introduced in court hearings or at Richards's trial or anywhere else. That extraordinary shopping list of goods (dusted with white powder and otherwise) the Mounties seized from Keith's rooms was never made known. It's amazing that Constable Hachinski admits that he and his fellow Mounties spent "approximately two hours" wandering through the Harbour Castle before finally locating Keith's and Anita's suites. (When I arrived at the Harbour Castle two days later, I managed to have the entire Rolling Stones rooming list maybe fifteen minutes after I checked in. How? By slipping a $10 bribe to a chambermaid. Do I maybe know something that the RCMP doesn't?) That gives the lie to the many later widespread rumors that there was an informant either within the Harbour Castle or perhaps within the Stones organization itself. It is also surprising that the RCMP made public immediately the fact that Richards had been arrested on the heroin charge and kept secret—for the time being—the matter of cocaine possession. Even Richards and his lawyer didn't yet know that he would later be charged with cocaine possession. Early press bulletins out of Toronto centered on heroin, such as this Associated Press file: "Keith Richards, lead guitarist with the Rolling Stones, has been charged here with possession of heroin for the purpose of trafficking. An ounce of heroin with an estimated street value of $4,000 was seized in a downtown hotel after a week-long investigation at Toronto International Airport by Royal Canadian Mounted Police and Ontario provincial officers, a police spokesman said." Hachinski's report also listed the RCMP officers making the arrest, without mentioning any involvement by the Ontario Provincial Police, who may or may not have been there: It remains a hazy matter which no involved parties are eager to clarify.

What Hachinski's report failed to mention is equally significant. First, of course, is the absence of any mention of the Ontario Provincial Police, whose (unnamed) officers accompanied the RCMP constables at the hotel. (Who actually decided to make the raid on the Harbour Castle?) And it doesn't say that when Richards was taken to a hearing before a Justice of the Peace, that Richards was taken back out to Brampton, which has jurisdiction over the Toronto airport but not over Toronto, where Richards was arrested. (Apparently, the reason was a simple one:

The Mounties had busted Anita at the airport and charged her in Brampton and it never occurred to them to do anything different when they busted Richards.) That would later cause court problems. The report also did not say that, when the constables finally located Keith's and Anita's suite, Keith was asleep during much of the search and thought—until he was arrested—that his visitors were executives from his record company. The police report also did not mention that Keith's name did not appear on the search warrant. That would also cause court problems later. It also did not say that the RCMP had put the Rolling Stones "under observation" three weeks earlier when Stones' advance men had started scouting likely spots for recording in Toronto.

Possession of heroin for the purpose of trafficking is a very serious charge in Canada. Conviction can result in a sentence from seven years to life in prison. The Justice of the Peace who dealt with the Richards case in Brampton didn't seem too concerned and released him on a $1,000 no-deposit bail. Which meant that Keith walked free without dropping so much as a dime. He immediately became a hot political issue in Canada. The RCMP, particularly, were furious that he seemed to be getting preferential treatment just because he was a rock and roll star and they were angry that this case seemed to be portraying the Mounties as ineffectual goofs who couldn't quite nail a drugged-up, scruffy, rich hippie who was giving the finger to the Dominion. High bail versus low or no bail for Keith Richards, drugged-up outlaw, was now a serious matter for the entire country to worry over. Richards's lawyer Powell discovered a hidden radio transmitter—a "bug"—in Richards's suite and decided to ignore it until such a time as he could use it for courtroom theatrics.

The rest of the Rolling Stones were said to be very angry at Keith and Anita (Anita had not been listed on the Official Rolling Stones List of those who would come to Toronto and perhaps therefore not anticipated by the people out there at the airport, who were not ready for the orange-haired lady bearing down on them with her twenty-eight pieces of luggage) and outraged that this apparently blatant disregard for ordinary, routine rules of the road might result in a premature termination of the Rolling Stones. One knew, after all, didn't one, about the proper methods of going through an airport in a foreign country and clearing customs without seeming to be a drug-laden rock star. A lot of serious questions that would never be answered (at least not for our purposes here) started getting bounced around in the Stones camp: Why hadn't Keith called his "holder" (note: an insignificant, therefore invisible, person on a rock tour who literally "holds" drugs for a rock star so that the cops don't notice what's going on)? Keith had apparently been clean when he cleared customs, so where did he suddenly score five grams of coke and twenty-two grams of heroin? After Anita was busted at the airport, didn't Keith have even a foggy notion that the coppers might be watching him? Whatever happened to caution? Or even good old-fashioned paranoia? Why hadn't the Stones' usual bodyguards been posted by the elevators to slow down and discourage unwanted visitors? Had the much-vaunted, tight-ribbed, leakproof Stones organization sprung a fatal leak? What happens to fools in paradise?

Things got serious, that's what. Mick Jagger, grim-faced, finally arrived from New York City, where he had been attending to his ill daughter, Jade, and he cracked the whip, as best he could after—well, you have to say something on the order of "killing the fox after all the chickens are dead." Mopping-up operations were in order. The Stones' lawyer most adept at dealing with governments, former U.S. Secret Service Agent Bill Carter, was beeped at the Dallas-Fort Worth Airport and he boarded the next plane for Toronto. Some of the Stones' beefy five-foot-wide security guys planed in to seal off sensitive areas of the hotel. Stones tour manager Peter Rudge finally grew a few gray hairs. Stones spokesperson Paul Wasserman skied in from Los Angeles to hand out the customary "no comments" until circumstances [more about that later] dealt him dirty. The lobby of the Harbour Castle filled up very quickly with as strange a mix of people as you will ever see: phalanxes of pressed-jeaned and crisply buttoned-down plainclothes RCMP agents trying to act un-RCMPy (even with the telltale police radio receiver earphones prominently in their ears); Rolling Stones security guys who were straining the seams of the Stones T-shirts and jeans that almost contained their four hundred pounds of pecs and lats and who were making no secret of who they were and projecting fierce defiance; reporters and photographers from the United States and England and Australia and Germany, all ready to kill each other in the quest to get the Obvious obvious story: Is this the end of the Rolling Stones? (The Canadian press isn't as keen on this. Yet.); fans and groupies and Rolling Stones crazies who hadn't left their niche in the woodwork since Altamont; and just plain crazies And ordinary citizens, finally taking that vacation after fifty-nine years on the assembly line at GM and here in Toronto they get—instead of the gold watch—the lobby parade of the fruitcakes. Runaway chicks with buns and tits hanging out everywhere. Wild-eyed hippies who have lived on nothing but pure methedrine (speed) since Altamont and MUST communicate with Mick immediately! (The runaway chicks will settle for anyone with a room in the hotel. Regardless of sex.) Crazed eternally drunk Limey reporters who will make up everything whether or not they actually talk to the Stones (and, truth be told, they would rather not be bothered with the facts). Stoned bikers who feel a kinship—Yea!—with Keith. A college professor with the—thank God!—predictable tweed jacket and horn pipe and a legal pad full of questions about the drift of American society. At least thirty-seven young Mick Jagger and Keith Richards look-alikes. Twenty-two coked-out songwriters waving smudged lyric sheets that they swear will "rescue" the Rolling Stones. (And this doesn't even include the deviates, I mean the real deviates, who get Messages from the lyrics of Stones songs and feel personally anointed by the Stones to carry out weird, twisted missions.) This is what the Rolling Stones have to face in real life, let alone what's coming up in court. What a thrill it must be to be a Rolling Stone.

Wednesday, March 2, 1977

So why am I here? I wondered as I stood before the window of my room at the Harbour Castle and watched the leaden light of another gray winter Toronto dawn slowly reveal details of the tableau before me: a sprawling, lifeless plaza that meandered down to Toronto Harbour, where a fireboat was churning through the dark waters and breaking up ice floes. In the plaza, there were seven desolate picnic tables on the dead grass and five dead trees poking up out of squat blue, yellow, and orange planter boxes. Enough of a palpable sense of despair and death to send one back to bed. Which it did me. Where I realized that death and despair had a lot to do with why I was here. I had heard from a very reliable source within the Stones camp that, now that Keith Richards had been busted and his passport taken away, he was in much more serious trouble than anyone was letting on and that the Canadian Government was going to do everything within its power to not only give him a life sentence in prison but to also move to rescind bail and jail him at his scheduled court hearing next Tuesday. That would effectively mean the end of the Rolling Stones. And it would also mean the end of a significant part of rock and roll music. And that mattered to me. The Stones do matter, after all—and not just to me.

I had also heard from that same source that Keith was slowly dying from his drug addiction. That source said he was glad, in a way, that Keith had finally been busted by the Big Boys—the RCMP—in a serious bust that he couldn't wriggle out of as usual. This one would either lock him away or end up forcing him to get clean.

And I had a selfish reason. My Stones source guaranteed that the band would play at least one night at the three-hundred-seat El Mocambo club in Toronto and I wanted to be ringside for that blowout. It would undoubtedly be the last chance ever to see the Rolling Stones be a bar band again. And, depending upon Canadian courts, it might well be the last chance to ever see the Rolling Stones perform at all.

Just after I had checked into the Harbour Castle, I met Stones attorney Bill Carter and we retired to the lobby's Quayside Bar—shielded from the Mounties in the lobby only by six-foot schefflera plants—to talk. He was uncharacteristically somber. "I'm afraid this is serious," he said. "Keith may well get life. We may be able to get him off or he may get life. I just don't know. We just can't figure it. Our local counsel [Carter, as an American citizen, could not practice law in Canada, so he worked with Toronto attorneys] will work on the warrant thing, but I am worried. They seem serious. We had absolutely no problem getting the Stones into Canada. But it may be a bit tougher getting them out. This thing Monday [a secret court hearing for Keith, whom court officials said publicly would appear on Tuesday] will be just preliminary, of course. But the Stones are desperate and depressed. They know that these are the last albums—the live one and the new one they're trying to work on. They aren't real happy with Keith."

Only a few minutes later, I encountered the second part of the Stones' three-pronged line of defense: nominal Stones manager Peter Rudge, the fast-talking, hyperactive Cambridge dandy who managed to manage both the Rolling Stones and the Who before his thirtieth birthday and never quite got over it. He blanched perceptibly when he saw me: He was obviously not overeager to have American reporters on the scene of what might well become his Last Stand. (Even before Keith's arrest, Rudge and the Stones had decided on a total press ban for the El Mocambo recording sessions and for the whole Toronto visit as well.) Half an hour later, he finally came over to the Quayside Bar to shake hands. (He is a gentleman, after all.)

"I forbade American press, you know," he said.

"I didn't get the message," I replied. "When are the Stones recording at the El Mocambo?"

He ignored the question. "We knew you were coming here. We saw your name on a travel list. Why else do you think you couldn't get a room on our floor?"

A good question. I had been saddled with a room on seven, Rudge was on thirty, and the rest of the Stones and entourage were somewhere between twenty-nine and thirty-four.

"I already have the rooming list," I told him.

"I'll bet you do," Rudge said, as he turned on his heel and walked away.

I had been bluffing only a little bit. I had gotten a list of the important Stones' floater rooms (Keith Richards registered as "Mr. Redlands" and Mick Jagger as "Mr. Waxley," for instance), thanks to the worldwide tendency of hotel chambermaids to trade information for cash. This one maid in particular went so far as to come back to my room with empty champagne and wine bottles that she said she had just removed from Jagger's suite, number 3216. She proudly presented me with two bottles of Paul Bouchard Chablis (1975) and one bottle of Taittinger Comtes de Champagne Reims Brut (1966). I had to pretend to be grateful for this find. "By the way," I asked her, "any excitement, what with the Stones staying here?"

"No," she said. "They keep pretty much to their rooms. I heard that one of them got arrested for something, though."

I trudged off to try to locate the third man in the Stones' defense: wily Los Angeles press agent Paul Wasserman, whose high-priced clients usually depend on him to keep them out of the press. I wanted to learn what he was not allowed to tell me. When he answered my knock on his door up in 3016, he sighed heavily when he saw me there, notebook in hand.

"Why didn't you call me from New York so I could have told you that you weren't allowed to come?" he asked, as he graciously ushered me in and opened a bottle of wine. "Exactly the point," I said. "I'd rather hear it in person. When are the Stones going to be recording at the El Mocambo? Now, I know that April Wine has booked tonight through Saturday night for a recording session there and I know that [radio station] CHUM has been running a write-in contest for tickets for a party with the Stones and I know that April Wine's manager is a friend of Skippy Snaire, who saved Peter Rudge's life in Montreal in 1972 when someone firebombed the Stones' equipment there and Skippy was the only person in Canada who was able to round up enough equipment in time to get the Stones onstage and I know that Skippy's here in the hotel. So the Stones will play the El Mocambo. When?"

He sighed heavily and poured more wine. "You know more than I do. It doesn't matter anyway. You can't get in. No press. And you can't talk to the Stones either. Your chances of seeing the band are zero. Peter is throwing a tantrum. Mick is very testy and so is Keith. And Peter's pissed off that you came here."

"Thanks a lot," I said. "I'll keep you posted on what's happening."

"Thanks," Wasserman said genially, as he opened the door for me to leave. "By the way, the Stones won't be at the El Mocambo tonight. There's a party here for Alan Dunn, which you are not invited to. If you mention any of this to Peter, I'll deny having said it. And be careful with the phones. We're all being tapped."

Since everyone seemed to be a little on edge, and since trying to crash a Stones party right away would likely not help grease the skids for future dealings, and since the atmosphere in the hotel was becoming increasingly stifling, especially with the crush of reporters and fans and police in the lobby, I decided to go check out the El Mocambo. I cruised down Spadina Avenue, finally locating a small crowd of people waiting underneath a neon palm tree. The front door was locked up as tight as the lobby of the Harbour Castle. I banged on the door. A tiny porthole opened slowly and a bouncer glowered at me. "Closed session. Whaddya want?"

I thought for a moment. There were a great many things I wanted at that moment, but getting into the club seemed to be the thing to do. I summoned up the name of a man I had never met (and hoped he didn't mind). "Skippy Snaire sent me," I said. It worked like magic. The bouncer even smiled. I went upstairs and watched April Wine play until closing time. The club looked to be a perfect spot for the Stones' return to bardom, dark and close and raucous, with a postage-sized stage decorated with a big orange cutout moon and black palm trees.

Back at the hotel lobby, the little parades continued. I talked a bit with one of the Stones' drivers. He volunteered a tip: "The Stones won't record till Billy Preston gets here." And when might that be? He closed one eye and laid a finger alongside his nose. "Friday," he whispered conspiratorially. I thanked him and headed for bed. At the elevator, he offered a final tidbit: "I hear this is the first time the Stones have let Anita out in public for years. And look what happens." He laughed.

Thursday, March 3, 1977

Incoming phone call from Wasserman at 5:00 in the morning: "Why won't you ever believe me?" he asked with indignation. "We know that you got into the El Mocambo last night. Why didn't you stay here and come to Alan's party?" He ignored my incredulous gasps and forged on. "If you wanted to learn when the Stones will record, you might call A&M Records and see what day Billy Preston arrives here. I didn't tell you that; I'll deny it if you ever say I did. By the way, I also didn't tell you that the bidding [for the Rolling Stones Records deal] is now down to MCA and Ahmet [Ertegun, chairman of Atlantic Records]. I just came from a rehearsal and the band is working on new stuff for the next LP, not just the live album. So they'll sleep all day. Carter and I are taking Anita to court this morning for her hearing, but there's no reason for you to go to that. They'll just remainder her hearing to the fourteenth. Remember, the phones are tapped. Ciao."

Well, what a pleasant way to start another day of the Stones Watch.

No Stones, as usual, to watch. No way to go back to sleep, though. Nothing to do but turn on CHUM radio, send for the morning papers, and order one of the "Breakfast Adventures" from the room service menu. What would it be today, Adventure No. 1, No. 2, No. 3, or No. 4? How about just asking room service to surprise me, for once?

They were happy to oblige. In fact, the entire hotel staff seemed to be getting the whole spirit of things. Having the entire Stones touring crew and legal staff staying here, but not really staying here, since they were registered—if at all—under *noms des pierres;* having a lobbyful of Mounties who denied they were Mounties; having sinister-looking unmarked cars prowling by outside periodically. The hotel, which is physically isolated from downtown Toronto, anyway, by the Gardiner Expressway and by its location on the harbourfront, took on a quality not unlike that of some strange outpost. I looked outside: same lowering gray skies, same ice-flecked harbour.

I scanned the papers and wondered why there was nothing in them about Keith's or Anita's cases. Then I recalled that, under Canadian law, the press cannot write about pending cases, other than to report any official actions taken in those cases.

There are other interesting items in the papers, though. Ontario Province Attorney General Roy McMurtry publicly apologized for having suggested yesterday that the province should go into the marijuana business and actually open up drugstores, since the courts were so cluttered with marijuana cases. An RCMP constable admitted in court that he had accidentally erased part of a phone wiretap that was used as evidence in a hashish possession trial. An RCMP chief superintendent replied to a Toronto *Globe & Mail* editorial that had challenged the power of the RCMP in issuing "writs of assistance" to officers, which, in essence, were permanent search warrants. In replying, Chief Superintendent R. R. Schramm wrote that, while writs of assistance were, in fact, no-name search warrants, the RCMP strove to preserve individual freedom and privacy.

Another reader, one L. E. Wallingford, had also written to the *Globe & Mail* about those RCMP writs and his view was quite different: "Acting on an informer's malicious, vague, and untrue 'tip,' some dozen or so RCMP from Fort Erie descended simultaneously on the homes of six members of the golf club to which I belong. Reconstructing what happened in the next hour or so is like something out of the Keystone Kops—only it loses its humor when it is being done to you and by police with such unlimited powers. The 'tips' concerned supposedly illegal golf clubs, but the RCMP used this as a lever for a 'fishing expedition.' In my case, I stood helpless and seething, while, ignoring my golf clubs, they searched my house from attic to cellar. Nothing too small or trivial—stereo, headphones, war souvenirs, and even one lone golf ball—you name it, they looked at it, all the time trying to trick me with leading questions. At another house they pushed past two teenagers whose parents were away, forced open a locked chest, thumbed through the lady of the house's bank books, and made off with two sets of golf clubs and some balls. Elsewhere, a photographer having his before-dinner nap was awakened to find a police officer towering over his bed, Out on the highway, a school principal with his son was driving out for an evening round of golf, unaware that two cars with five RCMP officers were trying to intercept them. In the end, none of these six people had done anything wrong or illegal. We were harassed, intimidated, upset, and humiliated, all because of an unfounded 'tip' and the Gestapo-like powers conferred on the RCMP by these obnoxious 'writs.' The only thing they cannot do is manhandle you unless they arrest you and thank God they have to have some valid grounds for that or we would all be in the jug."

Well. No wonder Mr. Wallingford was a tad irritated. It was a damned good thing for Keith Richards that he hadn't tried to bring his golf clubs into Canada with him or he might really be in trouble. Keith might be a junkie, but how far do you go . . . ?

I wondered why the Mounties who'd arrested Keith had even bothered with a search warrant (even though it did not have his name on it, after all). Why not just roam around with a writ of assistance? And what about those Mounties sitting patiently down there in the lobby and outside in their unmarked cars? How many writs did they have? What did they want?

I called up the RCMP and, after many runarounds and callbacks, received a very firm "no comment" about the Keith Richards case. The RCMP, I learned, were answerable only to the Federal Solicitor General's department. Prime Minister Trudeau himself, even if he wanted to, could not intervene in Keith's case.

I decided it might be helpful to try to talk to Mick Jagger about the band and its status, since no one else was likely to. And I knew that I wouldn't be able to reach Jagger through Rudge or Wasserman or Carter. And I couldn't get onto Jagger's floor because of the guards. And I couldn't call him directly. So I wrote him a little note and sent for my favorite Harbour Castle maid. "Take this note," I told her, slipping some greenery into her palm, "and make sure Mr. Jagger gets it." I held up my hand to stifle her protests. "Yes, I know he's not staying here. None of the Stones are. Just make sure he gets the note, okay?" She smiled and set off.

The noon news on CHUM confirmed what Wasserman had told me earlier: Anita had appeared in court and had her case remanded. CHUM's reporter referred to Wasserman as Anita's "large American bodyguard," which I was careful to point out to him when he called later. It didn't help his mood any, especially because the British press was really on his back now: to keep the reporters away from Anita, Wasserman had served as a decoy, while Carter spirited her out a back door and away. Now he was bearing the brunt of their spleen-venting. They were in a foul mood: packed away in that lobby all the time without absolutely nothing to do but interview each other, while their London tabloids kept screaming KEITH FACES LIFE, and no stories to go with the headlines.

"Oh, by the way," Wasserman added. "The Stones are recording tomorrow night at the El Mocambo, but if you show up I'll throw you out."

"Thanks a lot," I said. "I'll be there."

I called up Rudge and argued with him for a while, but he was clearly operating in some other dimension and cranking up his hysteria level. Check into the Harbour Castle and check your sense of reality at the door. Then I realized that I was registered as being from *Rolling Stone* and I wondered if the RCMP knew, even cared about the difference. I started occasionally searching my own room to make sure nothing had been planted. That level of paranoia spread, even though no one had found anything except the one transmitter in Keith's room. Still . . . it couldn't hurt to be careful.

Wasserman called back to reassure me that Rudge had just reiterated to him that my chances of seeing the band perform were "absolutely zero." He said Lisa Robinson, a syndicated rock columnist in New York, had been calling him from New York every two hours, frantic to come to Toronto but also desperate to have the Stones' blessing and permission. He said he was telling her every two hours that Rudge had forbade her to enter the country. "If Flippo shows up, you'll throw him out?" she asked. "Fuckin' A right!" was Rudge's reply.

Many hours later, in the early morning, two overdressed young women knocked on the door of Suite 3019. "Are you Peter Rudge?" one of them asked when he opened the door.

"Yes," he said. They swept by him and settled down comfortably on a couch. Rudge was, for once, set back a bit. "Who are you?"

"Look," one of them said. "You're Peter Rudge. We were ordered up here to do Peter Rudge and we were promised $100 each and we're not leaving till we get paid."

Rudge fled in his stocking feet to Wasserman in 3016. "My room has been taken over! Get the police! Get Carter!"

Carter went over to 3019 and knocked and they let him in. "Are y'all hookers?" he asked, knowing the answer all along. They were adamant about not leaving until they were paid. Carter negotiated a settlement with them: $50 each if they would leave quietly. Rudge finally retook his room. He never would find out who set the whole thing up.

Friday, March 4, 1977

This date was the sixth anniversary of the wedding of the former Margaret Sinclair to one Pierre Elliott Trudeau. Why was that a point of more than minor interest to the Rolling Stones and their entourage and their watchers? Only because he was still Prime Minister of Canada and she was still married to him and still the country's First Lady. Only thing is, she elected to celebrate the occasion by slipping the reins up there in Ottawa, where husband Pierre and three kids waited, and suddenly materializing in Toronto, where the temptation of the Rolling Stones seemed to be too much for a freethinking twenty-eight-year-old First Lady to bear. Maggie Trudeau checked into Suite 3219 (accompanied by a female RCMP officer) of the Harbour Castle as "Margaret Sinclair" (her maiden name). Why not? She could use any name she damn well felt like. It seemed more and more as if I was the only damned person in the hotel registered under a real name (that also happened to be my own).

So the freewheeling wife of the Prime Minister of Canada joined the free-floating Rolling Stones apparatchiks or remoras or camp followers or the growing army of weird people in and around the Harbour Castle who had a vested interest somewhere in the very presence of the Rolling Stones. There were record company presidents (Mike Maitland of MCA, Walter Yetnikoff of CBS, Ahmet Ertegun of Atlantic) wanting to sign the Stones; RCMP officers wanting to keep a sharp eye on the Stones (and maybe do more); shrieking London tabloid reporters wanting to debrief the Stones (and perhaps worse); wild-eyed Stones fanatics wanting to meditate (and more, much more) with their icons; every status climber in Canada desperately wanting a Ticket to the Show; many image-conscious dope dealers eagerly wanting to upgrade their status by becoming known as Supplier to the Stones; every flaky low-rent scumbag crazy acidhead who ever infected the front row of any Stones show; and (finally) down here at the bottom rung of the status ladder, your writers from the United States (of which I was still the only one present). Oh—somewhere off in an antechamber, there were your TV correspondents and your Canadian columnists, whose cobwebs were just beginning to think about rattling. And who didn't yet know that Maggie Trudeau had front-row seats for the Stones for both Friday and Saturday nights.

For shows that would be more than memorable for more than mere reasons: These would be the first club dates that the Rolling Stones had performed since at least 1964 (they themselves couldn't recall the last

time); these might well be the last public performances ever by Keith
Richards (should he be jailed, per RCMP schedule); and they might well
be the last concerts ever by the Rolling Stones. And everyone knew it.

At about 6:30 P.M. that day, the three hundred lucky ticket holders
met at CHUM, were not told their destination, and boarded buses that
dropped them off at the El Mocambo. They were passed through an
elaborate police barricade system into the club.

Back at the Harbour Castle, Rudge and Wasserman had expended
quite a bit of their energy and time and patience in explaining to me why
no representative of any press organization would be allowed in to see that
show that night: all this business of Keith's arrest had everyone on tenter-
hooks; the band needed to regroup in front of a real audience without
worrying about critics; and, hey, fellow, how 'bout givin' us a break? As
the ranking—and indeed, the only—representative of any publications
from the United States present for the argument and the occasion itself, I
decided to grant that concession. I do not feel I can be reprimanded for
my conciliatory decision. As a media representative of that percentage of
the United States population concerned with the activities of the Rolling
Stones—hey, I bit the bullet and made the choice and I was right. I also
knew that the Stones would be back the next night at the El Mocambo
and I knew no power on earth could prevent this foreign correspondent
from completing the appointed rounds. And all that.

So I felt pretty self-righteous and actually left my room (meaning my
telephone) for a while to try to eat something other than a room service
surprise. I might have known better (turn your back and they will all kick
the U.S. of A. while it's out trying to get a decent corned beef on rye).
After Rudge had smugly told me I was permanently, permanently barred
from the El Mocambo and I had relaxed the guard of the U.S. of A. while
studying a massive sandwich, I got a phone call from a friend at the El
Mocambo who told me the place had been practically been overrun with
Canadian reporters.

Well, that blew any trust. I raced down to the El Mocambo and
demanded to see either Rudge or Wasserman, which didn't work. My
New York City Police Department press pass finally did get me in and get
me a table, as the Stones finished their set. "Goddamn you," I hissed to
Wasserman as he sat down, "you lied to me."

"Well," he said, "Peter decided that since this is Canada, we had to
let some Canadian reporters in."

"The gloves came off here," I told him and Rudge, after Peter came
up and offered a marshmallowy sort of explanation for everything with no
promise of a resolution of any sort by even the next evening's Stones show.
Especially by then. That's when I pointed out to Peter that I had been

given his table and that his briefcase—stuffed to overflowing with Stones documents—had been practically in my lap.

"I copied everything in it, Peter," I told him, as I handed his briefcase back to him. He blanched. "I believe it," he said.

"It's only dirty laundry anyway," Wasserman—ever the optimist—said.

Meanwhile, during "Star Star" (better known as "Starfucker"), to whom does Mick address some spirited "Starfucker, that's what you are" lines other than our Margaret Trudeau, bravely seated at ringside. Earlier, downstairs in the beer locker which served as the Stones' dressing room, Margaret didn't flinch when she met Anita and Anita said, a bit loudly, "Fuckin' good to meet you!"

After the show (what little I saw of it), Bill Wyman came up to shake my hand and ask me what I thought of the concert. I said that the two and a half songs I managed to hear were good, despite Peter Rudge's having banned me for all eternity from any Stones' utterances—musical or otherwise. Wyman was just puzzled. "Why would Peter do that?" I had no answer.

Wasserman offered me a lift back to the Harbour Castle, along with my friend Richard van Abbe, the chief of United Press International's Toronto bureau, and Ken Regan, the Authorized Stones Photographer. Our Stones station wagon screamed down the alleyway behind the El Mocambo through a crowd of perhaps fifty fans and almost as many police officers and literally dozens of photographers, with their strobe lights winking furiously away at anything that moved. Regan had been the only photographer allowed in the club, as he explained at great length to van Abbe, as Regan laid down the Stones' ground rules for Official Stones Photographs being fed to UPI and how UPI could and could not utilize said photographs. Wasserman was a trifle glum during the ride back.

Back at the hotel, we went up to Rudge's suite. Rudge rather stiffly served wine and soon made it clear that he preferred that I leave. I asked him if the members of the Stones were totally aware of the exact nature of his dealings with the press, especially since he was speaking for the band. He didn't answer. I asked to meet with him the next day to discuss that. One of his lackeys called me a "sneaky bastard."

And so back to my Willy Loman Memorial Module. Along the way, I caught a scintillating glimpse of a woman who greatly resembled the First Lady of Canada. She wisped by in a white bathrobe. I had already promised myself that I would not ask Margaret Trudeau anything, even if trapped in a dumbwaiter with her for twelve hours. Nude. Or anything else. She appeared far too fragile for the kind of intense scrutiny and speculation she was obviously going to be sledgehammered with very shortly. Even as I regained my Module, there came a phone call from a Stones' insider: "Listen, Maggie's having a party in her suite. Mick's the one she's hot after, but Mick will not fuck her because he will only fuck people he wants to fuck." Enough of that.

Keith was due to appear in court on Monday and this was early Saturday morning. I called up attorney Carter and asked him how things looked. He said he thought Monday's hearing would be only a formality and that they could get at least a two-week stay. He said he and lawyer Powell would be working through the night, reviewing documents and precedents. He admitted, in response to my direct question, that they had not yet formulated a line of defense for Keith. He sounded very depressed.

I went to bed and riffled through my notebooks—ordinarily a fail-safe soporific. Not so on that night. I remembered one thing that seemed to have been already forgotten: the matter of the Stones' record deal, which was a major reason for their convening in Toronto. I had been unable to reach either Ahmet Ertegun of Atlantic Records or Mike Maitland of MCA Records. Both were in town and both seemed to be the finalists in bidding for the Rolling Stones' future. What I wanted to ask them, of course, was this: How much have the stakes changed since Keith was busted? A band's ability to tour is central to record sales. Now, there was much talk throughout the record industry that the Stones were damaged goods, as far as tour potential went. Even should Keith beat the rap, large portions of the world—especially Japan, Australia, and the Far East—were probably off-limits to the Stones. RSO Records two days earlier had withdrawn from the bidding. RSO spokesperson Anni Ivil said, "On March 2, 1977, RSO Records withdrew a $7 million offer to the Rolling Stones for their recording rights to the U.S.A. after protracted negotiations. The personal affairs of the band had no bearing on the thinking of the company. The decision was made strictly on commercial terms." The odd thing about that announcement is that it was unsolicited and that, greatly out of character for a record company, the announcement actually volunteered information: No one had asked RSO whether "personal affairs of the band" had anything to do with anything.

There was also the crucial matter of any Stones' capability of ever touring the United States again. John Ardway, of the U.S. State Department had told me that there are "certain types" of foreigners who cannot obtain visas through normal State Department channels, especially including individuals convicted on drug charges. Waivers for such individuals are handled on an individual, highly scrutinized basis. Verne Jarvis, speaking for the Immigration and Naturalization Service, said, "Mr. Richards has obtained waivers on prior convictions enabling him to tour the United

States with his band. Obviously, the more offenses you pile up, the harder it is to get a visa."

Saturday, March 5, 1977

When I opened my Willy Loman Memorial Module door to scoop up the newspapers and spied the headlines, I could kind of tell that all of a sudden all of the stakes here had been raised one hell of a lot. It didn't take much in the way of IQ, after all, to read the screaming, red-ink, redder-than-shame banner headline splashed across page one of the Toronto *Star*—MARGARET DROPS IN ON THE STONES, it shrieked to realize that a national crisis of sorts was springing full-blown out of a chance rock and roll liaison and perhaps (did the newspapers know?) from a white bathrobe and a late-night rock and roll party in Suite 3219 of the Harbour Castle. Toronto seemed to be turning itself upside down. What was amusing was that none of the newspapers knew that Margaret was staying in the hotel, even though the Toronto *Star* itself had its offices in a building just across the street from the Harbour Castle. The British reporters in the hotel lobby were in a virtual feeding frenzy.

Wasserman called to let me know that I was still banned from the El Mocambo that night. I thanked him for the courtesy and warned, "Wasserman, I'm going to be in that club tonight, no matter what it takes. You can't treat the press this way."

"No way," he said and I could almost see the weary shrug of his shoulders. "It's Peter's orders."

After a few hours of arguing with Wasserman and Rudge, I seemed to find myself being wheeled on a gurney down the bleak hallways of the St. Michael's Hospital emergency room, being wheeled past the Saturday night drunks and stabbing victims.

"Nerves and high blood pressure from arguments such as you describe could well lead to a nervous breakdown," said a crisp Dr. Wilkinson, who was attending to me. "By the way, who is this Rudge person you were raving about?"

I attempted to explain. She tsk-tsked and said it was a wonder that I was not down at the police station being booked for assault and battery. "I didn't know the Rolling Stones were even in town," said Dr. Wilkinson.

"They certainly are," I said, "and, in fact, the way things are going over at that hotel, you may well be seeing a lot of people pass through your emergency room here. They seem to have a few problems over there."

As Dr. Wilkinson ministered to me, I sent word to the hotel to let Peter Rudge know that I had just "been rushed to the hospital." Barely fifteen minutes later, as I sat up on my gurney and smoked a Dunhill contentedly and chatted with Dr. Wilkinson, the emergency room's swinging doors swung open to admit UPI's Richard van Abbe on a dead run. "Jeez, what happened to you?" he blurted. "Everybody thought you were killed or something."

I asked Dr. Wilkinson for my clothes and told van Abbe, "Let's get the hell over to the El Mocambo."

We stopped at the Harbour Castle, where I found waiting for me at the desk—not surprisingly—a pass for the El Mocambo, with no note of explanation. For the first time, as van Abbe and I headed for Spadina Avenue, I read my copy of the St. Michael's Hospital admission form. "Listen to this, Richard," I said, "for quote reason of admission unquote this says I was quote very shaky unquote." We laughed. "That could also apply to the Stones' future," I said. After a moment, van Abbe added, "Or to Rudge's."

We got past the police barricades on Spadina and slipped through the crowds and into the club with suspiciously little resistance, mainly by going through the back alley and through the stage door. There was only one slightly anxious moment, when we had to dive for cover as a huge black Caddy limo roared down the narrow alleyway and screeched to a halt by the stage door. Who should get out—alone—but Anita herself? Television camera crews perched up on the roof turned on their Stun gun lights and captured the magic moment. We got inside and settled down at a little table at stage front with Lisa Robinson and John Rockwell of the New York *Times*, both of whom had flown in at the last minute when Rudge's press ban on U.S. reporters had been lifted; which lifting, I of course knew nothing about, thanks to the Stones hierarchy's somewhat peculiar sense of humor and—more likely—notions of vengeance. (Later the Toronto *Globe & Mail* would write: "Saturday was a heavy day for those involved in the venture. Anybody who had done anybody in Toronto a favor in the last five years was demanding a ticket . . . Paul Wasserman, the Stones' Los Angeles publicist, was enjoying himself, allowing his grudge against *Rolling Stone* magazine to develop into a refusal, later recanted, to allow associate editor Chet Flippo into the El Mocambo. Flippo was spotted, very anguished, in the lobby of the Harbour Castle hotel. He was hustling everybody but the doorman for a seat." Well. If I was spotted at all, it was with spots of fury. The Toronto *Sun* was a bit kinder and just said that I was there because that was where I had to be. The Toronto *Star*'s coverage failed to mention me, perhaps because the night before I had maybe alienated the *Star*'s rock writer, who was lounging in the driveway of the hotel and wearing what looked like a chauffeur's cap and so I naturally swept majestically out the door and directed him to get me a car. Bad judgment, it seems now. But what the hey? Even as I was sitting down, Rudge yelled at Wasserman that he would have him thrown out if any American reporters got a table. Said Wasserman: "You can't throw me out. I signed my own pass. You didn't sign it."

Rudge visibly was grinding his teeth, but came over to inquire as to my health and to say, "I planned all along to let you in."

"Sure, Peter," I said. "I'll always believe you." With a nervous twitch of a smile, he was off to swirl up little pockets of hysteria elsewhere.

Wasserman leaned over to say to me, "The only reason you got a pass tonight is because Peter thought he had killed you."

"Well," I told him, "the only reason Peter thinks he killed me is because I intended to get into this son of a bitch tonight. By any means necessary."

I could see Wasserman's mind working as different expressions flashed across his face. He was clearly thinking: The bastard finally got even. Did he stage the whole thing?

The house lights went down and us bar band devotees, packed ass to elbow around little tables that might generously be described as the size of a dinner plate, ordered four beers at once (apiece) because you know how chaotic the service gets in a bar once the band starts playing. The band here finally straggled onstage in front of the mock-tropical backdrop just after 11:00 P.M. Keith Richards looked as if he belonged in the St. Michael's Hospital emergency room. He was hollow-cheeked, unshaven, gaunt, and he was so almost translucently pale that you automatically wondered how many years it had been since Mr. Sun had shined down on him. He smiled beatifically, though—almost as if he had just gotten out of jail—as he hit the first dead-note licks on his black Gibson guitar (with the design of a human skull on it) of the tortured introduction of "Honky Tonk Women." The decibel level of hanging notes and screaming bar band crowd was fearsome indeed. Talk about some kind of charged, crackling atmosphere between a band that usually counts its audience in the five or six figures and a raucous bunch of beer-drinking hell-raisers of an audience. Both rose admirably to the occasion. A version of Muddy Waters's "Mannish Boy," with its signature lyric of "I'm a rollin' stone," was as rock-bottom raunchy as anything the Stones have ever done: This was prime Rolling Stones before celebrityhood; this was music for music's sake.

Mick was wearing his little green- and white-striped jumpsuit, open in the front way down past his waistline and even lower, and red and white socks and white jazz shoes. He was loose and limber and ready for a tanked-up bar crowd that was prepared to take no prisoners. That show was as good a show as the Stones likely ever gave or may give again. It may have been rooted in desperation, but, nonetheless, the Stones pulled out all the stops. Even Mr. Rockwell of the New York *Times* wrote that the Stones "went back to their roots, knocking out raunchy British rhythm and blues in a smoky club. The only nagging fear was that it might have been the completion of a circle, coming back to the beginning at the end. Mr. Richards, who is the band's co-leader and co-songwriter with Mr. Jagger, was arrested last Sunday on a charge of possession of heroin for the pursuit of trafficking. The Rolling Stones would be inconceivable without Mr. Richards. Should he wind up in jail, it might mean the end of the band. But last night was more an affirmation than a denial. Given the energy, conviction, and sheer joy here, it was almost impossible to believe that this could be the end of anything." Well. Once the stolid, slow-to-move *Times* gets around to saying something, it's usually last century's news. How significant that even Mr. Rockwell could sniff out the odor of imminent destruction and death here. And he was certainly prescient about a "conviction" here. (Ha, ha. Sorry, Keith.) Still, the Stones faced down their demons on that night and played gut-bucket rock and roll with a fury.

The floor was awash in beer even before the second number, "All Down the Line," got off the ground and the very walls seemed to vibrate from the sheer wall of noise from the "Let's get fucked up" crowd and the Stones' own multidecibel output. Mick, obviously enjoying himself hugely, was defiantly prancing and strutting almost like . . . like . . . Mick Jagger! Two young women whom he quickly dubbed the "Feelie Sisters" were practically crawling across the low lip of the stage to grab his flesh. He grabbed one of the Feelies by the top of her head and shoved her back into the surging mob. She loved it and leaped back for more. Bill Wyman was over at stage left signing autographs. It suddenly occurred to me that this was the first time I had ever seen the Rolling Stones perform with none of them wearing any makeup whatsoever (even cherub-faced Bill Wyman usually used dark rouge and eyeliner to make himself look sinister). And what a statement about the progress of rock and roll their appearance made: haggard, lined faces, men aging totally ungracefully but happy to damn the consequences (and proud of the sobriquet "They only come out at night") and still setting the benchmark by which any rock and roll band must be judged and still sounding harder than Boulder Dam.

Jagger leaped up and hit the low ceiling at the spirited finish of "Hand of Fate" and then leaned over to stare at those of us clustered at the press table. "Are you critics enjoying it?" he asked, with a tad more sarcasm than he needed to make his point. "You all know that we're doing this show just for the critics." The crowd took his cue and gave us a resounding round of booing. He jumped into "Route 66," which is real vintage Stones material and not the sort of thing you will get from them in the arena shows.

"Are you havin' a good time?" Mick asked to a chorus of deafening cheers and whistles. "Cause," he continued, "we're gonna do lots tonight. We feel like dancin'." Keith and Woody alternated pulls on a fifth of Jack Daniel's sour mash whiskey and they all signed more autographs. "Aw right!" Jagger yelled, "I wanta hear you yell on this one!" He positively snarled the lyrics of "Star Star" (a/k/a "Starfucker") and took great delight in screaming "you're a starfucker, yes you are," first at Maggie Trudeau and then at your humble servants at the press table. Well, it was his show, after all, and he danced like a man possessed. He ended up on his back on the floor with one of the Feelie Sisters lying on top of him and reaching inside his jumpsuit. He was doing his part by caressing her ass. Great cheers from the weaving crowd. When he regained his feet, he just laughed and said, "This is our last night at the El Mocambo. It's been lovely." With that, the Stones were away to the races with a 90 m.p.h. version of "Let's Spend the Night Together." Even though everyone in the crowd had been searched earlier for tape recorders and cameras, I could hear entire phalanxes of tape recorders clicking back on under the tables. One heartless soul yelled to Keith, "Hey, drop dead, Richards," and I thought I heard subsequent muffled punches and groans from that general direction.

"Let's do another blues," Mick said. "This is Chollie"—as he pointed to drummer Charlie Watts. "And this is Ollie"—he pointed to percussionist Ollie Brown. "If you'd like to go back to the Harbour Castle with Ollie, you can meet his mother." Ollie just beamed. Keith and Woody picked up slide guitars and hit slashing, knifelike chords to kick off "Little Red Rooster," another American blues gem that the rock arena crowd doesn't get. The Stones fully reverted to what they actually were in the beginning: English schoolboys faithfully aping American Southern blues singers. If there were any way to get temporary skin transplants, these Limey boys would be black every night onstage. As it was, they played it a hell of a lick and still sounded surprisingly blacker than most white Limeys and than even a few gentrified, upwardly mobile American Negro singers who sensed that "the blues" was actually sung by field niggers not long off the ship. Better a marcelled hairdo and a drape suit and a record contract in Chi-cago or New York than Can't Bust 'Em overalls and a chaw of Red Man tobackky and kowtowing to the White Massa and moaning about staring up the backside of a mule on those endless plow rows instead of singing about dancing with some foxy high-yellow pussy at the Aragon Ballroom. Not a white experience—especially not a white and British experience. Still, even Mick Jagger, middle-class and socially grasping as he was, had the lungs and the soul to out-soul many brothers. And Keith Richards, who had no blood in his veins any more and whose soul had been stained blacker than black many years before by the same spirits that anointed the legendary Robert Johnson, glowed with an internal combustion that I'm not sure any scientist in the Western world could identify. Or would want to.

As if there was any possibility that this could have been the last Rolling Stones concert ever, Keith reached into his back pocket or somewhere for licks and notes he surely had not hit in years and in "Jumping Jack Flash" he seemed to have transcended his smack addiction and sounded again as if he was wired directly in to some pulsating black hole in space. He played good is what I mean to say and when Keith is on, ain't nobody can touch him.

The three hundred faithful in the El Mocambo were stomping the floor into splinters and there was a palpable smell of raw sex hanging in the air along with the ugly stink of a potential violence that said, "We might just tear this sucker apart." In other words, the women wanted to fuck the Stones and the men wanted to be the Stones—and since they couldn't, they wanted to beat the shit out of them. Elemental themes of rock and roll. How refreshing to see them resurrected for real after years of antiseptic music passed off as rock. Even the Stones seemed surprised that they had tapped into the cosmic pulse or whatever the hell it is that makes real rock and roll real rock and roll. You can't define it: It either is real or it's garbage.

As the Stones crashed to a runaway garbage truck sound to close out "Jumping Jack," I sensed a presence behind me. It was Peter Rudge. He was waving at Mick and pointing to our table. Rudge grabbed Lisa Robinson's hair and made sure she couldn't move. Mick responded by grabbing a two-gallon bucket of ice water and heaving it onto us at the press table. What a thrill. Still, the price was right: a free show and free beer on the Stones. And a free shower at the end. And free Stones' transportation back to the hotel.

The Stones and Margaret Trudeau screamed out of the alley in limos headed for a private party hosted by a famous Toronto hostess, a party which, of course, the press will never darken the door of. Back at the Harbour Castle, I had a drink in the lobby with Danny Marcus, who had just jetted in from New York. Marcus was director of artist relations at Atlantic Records, and the Stones of course were about to be re-signed by Atlantic. For some reason, Marcus was wearing a World War II U.S. GI helmet, a long military greatcoat over an olive-drab Army uniform and jackboots, and was carrying a swagger stick. He and Anita were the only two humans that I saw get genuine doubletakes from ordinary citizens in the Harbour Castle lobby. I asked Danny why, since he was director of artist relations at Atlantic, he wasn't out relating with his artists (viz., the Rolling Stones). He smiled knowingly, ordered more drinks (all charged to the Stones, of course), and just said, "I'm not sure that these artists *want* to relate."

Sunday, March 6, 1977

Reveille came late for this correspondent. The night before, Danny Marcus and Paul Wasserman made a dedicated effort to ensure that all visiting press representatives had an opportunity to sample the many and varied types of spirits that Canada offered. Obviously, it was a transparent ploy to keep us pesky types away from the Stones and to basically defuse us. And of course it worked perfectly. Wasserman was not handpicked by the Stones for no good reason.

Anyway, all I had managed to line up for Sunday was a 6:00 P.M. meeting with Peter Rudge. Naturally, he disappeared and stood me up. I stared out the window of my Willy Loman Memorial Module at that damn ever-gray dome of a sky pressing down against dead trees and gray ice and cursed the day that rock and roll was born. How thrilling it is for a grown man, who claims to be a legitimate reporter and writer, to spend day after day in a hotel bubble, while trying to track down some rich hedonists. How many times should anyone be forced to watch *Flesh Gordon* or *Little Girl, Big Tease* or *Young Playmates* or "The Best of the New York Erotic Film Festival" on cable TV when nothing else is on? No wonder Rudge went looney, I figured. This is no way to live.

Then the phone rang and I almost didn't answer it, since I was expecting some kind of lame apology from Rudge. Finally, my sense of duty prevailed and I picked up the receiver.

"Mr. Flippo? This is Mr. Jagger calling."

I was fuming. "Bullshit! This is Rudge or some lackey. Listen, I'm tired of being conned and furthermore—"

The caller cut me off. "Mr. Flippo, this *is* Mr. Jagger. I can prove it. You sent me a note saying you wished to speak with me. Well, I'm just sitting around waiting to be busted. Why don't you come on up? I'm in 3424."

Christ! I thought, it actually is Jagger! Bribing these maids really works.

Up on thirty-four, there were none of the usual beefy Stones' bodyguards flanking the corridor entrance. At 3424, the door was open and I spied Jagger, in tan suit and red boots, sitting alone watching TV. He waved me in.

"What happened to all the Stones' vaunted security force?" I asked.

"Oh, why bother," Jagger said. "Have a seat."

He was watching "Candid Camera." In a moment, Charlie Watts walked in and the two of them were soon giggling at a segment wherein a hapless woman in a beauty parlor kept seeing a demon in the mirror. Jagger finally got up and turned down the sound on the TV.

"Are you having a good time?" he asked.

"As good a time as you can have hanging out in limbo. How does it feel to be a bar band again?"

Watts answered, with a grimace, "A bar band? Awful!"

"Very nice," Jagger said. "It was a nice gig. It wasn't just people paying to come in, if you know what I mean."

"Was this," I asked, "your lowest-paying gig ever? Was it just for union scale wages?"

"Yeah, I guess," Jagger answered. "We got beer money—half the bar take, which was $371 the first night. So we didn't do it for the money, obviously."

"Why did you pick such a small club?" I asked.

"So we could get a good sound. And we liked the idea of playing a club. Toronto is part of North America and it just seemed easier to do it here. But it didn't turn out that way. Keith got busted. It won't be so easy for Keith. The club part of it turned out more or less how we thought it would."

"Well," I said, "I missed almost all of the Friday show—"

"Really?" Mick cut me off. "Why was that?"

"Because Peter Rudge is trying to do a number on me," I said. Jagger didn't crack a smile. "So what stuff did you play Friday?"

"Well," Jagger said, "we didn't do that many new songs. We did a lot of songs that we've never done—that we've recorded but have never done on shows. We did 'Let's Spend the Night Together' and I don't even remember playing that live, apart from once. And stuff like 'Little Red Rooster' that we haven't played for years."

"Have you," I asked, "heard the tapes from last night yet?"

"No," Jagger said. He poured fresh cups of coffee. "I heard a cassette, but it was a really rotten sound. So I haven't heard the tapes for real yet."

"It seemed," I said, "that a problem with the acoustics there was that your voice didn't always come up enough."

"I couldn't hear," Jagger said. "Where you were sitting was the worst place because it's a long room. The actual best sound was on the sides."

"Where I was sitting," I said, "was also the worst place because it was the easiest place for you to finally baptize the press. That was a lot of water you threw."

Jagger threw his head back and laughed. "That's because," he finally said, "you were sitting in the critics' circle. Actually, the sound up front wasn't very good."

"Yeah," I said, "but you spent a lot of time there, where those chicks were trying to rip your clothes off."

Jagger grinned broadly. "Oh yes, the Feelies, the Feelie sisters."

"Is there," I asked, "any considerable anxiety or worry within the group because of Keith's case?"

"I don't want to talk about it," Jagger said a bit testily, "because the more I talk about it, the worse it gets. I don't want to talk because they all read this fucking crap, these people, that's the trouble. Yeah, it's difficult, you know. You get busted all the time. It makes it very hard."

"Well," I wondered aloud, "was the problem that Keith should have come in here with the rest of the group rather than sailing in as he did?"

Jagger shook his head. "No. I don't think it would have made any difference. We all came separately. I don't think it would have made any difference at all."

A commercial for a Dr. Seuss book appeared on the TV screen. Watts spoke up. "I hate those books."

"Me too," said Jagger.

A long silence ensued as we studied the TV and sipped coffee.

And then we discussed children's books and finally agreed that Maurice Sendak's books were good for kids.

"How," I asked, "did Margaret Trudeau's interest in the Stones develop?"

Jagger grinned slyly "I don't know. She just dropped by. Someone said she wanted to come to the gig, so we took her. I had never met her before. But I guess she likes to go out to clubs and go rocking and rolling like everyone else—a young girl, you know."

"She's one of our mums," Watts said very primly.

And that was clearly that—and no more—on Maggie.

"Are you," I ask, "as the local reporters say, going to play the El Mocambo again?"

Jagger threw up his hands in frustration. "What am I going to say? No . . . never . . . what?"

"Well," I said, "the reason I ask is that a lot of Canadian reporters are calling me because they think I know everything about it and their bottom line is that the Canadian newspapers are going to say that last night's show could well have been the last Rolling Stones performance ever."

Jagger groaned. "Oh no, not again. Our Knebworth concert [on August 21, 1976] was supposed to be the last Rolling Stones performance."

"And there was another last one sometime in America," Watts added.

"We'll let you know when the last one is," Jagger said. "Or maybe we won't let you know."

"When my drums start to get blown up," Watts said, "that's the last one."

"Well, I think that's all rubbish," Jagger said. "That is just journalistic claptrap. That's just looking for a pathetic angle."

"Well, that's not what I mean," I said, "but the feeling that I got came from having to explain myself to a Mountie in the lobby when he saw the Stones logo on my suitcase from the '75 tour and then I was looking out the window at that damn frozen harbour and I started thinking about *The Prisoner of Zenda* and that you guys might never be able to leave here."

"Oh"—Jagger chuckled indulgently—"collective traits of paranoia. Now the lake is melting and it's all very well. Spring is on the way."

"Well," I said, "I could just see Ahmet buzzing in with the corporate jet to spirit everyone out of the country in a lightning-fast raid."

Jagger laughed. "It's not that difficult to get out of here."

"But didn't the Mounties take all your passports?" I asked.

"No," Jagger said. "Why? Why should they take our passports?"

"Well," I said, "that is what Wasserman told me. He said that twenty-eight passports were seized."

Jagger sat bolt upright. "Wasserman told you that? Why would they *possibly* take Charlie's and my passport?"

"I have no idea," I offered.

"They took Keith's passport," Jagger said, "but they didn't take ours. Why would they? Wasserman told you that? Are you *sure?*"

"Positive," I said.

"If I ask Wasserman, he'll deny having told you that," Jagger said with a note of resignation.

"Of course he will," I replied. "If I ask him, he'll deny having said it. See, that's one of your problems here. There is going to be a hell of a lot of crap written about all this, when even responsible journalists such as myself finally get to Wasserman and then that's all that I can find out from him. And of course Rudge is nuts right now."

Jagger leaned forward with interest: "Go ahead. Keep going. What else did he tell you?"

"What else did Wasserman tell me?" I asked. "Wait a minute! I'm telling *you* what you're paying *him* to tell *me*."

"Well," Jagger said, "I didn't tell him to tell you anything."

"Maybe not," I said, "but you're paying him to supposedly keep the press informed or not informed."

Mick lost interest. "Yeah, okay."

After some more TV viewing, I ventured to say that I perhaps had never seen the Stones play better than they had the night before.

Jagger jumped on that. "No, that's not true. I don't think the band played better than ever, but they did play pretty good. I mean, you know you can play in a club like that and you don't have to entertain. That's the advantage. There is a minimum amount of entertaining. You don't feel constrained to entertain, you know, so you can just concentrate on playing or singing or whatever you do. So I wouldn't say that this has been the best the band has played. It was pretty good, considering that this was only the second gig. In another five days it would sound a lot better, obviously. I mean, I'm not saying it sounded bad."

"Would the Stones tour without Keith?" I asked.

Jagger raised his eyebrows. "If Keith were in jail for a long time, a very long time?"

"Yeah," I said, "for more than a few months."

"Yeah, I should say so," Jagger said. "If they wanted to. I mean, if the Stones wanted to tour badly or wanted to go onstage, I think they'd have to. Obviously, we wouldn't if Keith was only in jail for a month or two months, but if he was in jail for a long period of time, I suppose we'd have to."

"For five or so years?" I asked.

"Yeah," Jagger said. "We can't wait five years. In five years, we won't be touring at all. Not much anyway, just a few lounges."

There was a knock at the door. Keith's guitar maker and guitar caretaker Newman Jones III stuck his head in the door and announced in his Arkansas accent that, "Hey, Mick, I'll have that new guitar for you tomorrow." He withdrew.

"What was that?" Mick asked. "I don't remember ordering a guitar. Apparently, I ordered one." He shook his head.

"Are you still going to try to tour the Pacific and Far East this year?" I asked. "What's your visa situation there, apart from Keith's situation? Can you just call those governments up and see where you stand?"

"Oh no," Mick said. "You won't get any clear answers out of any of them. They'll just say no unless you've got plans to say you are definitely going to tour there."

"But what if you have a definite tour planned?" I asked.

"No," Jagger said flatly. "I don't think you will get anywhere with that tactic. You can phone the State Department up and they will say that it is completely within their discretion. That's what they'll tell you. So, so what? If you phone the Japanese, they'll say no or maybe. The Japanese wouldn't let me in the last time."

"Into Japan?" I asked.

"Oh yes," Watts said. "He was the one they wouldn't let in."

"Anyway," Jagger said, "it's a different government now. They did that to McCartney, too."

"Are things here," I asked, "as serious as people make them out to be?"

"I don't know what people are making them out to be," Jagger countered.

"Well," I said, "all the London press can talk about is that Keith faces life."

"Apparently, he does," Jagger said wryly.

"But is that the story?" I asked.

"I don't think he'll get life," Mick said, getting up to pace a bit. "That's the sort of angle the London newspapers would write about."

"And," I said, "the Canadian press is interested only in Margaret Trudeau."

"Yeah," Jagger said with a tight grin. Silence ensued.

"And"—I decided to go ahead with another stupid statement—"the American papers want to know when the next album will be out and what will it sound like."

Jagger positively sparkled with his reply. "It's delightful. It will be out in March. It's a live one."

He was getting antsy. "Well," I said, "what is the band's future right now? It's not as if you can draw up a five-year plan."

"Well, no"—Jagger laughed—"we can't really do a five-year plan at the rate things are going at the moment. I did do a plan for two years, but that's going to be changed."

"Was that for touring Japan, Germany, Australia, South America?" I asked.

"Yeah," he said. "I did it in January. It was all planned. Now it is all different."

Charlie Watts tore himself away from the TV to say, "So you can never—"

Jagger cut in to say, "Still, you have to plan the tours."

"Oh yes, I know," Watts said.

"Because we don't play the same place every year," Mick added.

"We tried it in America and South America," Watts said.

"You still have to plan," Mick said. "You have to think about where you are going to go—"

"Well," Watts said, "what with five people like this, you can't—so we'll just do Vegas and forget it."

That was obviously their tag line, but I decided to try to stretch it a bit, foolishly. "That's right," I said, "a lot of groups are playing the Aladdin Hotel there now. I don't know what it seats."

"About 7:30," Jagger said dryly.

I can take a hint. "Brilliant, Mick," I said, getting up to leave.

"All right, Chet," he said with his most sincere crinkly smile.

What a thrill.

Monday, March 7, 1977

What was this going on in the Willy Loman Memorial Module? Its inhabitant, your humble servant, was, for the first time, in bed before midnight. I (for there is no longer any use in pretending; it is indeed me) had noble intentions to get a sound night's sleep, rise before dawn, cut a wide swath through RCMP headquarters before lunch, and then make short work of Keith Richards's court appearance in the early afternoon and subsequently sky off to Gotham City in time for a cozy dinner at Elaine's and be free of this wretched, frozen, paranoid mess for a spell. And the prospect of a Sunday night in Toronto in a hotel full of rock and roll deviates was perhaps as depressing a notion as jumping into the frozen harbour. For this reason: No alcohol was sold or dispensed or legally drunk in Ontario on Sundays in 1977. In World War II, armies marched on their stomachs; in the seventies, rock and roll armies swam with their livers. Cut off the supply of powerful spirits and you get some undesirable side effects. A lot of banging on doors to see who was hoarding stashes of Jack Daniel's. (A bootlegger could have earned ten times as much as the most beautiful prostitute in the world with that crowd.) Though it didn't advertise the fact, the Harbour Castle would discreetly supply a potent drink along with an order of food. If you knew about that. That's why when you walked up and down the hallways of the Harbour Castle, you were practically wading in piles of discarded room service trays and carts spilling over with all these crumbling cold hamburgers that were never meant to be eaten in the first place. One burger, one drink! The Stones' entourage could have fed the whole Third World.

So late Sunday in the Harbour Castle was a maelstrom of booze-seeking and bribing of room service and generally uninteresting behavior. In the lobby, security guards were discovering and evicting a new phenomenon: out-of-town Stones fanatics crashing on the floor in their sleeping bags. The Stones army was gathering to show its support for Keith.

Meanwhile, up in 723, yours truly was happily stacking Z's. Then, just after midnight, the phone rang. No one who has ever met a deadline can resist the temptation of a ringing phone: You never know who will be on the other end of the line. Sometimes, you learn, you should try to fight the temptation. I picked up the phone. It was sometimes Stones percussionist Ollie Brown.

"I'm ready for my interview, man," he said. "Come on up." This had been going on for two years. On the "Rolling Stones Tour of the Americas '75," I had mentioned to Ollie that I would like to talk to him sometime for a little while about what it was like to play with the Stones. Periodically, my chickens came home to roost. Now they were sitting on my head. I liked Ollie, though, and he was a genuinely talented musician whom I wouldn't mind helping if I could.

I went up to thirty-two, forgetting that it was also Keith's floor (as well as Maggie Trudeau's) until I was suddenly surrounded by Stones' bodyguard Bob Bender, who is as wide as Mick is tall.

"Hey, Ollie's got a chick in with him," Bender said softly. That was fine with me and I was ankling the scene when the door of 3226 opened and Ollie's head appeared: "Hey, man, come on in."

In the room, I was treated to the sight of a young woman buttoning her blouse and zipping her skirt up and then leaving. Ollie, in his feathers and beads, settled down on the couch and said that the lawyers, man, had forbidden him to mention the Stones at all, but that he really wanted to tell me all about his new production company (called Brown Sugar, of all things) and so on.

What a thrill.

Back to bed, to sleep until noon at least, since Keith was not due to appear in court until 2:00 P.M. Likely all that would happen, the lawyers had assured me, was that he would appear briefly at old City Hall and be remandered to a later hearing.

The Monday morning newspapers, as Paul Wasserman pointed out to me when his call woke me at 6:00 A.M., were full of Margaret Trudeau. Wasserman said he had really called just to let me know that I had made two of the papers myself: The *Globe & Mail* ran that business of me being "anguished" (Wasserman loved that touch; I accused him of planting the story) and "hustling" a seat to the Stones show and the *Sun* said that I had broken Rudge's ban on American journalists attending the concert. Another giant thrill.

Back to a fitful sleep until—glory!—actual sunbeams streamed through the window of the Willy Loman Memorial Module. I was so happy at the thought of the sun burning away all that grayness outside that I bounded out of bed, directed room service to send Breakfast Adventures No. 1 and No. 4—what the hell—and grabbed the morning papers.

The *Globe & Mail* was subdued, but the Toronto *Sun* splashed its front with a red headline reading: SUPERFAN MAGGIE GETS LIFT FROM THE STONES. Beneath that was a picture of Maggie leaving the El Mocambo. The caption read: "The rumor mills worked overtime yesterday, after Prime Minister Trudeau's wife Margaret showed up for the second consecutive night at the El Mocambo on Spadina Avenue for a performance by the Rolling Stones. Maggie, slipping into a limousine to return with the Stones to their hotel early yesterday, was under the watchful eye of Metro police security officers." Not all that watchful, maybe, since she was still upstairs at the Harbour Castle doing whatever it was she was doing. (The *Sun* ran a picture of Ron Wood with a towel over his head and the caption claimed that he was getting into Maggie's limo.) I did not like to criticize my foreign hosts, but it seemed to me that the Toronto press corps was a bit slow in figuring out certain things.

On its noon newscast, radio station CHUM announced that Keith would appear at 2:00 P.M. at old City Hall (and a later CHUM newscast would carry a complaint that too many citizens had tried to get into the courtroom and jammed the court plaza) and I heard later from more than two reliable sources that the RCMP had more or less encouraged CHUM to broadcast Keith's appearance as a come-on to the Stones army, so that the presence of this supposed hippie, ragtag band of Stones followers polluting City Hall would heavily sway public opinion in the politically correct manner. CHUM later claimed that a "Mountie informant" had called them and said that the RCMP intended to "make an example of Keith Richards." (By the way, that morning I ran across a CHUM document that you might find diverting. It is a letter dated October 27, 1964, from CHUM then-program director Allan Slaight to a listener who had complained because CHUM refused to play any Stones records. Slaight's reply: "Dear Gary: Many entertainers have personal habits that are not particularly commendable. In the case of the Rolling Stones, however, we believe that they or their publicity manager have deliberately attempted to exploit poor taste to a ridiculous extreme. I do not recall another phase of the music business in which the stars boasted that they did not like to bathe! If, at any time, CHUM is shown proof that this statement was publicized in error, or that the Rolling Stones and their management team have decided to improve the presentation of these young singers to the world, we will naturally be delighted to feature their music. Sincerely, Allan Slaight.")

I got down to old City Hall (it's called "old" to distinguish it from the new one, but the Canadians refuse to use capital letters correctly) at 1:00 P.M. and ran into a mob of several hundred young people milling around the imposing gray granite structure. Wasserman had promised the

Toronto press that Keith would arrive at the front door—and he did. He
was a trifle late. The band had rehearsed all night again, so, at 1:30 P.M.,
Anita had knocked on Bill Carter's door to borrow a razor for Keith. At
2:00, he emerged from a station wagon and marched up the old City Hall
steps with his head up and his white scarf flying above his black velvet
suit. He drew cheers from the crowd until he neared the doors, when an
unidentified photographer grabbed him by the hair and tried to wrestle
him down, while screaming, "Deport the Limey!" A willowy blond
woman, who later identified herself to me only as "Bonnie," screamed,
"Evil cocksucker!" at Keith and followed him inside to continue her
screaming. Neither person was detained or arrested by the Metro officers
and RCMP constables escorting Richards into court. The hearing was
immediately closed to the public, on the Metro police's suggestion that
there existed a "mob scene." In Courtroom 26, Keith and an audience
consisting of Wasserman, Bill Carter, yours truly, and Toronto reporters
listened to a brief session wherein Keith's lawyer, Clayton Powell, and
federal prosecutor David Scott agreed before Judge Vincent McEwan to
remand Keith's hearing on his heroin charge until next Monday. Then,
after the Canadian reporters were sent on their way, Keith was put in a
holding cell for half an hour while Judge McEwan held a private session in
his chambers with Scott and Powell and Carter. Scott dropped the bomb-
shell that a second charge was just laid against one Keith Richards, a
charge of cocaine possession. Scott said that the RCMP raiding party had
seized a white powder that laboratory tests had just established amounted
to one-fifth of an ounce of cocaine. Judge McEwan directed Powell to
produce defendant Richards in court in a secret hearing the following day,
Tuesday, to be dealt with on this additional charge. Prosecutor Scott made
no secret of the fact that he planned to ask for revocation of bail and to
move that Keith be jailed immediately. The Tuesday, March 8, hearing
remained an official secret: None of the Toronto newspapers or radio or
TV stations knew about it; it was not listed on any court docket; and no
one in a position of authority in old City Hall admitted to knowing anything about it.

Margaret Trudeau heard about it and told one Stones' insider that
she wouldn't let Keith go to jail, but the extent of her authority was quite
uncertain.

The Stones camp at the Harbour Castle fell into an absolute panic.
The odds were heavy that Keith, still a junkie, would be behind bars
within twenty-four hours and would likely never get out again. Wasserman
canceled a press conference, during the course of which the Stones' hierarchy had planned to allow Keith to appear for a moment or two. Tense
meetings went on throughout the Harbour Castle. The five Rolling Stones

themselves held an almost unprecedented band meeting, the minutes of which are still secret. I found out that, during this afternoon's hearing, Bill Carter had phoned Stones headquarters at the Harbour Castle with a direct order to assemble $25,000 in cash. As soon as he sniffed out prosecutor David Scott's intentions to revoke bail and jail Keith, Carter wanted to scrape up as much cold cash as he could get his hands on. The reason? The feeling in the hallways of old City Hall was that the RCMP wanted blood because they had busted a notorious figure who then got out on basically no bail. Keith Richards had, regretfully, tarnished the badge of the RCMP and must pay for that. The only possible and immediate defense, Carter decided, was to keep Keith out of jail by anticipating the prosecution and offering to have Keith's bail increased significantly and to have the greenbacks right there in court, ready to hand over. What better way to defuse the RCMP's anger about the humiliation of bail so low that it was a virtual insult to the Mounties?

I heard that WEA Records (Warner-Elektra-Atlantic) had apparently re-signed the Stones to a record contract and had provided the instant $25,000 in cash that suddenly appeared at the Harbour Castle. I also heard that WEA had offered another $200,000 in instant cash and that attorney Carter had spurned the offer, saying that anything above $25,000 in bail would amount to blackmail.

Wasserman called me at 5:25 P.M. to advise me to "change travel plans. The cocaine hearing is tomorrow. The hearing is supposed to be a secret. If you say I told you this, I'll deny it. Ciao." He called back at 6:30 P.M. and sounded worried. "I hear there will be no bail for Keith at all. I advise you to cancel all your travel plans."

A Toronto attorney, who must remain nameless, called to talk about the case. He had already heard, via Ottawa, that Maggie Trudeau had offered the Stones her assistance to keep Keith out of prison. "She has no influence at all," he said. He also said that the word in governmental circles in Canada was that "[Ontario Attorney General Roy] McMurtry is politically ambitious and wants to put Keith away to help his career. There is also pressure from the Mounties, who think they have to make an example of Keith. By the way," he said, "do you know what Marlon [Keith's seven-year-old son] called the Mounties who busted Keith? 'Worthless fuckers,' that's what!" He laughed. "It's a damn wonder they didn't bust Marlon, too!"

After another indescribable adventure of a room service dinner and many phone calls, I went down and wandered through the Harbour Castle's lobby. And ran into Peter Rudge and Bill Carter, conferring over drinks in a dark corner. Rudge, who was unshaven and visibly shaken, drew me aside for a moment and pumped my hand. "I know you and I have had our differences and our troubles," he said, "but do you realize how serious this is? If they put Keith in jail tomorrow, it'll be the end of rock and roll. We need your help. We need you to get the word out." He was pleading.

"Well, Peter," I said, "I've been here for a week trying to get the word out in spite of you. This is the first time you've talked to me as a human. You didn't need my help till it looks like Keith will actually go to jail."

"Look, look!" Rudge implored. "Something must be done. This is serious. Keith has been seeing doctors today. He knows something must be done. What can we do?"

"What you've always done," I said. Rudge understood that and we parted affably. I went off to have a drink with Carter, who was almost vibrating with nervous energy.

"Goddamn it! I'm pissed off," he said. "They're trying to put Keith in jail and I'm not gonna let 'em do it! I know they're gonna move to revoke his bail and lock him up. I'm pulling out all the stops on this one." We were sitting on one of the plush, deep, chocolate-brown couches tucked away by the water fountains in the lobby, safely out of sight (and sound) of the RCMP. Carter sipped his Jack Daniel's sour mash whiskey. "One thing they haven't realized here," he said, after a moment, "is that if they lock up Keith Richards here tomorrow, they're gonna have a riot. Those kids will go apeshit. They followed his car down the street today, cheering him. And they're still coming into town." That, I could confirm. I had made a late-afternoon taxi run through the streets that linked the Harbour Castle and old City Hall and I saw a significant number of obvious Richards supporters, with their ubiquitous backpacks and even more ubiquitous wine bottles. The Harbour Castle, itself, was beefing up its security at the doors.

Carter made ready to leave; he had legal work to do yet into the night. "Clay is going through the legal precedents right now," he said. "We're going for blood tomorrow. You know, there's one thing nobody much really knows yet. That's that the police fucked up when they arrested Keith. They took him out to Brampton's jurisdiction and that's why bail was set so low. The jurisdiction is actually here, in Toronto. We'll see about that tomorrow. Another thing the prosecution is complaining about is preferential treatment for Keith. We will have better security [because of today's attack], but I'll be goddamned if I'll ask for an armored car or any police help. The prosecution says Keith has always had special treatment. That's bullshit and I'll be goddamned if I'll ask for any. We'll walk in through the front door, just like we did today. And—if they actually put him in jail, I'm just getting in gear to really fight."

Tuesday, March 8, 1977

I had an extremely nervous breakfast down in the Poseidon Room with Peter Rudge, Bill Carter, and Paul Wasserman. They were all chain-smoking cigarettes, including Carter, who does not smoke. To say that they were not tense and anxious almost to the breaking point was to deny the evidence in front of my face that these three extremely powerful men in the world of rock music were worried sick. They couldn't eat and they gulped so much hot coffee that steam started palpably rising from them. Today, they feared, would be the day that Keith Richards would hear some massive jail doors slam on him. Never, perhaps, to un-slam again.

Our conversation was disjointed, to say the least. As a reporter, I was not supposed to know anything that was going on. Although, as a foreign reporter, I was not subject to Canada's stringent laws that severely restricted the press even beyond the point of dictating what could be written about: Even knowledge of forbidden information put one on shaky ground. A case in point: Keith Richards's court hearing on this date was an official secret. Since it was not listed on a court docket, it did not exist. There was no reason for the Canadian press to know about it; no First Amendment, no people's right to know. Spreading that information amounted to releasing a government secret and contempt of court and who knew what else. So, during the course of that breakfast, I received some very broad hints that Keith was due to appear that very day at 2:00 P.M. in Provincial Courtroom 26 before Judge Vincent McEwan. "Duly noted," I said.

Rudge shoved aside his untouched plate and pleaded with me. "We've got to get the story out that Keith is not a menace," he said, emotion making his voice quaver. "How old are you?" Before I could answer, he said, "Well, that's our generation that is now the Stones' fans and now includes lawyers and attorney generals [sic] and everybody else. We've got to get Keith and Anita to commit themselves, to admit that the music is more important." He turned to Carter to ask, "How much cash do you have?"

"Twenty-five [thousand]."

"That's not enough," Rudge said, "let's get two hundred [thousand dollars]."

"I won't pay them more than twenty-five," Carter said flatly. "They just want to punish Keith."

"Christ," Rudge moaned, "if they put Keith in jail today, they'll kill him by Monday. We need"—he focused on me and said with all the fervor of an evangelist—"we need the straight press. I want you to call *Time* magazine."

I was a bit taken aback. "Peter," I finally said, "I am sort of here officially representing *Rolling Stone* magazine. If you want *Time, you* call them. I haven't exactly seen them beating the bushes here the past few days trying to shake the story out and furthermore—"

Wasserman called for the check and rang down the curtain on that bit of folly. "The band rehearsed all night again," he said, "and in the studio next door there was part of a carnival troupe. All the dwarves came in together to watch the Stones play and Keith stopped the rehearsal and announced, 'I see that Wasserman has finally sneaked all of the press corps in here at once.'" That was supposed to be a joke. At least I didn't get stuck with the check, for once.

Shortly after noon, although none of the participants would ever admit to anything, first Rudge and then Carter conferred with the U.S. ambassador to Canada. It seemed fairly obvious that Carter, the visa and immigration law specialist, was maneuvering to get Keith admitted into the United States. After all, he had to go somewhere.

I made sure that I was an hour early getting into old City Hall's Provincial Courtroom 26, where Keith's nonhearing might take place. Court officers denied that he would appear. I looked at the docket: There was no Keith Richards listed. There were thirty-two drug cases scheduled for that day (fully half of them for intent to traffic) before Judge McEwan. A local courtroom maven told me that McEwan was known as "the menopause judge" because he had supposedly once, in a trial of indecent exposure by a male, questioned the female complainant's competence by asking her if she were going through "change of life." "A tough judge," said this maven.

At least half of the sixty or so spectators crowded into Courtroom 26 seemed to be young hippies, anxiously awaiting justice's determination of the futures of their friends/lovers/relatives/dealers/significant-others. I was squeezed in with a bunch of them. (Since, as I quickly learned, if you don't get a seat in a Toronto courtroom, then you are removed from the courtroom when the doors are locked. No standing room in those halls of justice. The hippies made room for me.) They solicitously asked me who "I had up."

"Keith Richards," I said and nobody believed me.

Judge McEwan came back from lunch and regained his high-backed red chair beneath the crown on the wall. The judge was wearing a green suit and bifocal glasses and was balding and pink-faced. He started his first afternoon case by severely scolding the attorney for a hippie defendant for being late. The hippie, seventeen years old and looking more like fifteen and as if he was about to burst into tears, pleaded guilty to possession of eight grams of marijuana, with intent to traffic. Subsequent police testimony revealed that cops had seized him after he had harvested eight grams of green marijuana plants from a city park that police had under surveillance. The hippie's hapless attorney tried to introduce as evidence Ontario Attorney General Roy McMurtry's public statements advocating the legalization of marijuana (or at least the opening of official grass stores) and Judge McEwan would have none of it.

"The attorney general of the Province of Ontario," he snapped, "has no jurisdiction in this court." The hippie got eighteen months' probation and a criminal record.

It was 2:20 P.M. and there was a stir in the courtroom. Keith, who had finally been awakened at 1:45 P.M. for his 2:00 P.M. court appearance, was escorted into the prisoner's box by a police officer. He had been rearrested, on cocaine charges, once he entered the courthouse and the Mounties now had possession of him. The day before, he had bravely marched into the courthouse with head high, white silk scarf flying, a man totally unafraid. Today he was a different man. He wore a dark suit with a light shirt and silver tie and he looked as if he had shrunk. He was plainly nervous and had lost whatever self-confidence he had impressed the crowds with a scant twenty-four hours earlier.

Rudge, Wasserman, Carter, and Clayton Powell trudged in and seated themselves at the defense bench. Judge McEwan roundly lambasted Powell for being late. Keith, in the prisoner's box, hung his head, his hands folded before him, and looked pathetic, vulnerable, and appeared—in a word—defeated. The hippies were astonished.

Crown Prosecutor David Scott rose in his blue pinstripe suit to mention the added cocaine charge and he started to complain about Keith's low bail when the judge cut him off, saying, "Bail is no longer a matter of dealing between defense and prosecution." No one was quite sure just what he meant by that and Carter and Powell exchanged uneasy glances.

Powell, a short confident man in a trim gray suit, stood to make a request that the judge prohibit any publication of the proceedings of this hearing in Canadian newspapers (or on radio or television news, etc.). That is a fairly routine request in Canada. Request granted. Keith remained standing, head down like a poleaxed bull.

The crown swore in as a witness RCMP Constable Bill Seward, who had been one of the Mounties who arrested Keith in the famous two-hour raid on the Harbour Castle. As Seward took the stand and prepared to testify about the circumstances of Keith Richards's Harbour Castle bust—the details of which the Stones' defense team was apparently very eager to keep out of court testimony—Clay Powell leaped to his feet with an apparently innocent request.

"Your honor," he said, "the two grams of cocaine charge arose out of the same search of the twenty-seventh of February." The court agreed. Powell continued, "Now, since your order—the court's order—to not publish this hearing does not apply to or cover reporters from the United States and since there is at least one reporter from the United States in this courtroom"—Powell looked over his shoulder directly at me—"I submit that we cannot today go through the facts of this second case of the cocaine matter." Judge McEwan agreed immediately and Constable Seward had to stand down without uttering a word of testimony. Prosecutor Scott slapped his own forehead in frustration. Powell had just defeated him with an end run. Powell and Carter smiled and winked at me. I had clearly been used: No wonder I had been told so many times when and where this "secret" hearing would take place. If I had not been there, the RCMP evidence of Keith's cocaine charge (that whole shopping list of things with white powder on them that were seized in Keith's suite) would have been introduced at length and obviously that would not have helped Keith's case. That shopping list would never make it into a court record in Canada. And that shopping list sounded fairly damning. Well, so be it. If I had chanced to oversleep, Wasserman and Carter would probably have hauled me into court, semicomatose, on a stretcher, to serve as a certifiably alive foreign correspondent whose presence, coherent or not, would compromise Keith Richards's legal rights in Canada. They later denied everything, of course. I would have been disappointed in them if they had not.

Momentum shifted to Powell immediately. Scott went back to his low-bail argument: "The present bail is $1,000, no deposit. Not only does it not look good, it is not a proper and fitting bail in these circumstances. The accused is in town for a certain length of time for business reasons. But not indefinitely, certainly not until a trial date. I submit there should be adequate bail to suffice, down to the time of eventual trial. I submit that in view of the additional [cocaine] charge and that the Department of Justice was not involved in the initial bail that there are insufficient facts. He has a residence in Jamaica and was a resident of London and we don't know that he maintains a residence in London." Scott seemed to be spinning his wheels.

Powell got up to say, "He owns property in both countries."

Scott said that he wanted an amendment to the charges to specify that the person charged was "Keith Richards of London and Jamaica."

Powell conferred with Keith and the latter smiled for the first time that afternoon.

Scott talked in circles a bit about where exactly did Keith Richards actually live, implying in broad strokes that Keith was a bad bail risk. He was still complaining about the $1,000 no-deposit bail.

Powell, almost too casually, got up to say that Keith was quite willing and ready to post a substantially larger bond, if his bail, as Scott suggested, was too low and "doesn't look good."

Powell said, "Keith Richards is ready to submit $25,000 in cash if that will make it look good to Mr. Scott and to be released on his own recognizance."

Judge McEwan leaned forward to ask, "Did you say $25,000 in cash?"

Prosecutor Scott leaped to his feet to object. "The man must be retained! It is too onerous on this individual to expect him to remain here until a trial."

Said the judge, "You are worried that he will leave?"

Scott scowled. "I don't agree with the $25,000 proposal."

"Well," said the judge, "I am not concerned with bail. Now, are you satisfied with $25,000?"

"Yes," Scott conceded. "I also maintain that his passport be retained and that he keep the peace and be of good behavior."

"We are satisfied," Powell said. Seizing the moment, he reached into his briefcase for an electronic device that he waved above his head. "I have here," he said triumphantly, "a Motorola transmitter that an officer left in Mr. Richards's room. If they want to claim it . . ." Judge McEwan had to gavel down the laughter. "Can we set a date now?" he asked impatiently.

"I submit the fourteenth," Scott said.

"March fourteenth, 2:00 P.M.," the judge said crisply.

Case closed for this date. In camera, the judge and Scott agreed to Powell's strong request that the RCMP return Keith's passport and allow him to leave Canada.

Downstairs, at the bail office, Carter counted out $25,000 in crisp new bills and winked conspiratorially at me. RCMP Constable Bill Seward, who had busted Keith, and Constable John Langley were waiting at the door to safely escort Keith back to the Harbour Castle. I had to ask Seward how he rationalized first arresting Keith and now serving as his bodyguard. "Well, sir," said Seward, "we are here as personal security. Yesterday someone hit him in the head with a camera. He is as entitled as anyone to protection. That's all I can say."

As Clay Powell left, he waved the Motorola transmitter at Constable Langley and said, "Hey, John, if you ever need new batteries for this, just let me know."

"Thanks a lot, Powell," Constable Langley said. He almost sounded sincere.

During the hearing, Margaret Trudeau had checked out of the Harbour Castle and flown to New York City. Mick Jagger and Ron Wood also checked out and flew to New York—separately.

Richard van Abbe, the UPI bureau chief in Toronto, finally decided to put Maggie's departure—as well as her stay at the Harbour Castle—on the UPI wire. "The roof caved in when I did," he told me later that day. He had to abandon his phones after certain offices in Ottawa and numerous tabloids on Fleet Street in London and gossipmongers in New York burned out his telephone lines. Some sample tabloid front-page headlines in London: PREMIER'S WIFE IN STONES SCANDAL *(Daily Mirror);* STONES IN A MYSTERY *(Sun);* MRS. TRUDEAU'S ROCK FOLLY *(Daily Express);* A STONES ROMANCE? YOU MUST BE JOKING *(Daily Mail);* and so on.

The Harbour Castle lobby really started to fill up with reporters, especially after the UPI bulletin finally convinced the Canadian press that Maggie had actually been registered at the Harbour Castle and may indeed have dallied with a Stone. A reporter, who mercifully shall remain nameless, cornered me in the lobby to tell me that: "I have found a maid who saw Maggie shoot up with the Stones. And I know that someone was carried out of this hotel Saturday night with blood dripping out of their arms. Now, who was it?" I could only laugh. Unfortunately, due to my lengthy stay at the Harbour Castle, I had become recognizable as a Stones Expert. Rue the day, the very day, I was thinking at the elevator bank when yet another reporter-come-lately aggressively nailed me.

"We know," he almost spat at me (Who's "we"? I wanted to know), "that today Maggie Trudeau left this hotel and disappeared after [Prime Minister] Pierre sent someone here to get her and we know that the Toronto *Star* followed Ron Wood to the airport and the *Star's* photographer was punched out by two bodyguards. So—what about it?" I was astonished. This was journalism? I stepped into the elevator and said in a confidential tone, "Maggie told me that she's been sleeping with her husband."

Over in the Quayside Bar, Wasserman was besieged by—by modest estimate—eighteen reporters with loud, angry accents. I went up to the rooftop Lighthouse Restaurant to try to get away from pack-rat journalism and ran into Bill Carter. We sat down over bourbon and steaks. "I can't talk about the case," attorney Carter said, but he was grinning so wide that it was obvious that Keith's victory today had been a significant one. Clay Powell came by for a drink and he could say even less about his pending case, but his smile was evidence enough that the Stones' defense team had pulled off a miracle.

On my way back to the Willy Loman Memorial Module, I stopped by Wasserman's table for a nightcap. There seemed to be an inordinate number of so-called "journalists" crowded about him, as if they were taking part in a "facts frenzy." Little did I know.

Wednesday, March 9, 1977

My head had barely fluffed the pillow when Wasserman started calling. "I'll deny ever telling you this," he confided in his first of many hourly dispatches, "but the amount of people leaving here indicates that there is no reason for you to hang around here. Why don't you get on the 9:45 to New York?"

He meant the American Airlines 9:45 A.M. flight from Toronto to La Guardia. I called American Airlines and then Wasserman. "Wasso, that flight was full weeks ago. No seats anywhere."

"Of course there are seats," he huffed. "Charlie Watts is booked on that flight, but of course is actually taking a later flight. Meet me in the lobby in the morning."

He called back in ten minutes. "I hear the government has a warrant out on me for allegedly tipping you off to that hearing. Ciao."

I was just dozing off when the phone drilled me awake at 5:00 A.M. How did I know it was Wasso? He was frantic. "Have you seen the *Globe & Mail?*" he asked. "It says Margaret ran off to New York with Mick and Ron. Jesus. Read it and call me back. We'll never get out of the country."

Before I could fetch my newspapers at the door, the phone rang. It was Carter, saying, "Why is that goddamn Wasserman calling every hour on the hour?" I promised to let him know ASAP and sat down with the papers. The front page of the *Globe & Mail* trumpeted the "news" that Margaret had "left Toronto yesterday to accompany Rolling Stones Mick Jagger and Ron Wood on a trip to New York." It was patent bullshit, of course, but we all know that there's no recalling of a front page of a metro newspaper. The article was a spectacular melange of fantasy, gossip fulfillment, quasislander against Pierre Trudeau, and standard Toronto scumbag excuse for real reporting. The alleged reporter had attributed almost all his scumbag quasifacts to Wasserman. Unfortunately, as I pointed out to Wasserman when I called him back, the alleged reporter was one of the scumbags that he had bought dinner for only a few hours earlier. I myself remembered this one alleged reporter because he had apparently never heard of the Rolling Stones and because, in the few minutes that I was at Wasso's table for a drink, this alleged reporter kept getting up and hitting the pay phone. I asked him once what he was doing. "Just filing two paragraphs of background," he had lied.

Wasserman was not encouraged by the revelation that he had bought dinner for the alleged reporter who was knotting his hangman's noose for him. Arthur Johnson is the alleged's name and the lead of his "story" alone libeled three persons: "Margaret Trudeau left Toronto yesterday to accompany Rolling Stones Mick Jagger and Ron Wood on a trip to New York." 'Nuf said.

Wasserman called me back shortly to say that Prime Minister Trudeau was announcing that Maggie was off to New York on "a special mission." "I wish Charlie Watts wasn't going on the plane with us," Wasserman said. "We may not make it." I said that I thought I was taking Watts's plane seat. Wasso ignored me. Carter called to ask me why Wasso's phone line was constantly busy. Pierre Trudeau had been buzzing the hotel, trying to get Wasserman and having to settle for Carter. Their conversation was confidential.

I couldn't possibly sleep, so I went downstairs and checked out. Wasserman was already pacing the lobby, ignoring the insistent phone pages for him. It was not yet daylight. Carter appeared and said we could not leave until he roused Charlie Watts and got him a guaranteed plane seat on a later flight. Wasserman half-ran back from the lobby newsstand waving the first edition of the Toronto *Sun*, with its angry red front-page banner headline: WHERE'S MAGGIE? The "story," such as it was, began: "The newest antics of fun-loving Margaret Trudeau are the hottest gossip in the nation's capital today . . . but the big question is: Where is Maggie? . . . Paul Wasserman, the Stones' press agent, when asked if she was still at the Harbour Castle yesterday, said, 'She left here about 1:10 P.M. today.'" "I said *that* . . . me?" Wasserman worried. Meanwhile, he had yet to get to the real meat of the *Sun*, which was its lead editorial page editorial, titled: C'MON, MAGGIE.

And this is what the *Sun* editorialized, as read to me nervously at dawn by Paul Wasserman in the lobby of the Harbour Castle: "Ever since Margaret Trudeau went to [the] hospital with emotional problems, the media—the country—has been sympathetic, understanding, tolerant of her periodic eccentricities. But there's a limit to this. When Mrs. Trudeau behaves erratically and inappropriately in a public place—not once but repeatedly—someone has to say something. And it might as well be us. Someone should control the lady. It is not only reprehensible, it is unacceptable for the wife of the Prime Minister to be cavorting with a group like the Rolling Stones. Most of them have, at one time or another, been charged with drug offenses. While Mrs. Trudeau was residing at the same hotel as the group she apparently admires greatly, one of them was being charged with possession of heroin for the purpose of trafficking and possession of cocaine. That's hard stuff. Lethal. The guy's girlfriend was also busted a week earlier on a drug count. The record of the Rolling Stones is studded with such incidents. Critics even reported that they seemed to be high during their two performances in Toronto (both attended by Margaret) on alcohol, nervous energy, or whatever. For Mrs. Trudeau to attend the performance on the arm, figuratively speaking, of Mick Jagger (another whose record is tarnished) is also wrong. A shoddy example—not only for the P.M.'s wife but also for the mother of three youngsters, to say nothing of her possibly being pregnant again. A spokesman in the P.M.'s office said Mrs. T. returned to Ottawa Sunday night. A Stones' spokesman [Wasso!] said she checked out at 1:10 P.M. yesterday. The hotel refused comment. Where is the truth? A curtain of secrecy has descended. It's not good enough. What Mrs. Trudeau does at 24 Sussex Drive in private may be her business. Her's [sic] and her husband's. If she's gone off the deep end again, for heaven's sake give her treatment. But she shouldn't gambol around with impunity, counting on the gallantry of the media to turn an indulgent eye to her peccadilloes. In her antics, Mrs. Trudeau is giving respectability to a lifestyle that is not only offensive but downright dangerous. Can you imagine the outcry if Mrs. Carter was behaving as Mrs. Trudeau? C'mon, Maggie, either behave with distinction or stay at home."

As he read the editorial, Wasserman became even more agitated. "I've got to get out of this fucking country before they find me," he said, perspiring heavily. "Carter, I'm leaving. Meet me at the airport. They threatened to arrest me for allegedly tipping off the press to that hearing. I've got to go. C'mon, Flippo."

I got into a cab with him, but protested that I couldn't get a seat on the 9:45 to New York, which he was on.

"Don't worry," he said, as he worried over the *Sun*.

"Well," I said, making conversation, "you've been here a week and you've disrupted this entire country and created an international incident and the Stones may topple the government."

"Yeah," he answered distractedly, mopping his brow, "not bad for a week's work."

We were finally joined at the airport by Carter, who said that Charlie Watts had elected to take a later flight and so his cancellation would give me a seat on the flight. The only problem was that Charlie Watts never cancels plane reservations—would you, if you were him?—and neither Carter nor Wasserman knew Watts's current airline name. Obviously, he is never Charlie Watts when he flies and sometimes even he doesn't remember what his flight name is, as opposed to his hotel name. So Carter and Wasso and I bounced around Charlie's travel identities. The ticket agents started getting very nervous as they listened to us try different names, as they should have: None of us had any luggage; we were flying under assumed names; and we were obviously either drunk or stupid or both.

We finally lucked onto Charlie Watts booking himself as "Charlie Sussex" and so I got his airline seat in that name. Just as we got through customs, we were stopped and Carter was pulled aside by a man with a serious-looking bádge. Wasserman forged ahead. "It's every man for himself," Wasso declared, throwing a serious forearm. We finally got on the plane and I asked Carter about the delay. "They were apologizing about detaining my client Mick Jagger so long last night before they would let him leave the country," Carter said.

"What?"

"Yeah. I had to come out here last night when Mick called the hotel and he said they wouldn't let him leave the country." He said it was actually touch and go for a while.

On this flight, there were in first class seven bona fide, self-important, wing-tip-shoed, brown-suited businessmen types who perhaps will never understand why they were afflicted with what got pulled down on them. At the last possible second, Carter and Wasserman and yours truly got onto the plane into the last three first-class seats. For some reason, the stewardesses threw in with our cause, as soon as it became apparent that the businessmen sector was openly hostile to the Rolling Stones crowd. Many drinks and flirtations attended Wasso, Carter, and your humble servant to the considerable chagrin of this group of men who had apparently spent over $1,000 each for ugly brown suits and matching brown gunboat wing tips and who thought that flying first class before noon made them citizens to be reckoned with. All it meant was that they had to get up before noon.

As soon as the plane took off, Wasserman, who surely hadn't slept in days, nodded right off. Carter immediately shook him awake. "Wasso, I hate to tell you this, but the Prime Minister just radioed the pilot to turn the plane around and go back to Toronto." Wasso gnashed his teeth and groaned in his sleep, to our great merriment. The gunboat wing tip crowd could only look on sullenly as the stewardesses brought Carter and me fresh drinks and perched prettily on the arms of our chairs and begged us to tell them how we had just managed to outfox the entire government of Canada and who was the large, suspicious-looking man whom we were guarding (and who was now twitching in his sleep). All of a sudden, without any warning, Wasserman rose up out of his seat like a massive avenging angel, threw back his head, and uttered a long, howling, blood-curdling scream. Just as abruptly, he slumped back down into his seat and went into a peaceful sleep. The plane seemed to suddenly drop a hundred feet. The ensuing silence was as absolute as a silence can be on a jetliner.

The rest of the flight was every bit as interesting—in quite a different sort of way—as the first part had been, but you don't really want to hear the petty details of the interrogation and search, now do you?

Thursday, March 10, 1977

How strange it was to wake up in a bed that was not in the Willy Loman Memorial Module at the Harbour Castle. And how strangely disquieting it was that I actually missed the Module in a perverse sort of way. No more early-morning panicky phone calls from Wasso, no more Breakfast Adventures from room service, no more shadow of death view of the frozen harbour. No more twenty-four hour a day obsession with the Rolling Stones and every breath they took, every move they made.

Instead of Wasso calling, I was getting the calls he should have gotten. Since I had been seen leaving the Harbour Castle with him, the press pack in Toronto assumed that I knew everything that was going on. Every cheap tabloid scumbag lavatory newspaper this side of Hong Kong had been calling for the past twenty-four hours to get the scoop on Maggie Trudeau and her fall from grace into the pit of fire with the unspeakable Rolling Stones. I unplugged the phone after one scumbag Toronto radio station offered me $500 if I would tell them where Maggie was. As it happened, I knew where Maggie was staying (with her friend Princess Yasmin Khan on Central Park West), but I didn't think it was my lot in life to hand out road maps to the hell hounds. Maggie had enough trouble as it was. Everybody in the world, it seemed, was after her.

The night before, she and Yasmin had gone to see Mikhail Baryshnikov dance at the City Center on West 55th Street and the mob of reporters and photographers outnumbered the audience. The omniscient New York *Post*—driven to new heights of hysteria in celebrity coverage—began one piece thusly, "Margaret Trudeau, sitting fourth row on the aisle at the ballet at City Center last night, took one look at those headlines saying she had gone 'into hiding' and tossed the paper into the row ahead. 'I say, f—— to all those papers,' she said in a tinkly finishing school voice. Her friend Princess Yasmin Khan put hand to mouth in mock horror and whispered, 'Oh, don't say that.' " Verily, not a whisper shall be whispered upon this earth that is not overheard—and printed (but not necessarily confirmed)—by the New York *Post.*

Even the staid New York *Times* seemed to be compelled to say something, at least, about L'affaire Trudeau. The *Times* piece, although buried on page sixty-nine, was such a precious and perfect example of the *Times'* white-gloved treatment of this sort of seamy, pop-culture scandal that you should be treated to it in its entirety: "Margaret Trudeau, the wife of

Canada's Prime Minister Pierre Elliott Trudeau, flew here from Toronto yesterday to continue what she described as a long-planned vacation devoted to photography. 'I plan to take a lot of pictures while I'm here,' explained the twenty-eight-year-old Mrs. Trudeau, who said she had begun the vacation last Friday and would return to Ottawa next Monday. A photography student at Algonquin College in Ottawa, Mrs. Trudeau said she planned to spend most of today at Richard Avedon's studio here. Mrs. Trudeau, who said she was staying with her friend the Princess Yasmin Aly Khan on Central Park West, was interviewed at the City Center on West 55th Street, where the two young women were mobbed by reporters and photographers when they arrived for last night's performance of the Eliot Feld Ballet starring Mikhail Baryshnikov. Mrs. Trudeau, who has been the subject of widespread press comment in Canada because of her association with the Rolling Stone [sic] rock group there, denied any romantic involvement with any of the Stones. 'They're great musicians and I was excited that they could come to Canada,' [said] Mrs. Trudeau, who was reported to have attended two of their performances in Toronto last weekend and to have stopped [!] at the same hotel there. Mick Jagger, the group's lead singer, and Ron Wood, one of the guitarists, also came to New York during the day. Mr. Jagger said he had come to be with his wife and daughter. Last night, in a message relayed through a friend, Mr. Jagger denied any romantic link with Mrs. Trudeau."

A perfect *Times* story. All innuendos intact and still very proper and quite above all this sort of vulgar carrying-on.

I finally plugged my phone back in because I had finally persuaded Peter Rudge to sit down and talk on the record and he was due back in town from a quick trip down South for a meeting with .38 Special, a band he managed.

The phone rang immediately. It was Carter, calling from his home in Little Rock, Arkansas. "How crazy is it there?" he asked and just laughed when I told him. "Shit," he said, "by the time I got home yesterday, everything was crazy. Mick called me first thing. He's really pissed off about this whole Margaret thing. I told him it was time to take the damn gloves off, that it's time for him to come out of hiding. And Rudge called. He's scared to death. This thing with Keith is serious, but I think it can be handled if we do it the right way."

Mick apparently heeded Carter's advice or maybe followed his own lead. At any rate, in a move unprecedented for him, he called up the dreaded New York *Post.* Let's review highlights of the *Post*'s story (which only made page two): The headline read: FROM AN 'INSULTED' MICK. The kicker read: A DISCLAIMER OF ROMANCE.

And from the "article" itself: "Rock star Mick Jagger has called the

Post to say he and Margaret Trudeau have no romantic ties, just a 'passing acquaintance for two nights.' Hints to the contrary are 'insulting to me and insulting to her,' the lead singer for the Rolling Stones declared last night with an injured air . . . Jagger, calling from the office of his tour manager, Peter Rudge of Sir Productions, said he was annoyed at such 'libelous' stories . . . Jagger went on, in his best street-swagger tones, 'She was very charming . . . nice and polite. She just wanted to be introduced. Princess Margaret wanted to be introduced to the group in London. Lee Radziwill followed us. All these ladies are very charming to have around and there is no suggestion of anything other than that. You Americans think we are a bunch of male chauvinist pigs. We can't talk to a woman without being romantically attached to her. And you [American] women have a worse attitude than the men. You think we can't say hello without wanting to be in bed with them.' Jagger said he had come to New York to 'speak to my wife and child.' His daughter, Jade, five, had been hospitalized for stomach pains last week. And Jagger's wife, Bianca— known for her own independent streak—said she and Jagger had 'laughed' about all the furor. Chatting briefly with the *Post* outside their East 73rd Street townhouse yesterday, the willowy Mrs. Jagger said the couple had been deluged with calls about Mrs. Trudeau and Jagger. 'We laughed about it. We thought it was very funny.' "

Mick was actually catching hell from Bianca about it and that was the beginning of the end of that marriage, just as it was the same for Pierre and Margaret Trudeau. And Mick never laid a finger on her. I told him once that there was an old Texas saying to the effect that once you're accused of raiding the henhouse, you may as well go ahead and sample some of the flesh. He laughed sardonically. I was sorry that Mick never got to meet Lyndon Johnson. They would have hit it off famously.

Wasserman finally called. "Well," he said, "we're toppling the government. Pierre just went on the CBC to say that 'If my wife likes to go to rock concerts and you don't like it, then that's too bad. If my wife's musical taste has anything to do with my ability to govern, then don't vote for me.' He's finished in politics in Canada; he's wearing horns. The London reporters all followed Woody [Ron Wood] to L.A. They're after the Woody-Maggie romance rumors. I didn't tell you that. I'm denying everything these days. By the way, although I didn't tell you this, Maggie asked me if I could get her into 'Saturday Night Live' this week. I'll figure out some way to dissuade her. Ciao."

Richard van Abbe called from his UPI bureau in Toronto. "It's settled down a little bit here," he said. "Of course, it's still front-page news. Off the record, I hear that the Mounties may try to lay another charge on Keith. It's a big secret. There's a split. The prosecution is arguing that another bust might play into the Stones' lawyers' hands and prove harassment of Keith."

Peter Rudge finally called and invited me over to his offices. His Sir Productions filled two floors of an office building on West 57th Street. A blackboard listing tours of his bands covered one wall of the entryway: The section underneath THE ROLLING STONES was conspicuously blank. In his airy two-story office overlooking 57th Street, Rudge appeared harried. The lawyers had already told me there was very little I could ask him, in light of the pending court case (just as my petition to interview Keith was met with hoots of laughter), so here was a quick talk, mostly off the record.

Me: "Will the Stones tour without Keith?"

Rudge: "No! At the moment, they will not tour without Keith Richards. It would not be the Rolling Stones without him. I can make no comment about the repercussions of the charges against Keith that have been made by Canadian authorities, but should the courts find him guilty and the resulting conviction end in anything as severe as a jail sentence, then it would probably result in the end of the Rolling Stones. I'm sure there are millions of people around the world who would be very much affected by that decision."

We talked for a while. Rudge's greatest fear was that the Canadian Government intended to try to revoke Keith's bail and jail him as soon as possible [and he was right about that]. He said that the other Rolling Stones planned to hold a band meeting in New York City the following Tuesday, the day after Keith's next court hearing in Toronto, and that the future of the Rolling Stones might be decided at that meeting.

"It's funny," Rudge said, "we picked Toronto because it has a great musical history. It's a good club town and the atmosphere is right and it's close to New York. Keith, at the time, was unable to get into America [the United States] anyway [because of his most recent drug arrest]. So we decided to go play the club. Despite everything, we played the club, although that seems to be forgotten now. It was probably one of the most unique music events ever. And it could very well have been the last time that anyone will see the Rolling Stones."

Friday, March 11, 1977

The New York *Post*, which I had always thought could not surpass itself in terms of sheer bullshit, managed to do so today. "Page Six," its gossip column, reported—under a headline reading DRUG DOC FLIES TO ROLLING STONE—that "A top Hollywood doctor, who has helped many stars strung out on heroin, has flown to Toronto to aid Keith Richards. He has the star 'doing a heavy methadone trip,' according to our sources in the Rolling Stone camp. If Richards gets off the charges of possession of heroin and intent to traffic, he plans to return at once to Britain, declare himself an addict, and enter a government drug rehabilitation program. Whatever happens, the Stones will give up touring for studio work because Richards is unlikely again to be admitted to the United States." Total bullshit. There was not a shred of truth in that item and I actually tracked down the persons responsible for it and will not name them because that might lend some legitimacy to their hackwork.

This was a great day for journalism. I unwrapped my air-freighted copy of the Toronto *Sun* and was delighted by the lead editorial. It was titled ROLLING STONED. This is what it said: "Perhaps the most scandalous thing about the whole Rolling Stone caper in Toronto was not Maggie Trudeau's bizarre antics, but the treatment Keith Richards of the Stones got from our courts. Richards was charged with possession of heroin for the purpose of trafficking [!] and later with possession of cocaine. That's pretty serious stuff. Especially for a guy with his record—make it the group's record, which is long and awful. For the first offense Richards was released on $1,000 bail, which some call 'disposable bottle bail'—no deposit, no return. And $25,000 bail on the second charge is ridiculously low too, considering his millionaire status. Police say that normally bail for a foreign national, involving possession of heroin or cocaine, would be denied—or set at a very high figure. One can only conclude that there is indeed one law for the rich or renowned and another for the people—contrary to all our principles of justice. The Rolling Stones and Richards in particular have a history of offenses—and of getting favored treatment. Only in January a British court convicted Richards of possession of cocaine and specifically didn't give him a jail sentence because it would interfere with his right to come to Canada and earn his living. The effect of this misguided leniency was to enable Richards to come to Toronto, where he was charged with possession for the purpose of trafficking! Thanks a lot, England. Reading the file clippings of the Rolling Stones, you see time after time where political pressure seems to have been applied to get them off or to get them lenient sentences. Authorities seem petrified of adverse fan mail. Yet Canada is no better than anywhere else. We too pamper them, dabble in double standard. If Richards skips bail, we trust extradition proceedings will commence. Let him receive the same treatment your kid, your brother, or your friend would receive if they were charged with possession of heroin for the purpose of trafficking!"

Wasserman called to ask if I had made my room reservations at the Harbour Castle for Keith's next court appearance on Monday. I told him I wouldn't miss it for all the coke in Keith's carpet. "By the way," I asked Wasso, "how's my request for an interview with Keith doing?"

"Well," Wasso said, "I'm in favor of it, Keith's in favor of it, even Rudge is in favor of it. The only problem is that the lawyers say 'No way.' They said to tell you that you can interview Keith for as long as you want, as long as you don't ask him any questions at all."

I pondered that for a while. "Please resubmit my request, Wasso," I finally said.

"I'll see you in the Poseidon Room," Wasserman said. "Ciao."

Sunday, March 13, 1977

What a pleasure it was to be back in the warm, cloying confines of a Willy Loman Memorial Module at the Harbour Castle, with that reassuring view of the ever-gray harbour. I was back to attend Keith's next court hearing on Monday and to twist the lawyers' arms to let me get some kind of an interview with Keith. Just in case that happened, Annie Leibovitz, *Rolling Stone* magazine's chief photographer, was scheduled to sky in on Monday to shoot a cover session with Keith—provided, that is, that he was not thrown into jail after Monday's hearing, which was what the crown still seemed to want to do. Like all great photographers, Leibovitz is both aggressive and a bit reckless and I had forbade her to hit town until I had gotten to Keith, which was an extremely delicate matter. What with his legal mess and drug addiction and the incredible pressure of literally dozens of reporters from around the world trying to get to him and the caution of his lawyers, my chances of interviewing him were slim and depended on persuasion and negotiation. Naturally, I should never have told Annie that.

At any rate, the staff at the Harbour Castle welcomed me back warmly and sent up stacks of newspapers and a fruit and wine and cheese basket. I was practically glowing with bonhomie as I uncorked a bottle of a modest Chardonnay and flipped open the Sunday Toronto *Sun.* What a rush of pleasure I felt upon being visually assaulted by the flaming-red banner headline screaming: MAGGIE IS BACK IN TOWN FINALLY. Filling up the rest of the front page was a grainy, out-of-focus, divorce-court-quality photograph of a very glum-looking Margaret traipsing down the exit stairway from an Air Canada plane in Ottawa. Page after urgent page of the *Sun* was filled with speculation about Maggie and rehashes of Keith's bust and analyses of the savage, "sensual" appeal of the Stones' music. A whole double-truck spread of the paper was bannered MAGGIE AND . . . THE STONES with two kicker headlines underneath: MARGARET: WHY SHOULD SHE BE A BARBIE DOLL? and ROCK 'N' ROLL: STONES REPRESENT A GENERA-

TION. What great tabloid sensationalism. A separate section, called "Armchair Critic," invited ordinary citizens to answer the burning question: "Should Maggie be left alone?" Most readers said yes and by the time I had scanned the newspapers, I quite agreed. She had been hounded by the international press as if she were a fugitive on the lam. Enough was too much. A Toronto *Sun* columnist with an acute case of cute writing wrote a plodding open letter to the Stones, ending thusly, "Hey, Mick, have a good time. You too, guys. Say hi to Margaret if she's there. Send her back if she's not. See ya in court. Bye for now, bunkies." Fairly tedious stuff after a while.

I went down and cruised through the vast lobby. It was almost devoid of humans. A week before, it had resembled a hippie refugee camp.

Went back upstairs and took a nap and then met Carter and Wasserman for dinner in the Lighthouse, a revolving restaurant up on the hotel's roof. Carter would not say what the legal strategy would be at Monday's hearing—he had just come from a meeting with Clay Powell and Keith—but there was a palpable absence of the tension that had marked all our earlier meetings. Wasserman joked about the newspaper stories that had called him the "press agent for a government-in-exile."

"I'll probably be here all week," Carter said leisurely over his steak, "till I can get Keith out of the country. I think we'll get Anita off [her arrest] without much trouble."

"By the way," Wasserman told me, "I see you're working your way up. You're on the ninth floor this time."

I was, in fact, staying in a ninth floor Module.

Carter laughed. "Wasserman did make sure you were stuck on seven last time, you know."

"We fixed you," Wasserman said. I joined in the laughter. We were gentlemen—of sorts—after all.

A pleasant dinner, a rosy glow from a cognac or two, and I was off to an early bed. I had twisted their arms to the extent that Carter and Wasserman said that I could likely interview Keith after his court appearance if I allowed one of his lawyers to be present. Fair enough. Off for a good night's rest before Keith's day in court.

At 11:00 P.M., Pam from the message desk downstairs called and rolled me out of the sack. "I hate to bother you," she said nervously, "but a customs officer at the airport wishes to speak to you. *Now.*"

I sighed and got on the phone. A very officious-sounding woman informed me that she was holding "your colleague, Annie Leibovitz" in customs until Annie paid an import tax of $301 on her cameras as "tools of her trade." I knew that Annie had absolutely no credit cards and usually traveled with about 75¢ in her pockets—depending on the kindness of writers to bail her out. Obviously, she had told customs that she had come to work, rather than saying she was a tourist, which is what you always do. Still, I was angry at the officious customs lady, who kept telling me, "That photographic equipment is commercial property, the property of her employer. She may either pay $301 tax to bring in the tools of her trade or she may leave them here and rent Canadian photographic equipment if she is going to work here."

"Bullshit, lady," I said, "if you knew Annie, you would know that she owns that stuff. That is her personal property. If that is not released immediately, my attorney will be there to see that it is."

"Fine," said the officious lady. "I'll be waiting."

I went off to find Carter to raise some legal hell. The big problem was that I didn't have $301 and Pam downstairs said the hotel's cash supply was time-locked for the night. I also didn't want to pay what amounted to blackmail. Unbeknownst to me, Annie had already taxied in to the Harbour Castle, gone up and borrowed $301 from Keith, taxied back out to the airport to get her cameras, and—before I got back from Carter's room —had moved into my room, since she had no credit cards, etc.

I was suddenly relegated to sleeping on my own couch. "Just one thing, Annie," I said firmly before nodding out. "Don't try to shoot Keith until I get my interview. This has been absolute hell to set up."

"Sure," she said.

Monday, March 14, 1977

At 9:00 A.M., the phone's insistent ring roused me from my couch. It was Carter and he was coldly furious. "You have just lost any chance of an interview," he said. "Your photographer kept Keith up all night posing for pictures and I'm supposed to deliver him in court in an hour." It seemed that Keith, after many jolly hours of posing for Annie (who had charmed him into an all-night session), had just toppled over with a needle in his arm and the odds were three to five that he would make his court appearance with his eyes open. What a great impression that would make on the judge. (Thanks a lot, Annie.) I called Jann Wenner in New York and woke him up to tell him I was fed up with all this prima donna bullshit—how many hands did I have to hold, after all? Then I called Bill Carter back and told him to have Annie Leibovitz deported immediately, on any grounds he wanted. She would be the last superstar photographer to step on one of my stories.

Even Carter seemed to think that was a bit extreme. I said I would call the RCMP myself and press some kind of charges against her for wiping out weeks of my work in an instant and I woke Jann up again to tell him that his star photographer was about to be thrown out of Canada, praise God! I was not quite frothing at the mouth, they said later. (The Grand Jury upheld me.)

(After I was persuaded to not have Annie deported, she offered a sort of apology by having room service send me a fifth of Jack Daniel's Black Label, along with a bottle of Taittinger Comtes de Champagne Reims Brut for herself. She charged both of them to me, of course: $23.00 for the Black Jack and $41.75 for her champagne. Thanks a lot, Annie.)

(And then there was the ugly episode when Carter and Wasserman pushed their way into the room, while I was asleep on the couch in my Jockey shorts and Annie was asleep on the bed in   whatever it was that she slept in. Annie and I were both dazed as Wasso and Carter burst in, waving "exclusivity contracts" that they demanded we sign. "All right, Flippo, we know you two are shacking up!" Wasso said. "Just sign here. This just means you will never mention the Rolling Stones again without their strict approval." Even I was hip to such an unsubtle attempt at sledgehammering.)

In court, in the morning, Keith did indeed nod out. But it didn't really matter. There was again a mob of hundreds of Stones fans outside old City Hall. On my way to Courtroom 26, I ran into Clay Powell, who had just gotten Anita off with only a $400 fine. Nice work. He was still a bit worried. "I have Keith's passport in my pocket here, but they kept Anita's. I think they're going to start deportation hearings on her tomorrow."

I had to argue my way into Courtroom 26. Inspector McGowan was personally screening everyone who wanted in and he didn't want to hear from any disrespectful foreign correspondents, so I had to become a tourist. Keith's hearing took perhaps twenty seconds. Crown prosecutor Scott walked over to a calendar hanging on the wall, leafed idly through it, and stuck his index finger on June 27. He returned to the bench and proposed that June 27 be the day that Keith would be remanded to court, at which time a plea might be entered and at which time an actual trial date might be set. Agreed by all. As Keith and Powell and Carter started out, the judge instructed the bailiffs to "Give them a sixty-second headstart before you let the crowd out." And, indeed, there was a mob outside waiting to cheer Keith as he marched, head proudly up, to a station wagon waiting to whisk him back to the Harbour Castle. And bed. It was a good thing he hadn't needed to be awake for this hearing.

Tuesday, March 15, 1977

Just after midnight, I finally got the clearance from the batteries of lawyers and advisers to go talk to Keith. Everyone was now apparently kissing and making up. Wasserman phoned with the regal summons.

Up I went to 3424, into Keith's chambers and into a world that few —if any—of the tranquil Harbour Castle's visitors could even fathom existed within their midst. The central living room was a whirlwind of activity. Room service came and went almost nonstop; the phones never stopped ringing; Stones aides-de-camp rushed in and out with urgent messages; "Honky Tonk Women" howled from a bank of speakers next to a TV set showing a church service; guitars and amps and tape recorders were stacked everywhere; room service carts and trays lined one wall; neatly suited-and-tied attorneys sat talking with T-shirted and blue-jeaned Stones aides. As had been Keith's custom for years, all the lamps were draped with colorful Moroccan scarves, casting an otherworldly light on this tableau.

The obvious impression, albeit a highly romantic one, was that of the headquarters of a rebel-in-exile. A people's revolutionary on the run, hounded by the relentless authorities who are determined to quash this revolutionary and the insurrection he was attempting to foment. The image flickered of a rock and roll Che Guevara, racing narrowly ahead of the tribunal's dogged storm troopers. Could then a firing squad for this rock and roll Che be far behind? Of course it could. Che had no high-powered lawyers and moneyed international record companies eager to protect a valuable asset. Even so, the image was perhaps very real for the ragtag Stones army that had surrounded the old City Hall and had seemed ready to tear up the very paving stones and start hurling them if their spiritual El Jefe were to be locked away forever. For a generation whose politics and ideology—such as they were—were forged by the sound of a backbeat at 110 decibels, perception is reality. The power of rock and roll to generate and especially imprint a common international perception and identity has been vastly underrated, I was thinking, when I was interrupted by the great man himself.

Keith strode in to shake hands. He was wearing jeans tucked into suede boots and a red shirt and a red and blue short-billed soft cap. Anita drifted in and out in a nightgown. Young Marlon Richards sat on the carpet with some coloring books. Keith and I sat down on a couch. For a man who has lived several hard lifetimes already, it seemed, he did not look that bad. And it was mainly his eyes that told me that; the unflinching dark eyes of a man who will not give up or be beaten.

"These are the Paris tapes," he yelled to me. "These are good, but

I'll play you the El Mocambo tapes. They're better, in some ways." He got on the horn to room service to order some more Jack Daniel's and we went off to a quieter room to talk. We sat down with tumblers of Black Jack and with attorney Carter, since the only way I had finally persuaded the Stones organization to let me talk to Keith was to agree to have one of his lawyers present, who could strike only any material prejudicial to Keith's court case. Not that I was interested in solving it.

So what I faced was a music interview, albeit with one of the most interesting and significant people in rock and roll history.

"Basically, Keith," I said, "I have to be very careful in what I ask. So what are you doing musically here in Toronto?"

He smiled slyly and took a sip of Black Jack. "Well, since I have been stuck for a week in Toronto by myself, after everybody else drifted off as stealthily as they could during the week, and since we had the studio time booked anyway, I've been getting some rough mixes down from the El Mocambo gigs, in which the second night is where we recorded some good sounds. The first night had a really great sort of ambience throughout the crowd, but the band sounds like it was playing for something in New Delhi; there were these weird sort of quarter tones, out of tune, very frantic. It was all adrenaline."

"Playing in a club again," I said, "brought out a lot of the best of the Stones, I thought. Playing again with people a foot away from you—or on you."

"It was dead easy to get back into it," he said, with his husky laugh. "I mean, we haven't played a place that small since '62. But it all fell into place. Because we were used to it from those early gigs, it felt very natural, you know. I mean, it has been a long time since I've had my legs stroked while playing, you know. I'd forgotten all about that."

"It was the first time I've ever seen you and Charlie and Bill smile onstage at the same time," I said.

He smiled and lit another cigarette. "Yeah. It felt really good. But it's the same with the stuff we recorded on the European tour, you know, all the best stuff came from Earl's Court [in London] or from Paris. The reason being, it's pretty obvious that if you are in the same auditorium for four or five nights and everybody sort of gets hotter and hotter every night, the engineer gets the sound better and you get to know the hall and how to handle the sound better. The same here. It's pretty obvious that the second night was going to be technically superior. The whole reason for coming here and doing the shows, as far as all that is concerned, is a total success. Because we came here to record songs that we don't usually do on the stage, the usual stage, and to also do some songs that we have never touched before."

"What about any of your own stuff?" I asked.

He cracked another fifth of Black Jack and poured a round. "The other thing that I have been doing," Keith said, "is that I got time to put down on tape all these songs I learned from Gram Parsons. I was very tight with him for a long time. I've never really done anything, in the eight years since he taught me, anything more than put them on cassette to just remember the lyrics. So I thought I would put them down, as a dub sort of thing. It's mostly country songs, Merle Haggard and George Jones. Stu [Stones pianist Ian Stewart] and I have cut 'Worried Life Blues' together and it has rather a Big Maceo/Tampa Red feel to it. Mick and I play them whenever we get together and if we want to do them, then they are now half-ready to go, you know? So I took this opportunity to sort of rack my brains and put down everything I had floating around in my head: songs, half-songs, riffs. I got it all on tape, which is very efficient for me. I have been meaning to do it for ages, but at sessions, you know, everybody is there usually and so you don't get the chance to do it. So that killed some time in Toronto."

"When you," I asked, "work on what will be a Rolling Stones song, do you consciously put down what would be the Richards half of the Jagger/Richards composition?"

"Yeah," he said, "I put down the Richards part of the song because it could well be that Mick will play me a song and say, 'Let's put that bit onto the middle of your bit.' "

We took a cigarette and Jack Daniel's break and listened to rough mixes of the Stones at the El Mocambo, Keith pointing out things that I had not heard, as close to the stage as I had been. That's why he is who he is, etc.

"What about the future of the group now, Keith?" I asked.

Keith looked over at attorney Carter, who nodded assent.

Keith spoke softly in his husky voice, so softly that I had to lean forward to hear every word. "I don't think that I feel any differently about it, as far as I know it is just going to go on. I mean, it will go on because it feels good to go on right now. There is no reason for it to not to. I mean, they can do what they like. If someone is unable to be with the others for a while, for one reason or another, then there will just be a gap, but it will go on. I don't think it will come to that. As long as people are going to come and hear, the Stones will go on. I mean, Charlie is getting better and better, man, you can't just let that go when things are improving all the time. For the band, in its own perverse way, we all feel it's getting better. We are learning and understanding more about what we are playing and, from that point, it will go on. I mean, there was a time when nobody thought an act could last more than two years. You had that sort of planned obsolescence. Especially when we started. Two years, forget it! But Muddy Waters has just put out a great new album. There's no reason that rock and roll has to be played by adolescents and juveniles. It was great when it was played by them, at least when I was one. It still feels better from this end, you know. Fred McDowell, all my favorite cats like that kept on playing till they dropped—seventy, eighty years old. It's like wine, man, they just get better."

"But," I asked, "given the sink-or-swim record company approaches to new bands, can groups like the Stones or Beatles or the Who have time to develop into what they will be?"

"I just read in *Sounds* [British pop music tabloid] the poll for awards," Keith said, shaking his head. "For best songwriter, it said, Robert Plant, Jimmy Page, followed by Ritchie Blackmore and some amazing people I don't know. England is very strange, as far as its music goes. There just used to seem to be so many bands. I just wonder if there's anybody managing to lurk in some backwater and getting something together. Just being allowed to get the sort of basic thing together before—it seems that everybody is sort of sucked in whether they are ready or not. I don't think there will ever be any more sort of Beatles, Rolling Stones, any more sort of huge things. Everything these days is more like boiling pots of influence. In ten or fifteen years, you might be able to say that reggae, for example, was on a par with the Hula Hoop or the cha-cha-cha. Flashes in the pan maybe. I think the days are over for a big thing like the Beatles."

"What then," I wondered, "lies in store for a hugely successful band like the Stones, who were nurtured in such bars as the El Mocambo? And now come back to such bars. Can you go back to the rock stadium circuit?"

"Well," he said, "it is a full circle for us. Maybe it means we are going to start playing a whole lot of bars again. It felt good. I know the band wants to do it. And not just our band; a lot of bands would like to break this system of these enormous tours. It's so hectic: Three months, then everything explodes just as it's getting good and it's starting to go to a top gear that you didn't know was there." He snapped his finger for emphasis. "Then it stops! No gigs for nine months. If every band could only play three or four gigs a month. But it's not structured that way. How can you get a crew to work that way? They're all contracted. You constantly come across the ins and outs of obstacles every time. Our band is just as happy playing the El Mocambo as Madison Square Garden. If we could just play one of those every month to stay in shape. This system of tours and huge auditoriums is really a very unprofitable way of using the available energy. It can't go any bigger, you know. It's going outdoors. It's only now that we can find a way to make it pay for itself, but also to be able to play sensibly sized places where the music fits. Whereas, with any sport, okay, they build a special place for you to play that game in. If you play football, you go to a football stadium. With rock and roll, you don't get a rock and roll building. You know you'll have to play in a fucking football stadium. It's strange. Everywhere else, they have their venues specially made for what they do. But there is nothing for us. So we have clubs like the El Mocambo, but that's not going to buy any of us a Rolls-Royce, is it? What do you do? Play for three years at the El Mocambo? It's not possible. There has got to be a way to do it in between."

Marlon came in with his crayons and coloring books. "Shh, son," Keith told him, "Daddy's working right now."

"For the meantime," I asked, "if you have trouble getting into certain countries, will the Stones keep touring?"

"Oh yeah!" he said. "Because we will keep on trying to get in and eventually we will. If they want us in bad enough. There's that to be considered, too." He laughed.

"This may be exaggeration, but I don't think so," I said. "Why do entire governments regard you as the devil incarnate?"

"It's convenient." He shrugged. "They don't have to look any farther. I really can't answer it. I've seen simple little tiny court trials where the prosecutors . . . for some reason it becomes enormously important to them to have to prove themselves. That's some of it, but it's not all of it. I feel that they always want to show that kid that they have got some balls. That's one attitude I come across an awful lot. It's like Lenny Bruce. But once they start on something, man, they don't let up. They just don't. Elton John came to Toronto to record and no one noticed. David Bowie came here and no one noticed. The only thing they've really got going here, and the reason that people are coming here to record, and the whole idea behind building all these recording studios is that they have only a 10 or 15 percent withholding tax here. These studios might become mausoleums, no matter how good they are."

"But why do you think it is," I asked, "that an Elton John can cross a border like a nun, but if the Stones are coming it's the huns and a red alert is declared? Your history or just the notoriety?"

Keith laughed grimly. "There's all this incredible rivalry that goes on between different branches of the legal department—even on the international scale. It's like 'If the English cops can't do the job, then let's show them!' It's their show. I guess also by popping me, they think I'm worth popping a hundred and fifty or two hundred ordinary people. It shows people that your police are really on the ball—'We're doing our job' sort of thing—from a public relations point of view. For all I know, the public relations office decides who they go after, but it's always [press] coverage if you bust so-and-so. Police: they are basically in the business of crime, you know, and that's there in the game. There's criminals and there's police, but they're in the same business. They both think the same way. If there is a criminal mentality, there has got to be a police mentality and it has got to be pretty much the same, since they are in the same business. I mean, it's no different than a wholesaler and a retailer in dealing in the same product. It's crime. They are both in it and there is really not much difference except what they want to put on as a really good guise. But it's still the same job. It's big business."

"But," I said, "you are not an ordinary citizen."

He smiled and lit a cigarette. "I know, but I was thinking that, like everything else in the world, the immigration department would get younger people coming to work there. I don't know. It doesn't seem to have affected that area much. Whereas, in my last [court] appearance at Aylesbury assizes, the jury was incredibly young. I had been expecting a whole panel of housewives. But most of them were young and one chick was crying."

"Well," I said, "do you think you're still the most visible target of rock and roll as corrupter of youth—the old story?"

"Sure!" he said. "They still think rock and roll is going to go away, you know. It's like that old Tin Pan Alley attitude when rock and roll came on the scene in the fifties. They kept telling themselves, 'Oh, it's only a fad. It's not gonna last.' That was all you heard for eighteen months after Little Richard."

We talked about the fifties for a while and went to the bathroom and made fresh drinks and told bad jokes and played a few tapes.

"Would you ever," I asked, "do a solo album? Or does this stuff you're cutting alone now belong to the Stones?"

He thought a moment before answering. "I'm not really interested in doing a solo album. I haven't got an album's worth of stuff that I think I can interest people with anyway. Myself, that's what I think. I don't think I want to put myself in that position of writing a song, see—that position of 'Do I keep the song myself or do I give it to the Stones?' It would cut us all in pieces and I don't want to put myself through that. I can do nearly everything I want to do with the Stones and what I can't do with the Stones I'm not good enough at doing. There is probably going to come a time when I will do one, but it won't be a decision of mine. It will just come about through having recorded tracks and after two or four years that . . . it may happen. I just haven't meant to put myself through that trip of 'Well, do I give this to the Stones or do I keep it for myself?'"

"What about," I said, "the Gram Parsons stuff that you're working on?"

"Let me play you some," Keith said excitedly, getting up to rummage through piles of tape boxes. "These are songs that Gram taught me. There's a few cuts by George Jones that were written by Dallas Frazier. 'Say It's Not You,' 'Apartment Number Nine.' 'Sing Me Back Home' by Merle Haggard. 'Six Days on the Road.' And a couple of Jerry Lee's [Lewis's] things. 'She Still Comes Around to See What's Left of Me.'" He laughed and raised his glass. "I used to spend days at the piano with Gram, you know, just singing. I did more singing with Gram than I've done with the Stones. He taught me all the Everly Brothers stuff and the cross harmonies and shit like that. We lived together when we cut *Exile on Main Street.* He was living with us then for two or three months. He wrote songs, man! He kept going; he would go all day without ever repeating himself."

We talked some more nostalgia and drank some more.

"What do you see in your immediate future?" I finally asked.

Keith chuckled humorlessly, sipped Black Jack, and answered: "Finish this live album, beat this rap, hopefully do some gigs in the States later on this year. South America: I'd like to bust that one wide open. I look at South America and I think of the rock and roll business's potential audiences that are ignored. It's not really the musicians' fault, although they could push, but it's the promoters and the agents, because it's a hassle to break new paths. I mean, there's people screaming for rock and roll. It's like BP [British Petroleum] not going and tapping some huge oil field, you know, just not bothering. Can you imagine that? The audiences are equivalent. They'd be down there like a shot after the pipelines. Rock and roll is ignored. There are thousands and thousands of record buyers. They should be knocking on Moscow's fucking door; they should be hitchhiking down to South America. You could even go to New Delhi or Calcutta; there are thousands of street kids there. Africa is another place where we could get it together. More and more I think about how long we've been on the road and how many tours we've done around the world and how the itinerary, with the exception of four or five cities here and there, is identical. You go around like nomads on these well-beaten paths. Meanwhile, there are all these other people screaming for it. So that's another thing that we will definitely try to do; break open a few new areas. It's essential."

More Jack Daniel's flowed (in case you have not guessed by now). I said that Robert Johnson albums must be heard worldwide.

"You have to go ahead of where he [Robert Johnson] is going to strike," Keith said with some emotion. "I mean, if Leningrad goes potty over Cliff Richard . . ." We talked for a great long while about foreign countries and rock and roll and the problems of combining the two.

"I can't believe," Keith said with some fervor, "that a government would spend two seconds of its time worrying about what rock and roll band is coming to its country. But they do. They spend precious taxpayers' money worrying about it."

"Have you thought," I asked, "about the possibility of what a country might do if it jailed you and then saw 50,000, say, young people demonstrating for your freedom?"

Keith smiled at the prospect. "That particular idea has to be put next to the one of 'Let's grab him!' So it comes down to political outlaws. There really isn't any way that anybody in our position—or my position—can really get a fair trial because the image—or the prejudice or whatever it's called—is already cast against me."

"For better or for worse," I said, "you are the spirit of outlaw rock and roll and the old rebellion."

"Illegal," he spat out the word. "They are really out to make rock and roll illegal. Really, it would be illegal to play the goddamn music. That's the basic drive behind the whole thing. They are just scared of that rhythm. That disturbs them. Every sound's vibration has a certain effect on you. You can make certain noises that automatically make you throw up. And there is nothing you can do about it. Certainly, every sound has an effect on the body and the effects of a good backbeat make these people shiver in their boots. So you are fighting some primeval fear that you can't even rationalize because it has to do with chromosomes and exploding genes."

We nursed our drinks for a while. Attorney Carter had completely given up on us, although he still tried to track the conversation.

"Well, Keith," I finally managed, "the impact of a Stones song like 'Satisfaction' would still have the same impact today as it did in '65 because it is the anthem of a generation and it won't die because it represents what a generation felt and thought. Maybe that's oversimplifying it."

Keith seemed pleased and modest. "But over the years, it's the simplifications that stand out."

"Still," I said, " 'Satisfaction' stood for a hell of a lot for a lot of people and that will never change. Which puts a lot of responsibility on you as a songwriter."

"Songs," Keith said, pouring more Black Jack. "Songs. People think you're a songwriter. They think you wrote it, that it's all yours, that you're totally responsible for it. Really, you are just a medium, you know. You just develop a facility for recognizing and picking up things and you just have to be ready to be there, like being at a seance. Whole songs just come to you, you don't write them. Songs come to me en masse, virtually out of the air. It's more of being a medium of the thing coming through you than of you actually creating it. I always get the feeling that it has been on its way, anyway. 'Satisfaction': I just happened to be awake and to have a guitar in my hand when it arrived."

7 Chop, Chop, Chop

Chop, chop, chop, chop, chop. Scrape. Chop, chop, chop, chop. Scrape. Chop. Pause. The brittle impact of a PAL single-edged razor blade slicing through a glittering pile of white powder and striking the small hand mirror upon which the pile gleams is the only sound in the room. Chop, chop. The chopper is very thorough. Determined to leave intact no powder chunks that might congest and thus foul up the internal passages eager to receive the shining white powder. Chop. The snowy crystals break apart into tiny billowy drifts. Chop. Scrape. The chopee scrapes the snowbanks into two thick lines and eyes them longingly, as one might let his gaze linger over the waiting, eager body of a lover. Then the chopee and scrapee hauls out a two-inch length of powder-encrusted transparent straw and inserts one end of it into the right nostril of his wide proboscis and the other end into a fat white line and—with a loud honk—proceeds to suck about $60 of what I hope is lactose and Procaine into his sinus passages. He does not offer me any—hey, no big deal, who wants the stuff?—as I sit watching. Then he tilts his head back to let all the luscious grains penetrate every cavity in his moneyed head. Then—and only then —does Mick Jagger look up at me, tap his nostril, smile his crooked grin that shows off the diamond in a front tooth, and speak. "You do smoke, don't you?" he asks in his most charming man-of-the-people voice.

"Depends—" I start to say and, without waiting for a reply, the most famous man in rock and roll reaches into a desk drawer and produces a baggie of some green leafy special tobacco and a packet of rolling papers. He turns his attention to cleaning the special tobacco and discarding its peculiar "seeds" and assembling a homemade cigarette. I look around the room. I'm in no hurry to leave. It's about 4:00 on a balmy Sunday afternoon, April 7, 1979, here in Mick's apartment overlooking New York's Central Park. He was then living just up from John Lennon's aerie in the Dakota at 72nd. Mick's building was nothing special and his apartment wasn't either. His view was of the street and the trees across the street. And the noise level was considerable: A second-floor Manhattan apart-

ment overlooking a major artery such as C.P.W. may as well be inside a
ghetto-blaster. Still, it was airy, and roomy, and pleasant, and homey, as is
any living space that was put together to live in comfortably, rather than
to impress visitors. Why was I there that Sunday instead of staying in bed
and drowsing through the six pounds or so that was the Sunday New York
Times? I didn't know myself. I had written articles for years about the
Rolling Stones. Not all of those articles had been what you might call
"positive." I had, in fact, been thrown off the Stones' 1978 American
tour, only the year before. I had, however, tried to write honestly about
the band. Maybe, I pondered there in Mick's sunny sitting room that
Sunday, honesty will earn me a Stones Gold Medal or something equally
ludicrous. Mick, bent over, kept rolling his special cigarette.

I had gotten a call that morning from Jane Rose, who is the Stones'
very effective interface with the real world. "Can you meet with Mick this
afternoon?" she asked enigmatically. "Sure," I said. What do I have better
to do? So I head up C.P.W., past John Lennon's gothic Dakota, and the
doorman at 135 C.P.W. sends me right up to 2N. Up a circular marble
staircase. Mick, in stockinged feet, jeans, and open-necked sport shirt, lets
me in the door. "Can we go in here for a bit?" he asks, ushering me to a
small living room overlooking C.P.W. The focus of the room is a Sony
Trinitron sitting on the cardboard box it arrived in. Mick and I sit stiffly
on a couch and run through the channels on the TV. Linda Ronstadt and
Jerry Brown are off to Africa, we learn. "To rescue Idi Amin?" Mick asks
sarcastically.

Since Keith Richards is about to play the Canadian benefit for the
blind concert that was part and parcel of his sentence for being busted in
Canada with a snootful of smack, I ask Mick if he will join Keith's New
Barbarians group at the show to make it a full-blown Stones event.
"Yeah," Mick sneers, "if we can find a way to mark the tickets to keep the
'blindies' from scalping them." We trade tasteless cripple jokes for a while.

Finally, the focus of Mick's delay arrives. Jade Jagger, radiant, comes
in roller-skating across the wood parquet floor to hug her daddy. Just
behind her is Jerry Hall, huge and gorgeous, out of breath from a quick
shopping trip. She says she didn't have enough money to buy herself a pair
of roller skates. "Why, they cost $157 and I didn't have the money and I
didn't have any checks left in my checkbook," she says in her charming,
disarming Texan drawl, as she beams a sunshiny smile at Mick. He hugs
her around the ass and grins. "They won't give you any credit cards, huh?"

Jerry and Jade leave to walk and skate in Central Park and Mick
invites me into the corner sitting room. "There's nothing in the house,"
he apologizes. "What would you like?" He calls down to a deli for beer
and soda to be sent up. While we wait, we exchange small talk. He wants

to know what Dylan and Lennon are up to; I want to know what he's up to. Verbal sparring. Finally, the delivery boy comes, who of course recognizes Mick, to their mutual delight.

We settle down with cold bottles of Heineken and go through Mick's rituals of the razor blade and the rolling paper.

He licks down the seal on his fat special cigarette, lets it dry, fires it up, inhales what must be a lung-busting toke, and hands it to me.

"We want to go to China," he finally says, after exhaling a thick plume of smoke toward the open windows facing the park.

I am temporarily befuddled, whether from the apparently harmless funny cigarette or from this sudden, unexpected camaraderie with a rock and roll giant with whom I have clashed before. I take a mind-clearing sip of beer and venture, "You want to go to China? So where do I fit in?"

Mick leans forward intently. "The Stones want to play China. We'll never get Russia. But the Chinese Government is interested." He smiles a smug smile. The Stones want everything, after all, but they have never gotten closer to penetrating the world of communism and corrupting as yet uncorruptible upright Communist youth than playing Warsaw, Poland, on April 13, 1967. China! What a virgin territory. Untold legions of rock and roll converts just waiting to be converted.

I mull that over as legions of ghetto-blaster-toting youths parade beneath Mick Jagger's windows. None of them are playing Stones songs. "Why me?" I finally venture, as Mick hands back the funny cigarette.

"The Chinese Government really doesn't know who the Stones are," he says with his crinkly grin, which is supposed to let you know that you are a favored Stones' insider. Big deal—if you think it is. "What we need," he continued, "is a concise, detailed history and description of the band to present to the Chinese Government. Something that explains to China why China needs us." The heavy emphasis on the word "needs" hangs heavier in the still air than does the thick smoke. "That's what we need written. Can you convince the Chinese Government that they need the Rolling Stones?"

Well—hell yes! Can you name me anything that would be more fun than trying to get the Stones into China? Than trying to match these misanthropic millionaire misogynist paragons of capitalism and decadence with the Chinese revolution? Amazing? I burst out laughing. Can't help myself. Mick is puzzled. The first thing I ask him actually surprises me because it is not a normal concern of mine. "Mick, there isn't enough electricity in China to run 'Jumping Jack Flash' outdoors." He looks relieved. "Oh well, then, we'll just take a jenny [generator]."

Okay. If you believe it'll work, I think. Aloud, I ask Mick where things stand with the Chinese. He becomes very serious. He had met, he says, with the Chinese ambassador-designate in Washington and the meeting had gone very well. A frank exchange of views and all that. The only problem was that the ambassador-designate was a little apprehensive that the Stones' presence might develop into a disruptive influence on Chinese young people heretofore unexposed to such influence. Mick said, though, that he felt he had won over the ambassador-designate. Who retained only one caveat: He needed a persuasive argument on paper to send to Peking regarding the worthy Rolling Stones and he needed it soonest. Fast.

"What exactly do you have in mind?" I ask Mick, after we get fresh beers. "Wal," he drawls in his fake Southern drawl with the crooked grin that is meant to be boyish charm (and which usually works), "can you tell China that they must have us?"

He is as serious as I have ever seen him be. Even so, neither of us—I think, anyway—feels that this is some kind of historic moment. We pass the funny cigarette and get some more beers.

"I can give it a whirl," I tell Mick in response to his question about China and that they "must have us."

"But," I say, "I can't sugarcoat you guys. You do have a checkered history [you do talk that way after smoking those things] and I don't think that the Chinese are naïve enough to think that they're getting the Trapp family."

Mick laughs exuberantly and gets up to fetch more beer. "I know that," he says when he returns. "Just haul out the good stuff about us. Quote the right lyrics. Explain why we are what we are." Chop, chop, chop.

We talk for a couple of hours about the benchmarks in the Stones' career, about the band's place in the history of American popular music (not British, interestingly), about the significance of the blues tradition, about the substantial constituency the Stones maintain worldwide, about the phenomenon of the continuing rock and roll revolution in youth culture, and on and on. A stimulating discussion of pop culture and its role and impact and all that.

Then I look him straight in the eye and ask him the one question that I know I have to ask: "Mick, what about Altamont?"

The question hangs in the air like a huge dust mote on this sunny afternoon. A chunky disco beat from a ghetto-blaster down on the street dances through the open windows. Mick looks away and laughs nervously. Then he summons up his most charming and fetching smile and trains the 300-kilowatt look on me: "Why do you have to mention Altamont at all?"

I fall silent for a moment. Finally, I say, "It *is* a matter of history."

Mick grins. "Wal, no need to sensationalize it!"

We seesaw back and forth a while, both half-drunk and half-stoned, both spouting half-assed philosophy. I leave finally when Jerry and Jade come home.

I go home to try to tell my wife, "Guess what I did today, dear."

She is not impressed. But I do stay up for the next two nights writing one motherfucker of a defense paper for a renegade rock and roll band that probably should not be allowed within a thousand miles of the Chinese border, much less hugged to the bosom of the continuing revolution. The Rolling Stones own total rights forever to this historic document (for which they paid me $500), so I can't reprint it and you'll never read it. But the fucking Chinese swallowed it! They were going to let the Rolling Stones in! Going to let this insidious capitalistic deviationist agent of sloth and sin infect correct youth with the incorrect ways of Western poison. Here is an excerpt from the October 17, 1979, Starship Radio bulletin: "Stones to Tour China; The Rolling Stones are to tour China next spring. The invitation was extended to Mick Jagger as he chatted over a cup of tea with a Chinese ambassador in Washington. It's a remarkable break- through for the Stones, who have always been considered by Iron Curtain countries as symbols of Western decadence and a threat to Communist youth. Now it seems that China is eager to welcome them to build up an image of openness and liberalism."

Well. That's nothing compared to what I tried to whip up in that little Stones manifesto. Working-class heroes? You got them right here. Champions of the underdogs? Guess who. Who are the true revolutionar- ies in rock music? Not the Beatles. Guess who. Which rock group consis- tently attacks upper-class hypocrisy and decadence in Western society? I think you know. I even clinched the deal, I hear now, by celebrating the fact that Charlie Watts was the president of the North Wales Sheepdog Society. Actually, it was a fairly sober document that showed the Stones, warts and all (Altamont included), as the most Western of Western bands that the Chinese would appreciate. So I typed it up and sent it over to Jane Rose at Rolling Stones Records in Rockefeller Center and she had it translated into Chinese and fired it off to the ambassador-designate in Washington, who relayed it to Peking. And everyone sat back to see what would happen next. Keith Richards got his copy of the thing at his estate in Jamaica and he called me at home to tell me how much he appreciated it and, by the way, to ask what the Stones song was that I quoted from that was so democratic ("Salt of the Earth").

Peking was pleased, it seemed. Newspaper articles began appearing about the Stones' projected tour of China. Then Mick was invited back to Washington for a meeting with the ambassador-designate and other Chi- nese officials to discuss the realities of such a tour. Mick will not discuss what happened, but apparently the meeting was a mess and the Chinese were horrified by some of Mick's remarks. I heard from within the Stones camp that Mick gave the ambassador-designate rather a hard time and that they reached no meeting of the minds and that it developed that, rather than the Stones touring China next month, that it appeared that the Stones would tour China when, in fact, hell freezes over. The opinion within the Stones camp was that Mick blew it. Deliberately. Everyone close to the Stones knows that he does that now and then. What no one knows is why he possesses such a penchant for self-destruction, for so strong a sense of self-doubt that it amounts to nihilism.

8 Canada Revisited

"Life is truly stranger than publicity" department: I was sorting through my pounds and pounds of newspaper and magazine clippings on the whole Toronto and El Mocambo and Maggie and Anita and drugs and the RCMP episode (truly the most amazing in the Stones' chronicles of their being able to influence history simply by being alive) when I chanced across a thoughtful, chin-stroking, two-pipe essay by Roger Rosenblatt in *The New Republic*. Rosenblatt stroked his chin at great length, of course, but what caught my eye was his essay's title: "Maggie and Wilbur." He of course compared Margaret Trudeau's plight with that of former Ways and Means Committee Chairman Wilbur Mills. Two similar falls from grace. Both falls, apparently, stemmed from pristine intentions and pressures of an unwanted fishbowl existence. What struck me as extraordinary was that (and Rosenblatt could not have known this) Wilbur Mills had been the man who had introduced the Rolling Stones to their current champion defender, attorney Bill Carter, when Mills had heard via mutual friends that the Stones needed visa and immigration help and advice. At a time when Southern politicians such as Strom Thurmond were privately twisting White House arms to get John Lennon deported from the United States, a Southern politician such as Wilbur Mills sought to get the Rolling Stones a fair shake in Washington. He deserves a round of applause. At any rate, essayist Rosenblatt concluded by observing that Wilbur Mills and Maggie Trudeau were made for each other. And he was dead right, although he didn't really know why. He said that they were public figures who became "swingers." (Wilbur had picked a stripper; Maggie, the Stones.) Too simple an answer. They were both just Rolling Stones' groupies, who both reached the point where they just couldn't hold it in any longer.

June 8, 1977

In a secret move, attorney Clayton Powell got the Supreme Court of Ontario to declare invalid the RCMP's search warrant, under which warrant Keith Richards had been busted. Why? No specific officer had been listed on the warrant. There was much gnashing of teeth at the RCMP. Carter, meanwhile, had whisked Keith and Anita to New York City and enrolled Keith in a special camp on Manhattan's chic Sutton Place where you learn to not shoot heroin. Keith was doing real good in camp. He was practically wearing a Boy Scout's uniform.

June 27, 1977

This was to have been Keith's day in court. He didn't show. A bench warrant was issued for his arrest. In a highly irregular move, crown prosecutor David Scott called, in camera, for a 5:00 P.M. meeting that day with RCMP arresting officers, the Staff Superintendent of the Ontario Provincial Police, an RCMP superintendent, and the director and deputy directors of the Department of Justice. At the Department of Justice. No one who was there will say what happened, but it apparently was a very heated meeting. Angry words were exchanged. Ultimately, in a secret discussion, the Justice Department ordered that Keith's charge of possession of heroin with intent to traffic (potential life sentence penalty) be reduced to simple possession of heroin (slap on the wrist time). RCMP Superintendent Heaton angrily argued against the lighter charge. He was effectively muzzled by the Department of Justice and told to shut his mouth and follow orders. Keith's skids were starting to get greased. And this was still a big secret. The question must be asked: Was the fix on? What do you think?

Keith missed that court date, as well as three others (July 19, 1977, February 6, 1978, and March 6, 1978) and the RCMP was upset that the crown prosecutor made no motion to have Keith's bail forfeited for failure to appear. On October 31, 1977, the RCMP asked the Department of Justice if it could introduce Keith's (lengthy) criminal record at the preliminary hearing. The new federal prosecutor, Paul Kennedy, said that the RCMP could not do so. Keith would, in effect, appear in court as a virgin.

On February 15, 1978, chief RCMP arresting officer William Seward was killed in a car wreck. He had been in charge of the exhibits and evidence in Keith's case.

Although the RCMP had compiled a lengthy list of Keith's previous arrests, it was informed by Justice that said list could not be introduced in court. Prosecutor Kennedy advised the RCMP that Keith would plead guilty to simple possession of heroin and that that plea had been "authorized" by the heads of the Department of Justice and the RCMP. Keith's cocaine possession charge would be overlooked. Was there a fix on?

I wish I had had an answer to that when I went to Keith's trial at 10:00 A.M. on Monday, October 23, 1978, before York County Judge Lloyd Graburn and about seventy-five spectators in Courtroom 5 of Toronto's County Court Building. Canadian and British reporters were laying me five to one odds that Keith would serve at least—as the merest hand slap—a year of hard prison time for the trafficking charge. None of us knew that the charge didn't exist any more. Even so, simple possession of heroin could draw seven years. So the betting was heavy.

So was the press coverage. UPI had the airport staked out when Keith had flown in by private plane on Sunday, October 22, for his preliminary hearing on Monday. The Toronto *Star* had two reporters checking every hotel in town to see where Keith was. He got to the Four Seasons Hotel at 9:30 P.M. and spent the next couple of hours trying to get a drink. He had forgotten about Toronto's Sunday laws. Not even Keith Richards could order a drink. He finally, as any sensible man would, ended up bribing a bellboy to fetch him some hooch. Hard for a condemned man to get that last drink.

There was almost no crowd outside York County Courthouse in the morning and Courtroom 5 was not jammed. A clutch of hungover Brit reporters regarded the crown seal with its *"honi soit qui mal y pense"* admonition. By 9:30, jury chairs were being moved down to handle the press overflow. What was afoot? No jury? No trial? Keith arrived at 9:40 at the building with Austin Cooper, a lawyer with (as a Brit scribe said) a "golden dome" (a reference to his glowing pate). At 9:59, just as the courtroom was being warned against gum chewing before Judge Graburn's entrance, the press corps noted that there was only one jury chair left that had not been given to a spectator. The obvious message: No jury would be seated. Suddenly, all bets were off. Judge Graburn swept in at 10:07 in a purple-sashed black robe. "Oyez, oyez, oyez." All stood. Keith came in, three minutes later, in a very uncharacteristic three-piece tan suit. He was accompanied by Wasserman, Stones' cornerstone Jane Rose, bodyguard Bob Bender, and—surprise!—producer Lorne Michaels and Dan Aykroyd from the TV show "Saturday Night Live." Keith stood alone in the box and tugged at his silver earring as the heroin possession charge was read against him. He was told the RCMP searched his rooms while he slept and when he finally awakened he had told the arresting officers that the drugs were his and that he had been a "heavy user for four years" and that he "purchased in bulk to reduce the risk of detection." A doctor testified that Keith and Anita were in "desperate condition from opium abuse."

An affidavit signed by Rolling Stones financial adviser Prince Rupert Low-enstein advised that Keith's casual spending had totaled $175,000 in 1975, $300,000 in 1976, and $350,000 in 1977. This was to establish legally that he was wealthy enough to not have to commit crimes to get drugs. Austin Cooper said that Keith had told arresting officers that he had tried to kick heroin but was on tour and didn't have the time to complete the cure. Cooper said that police said that Keith had been a "real gentleman" during the arrest. Keith laughed derisively.

The judge said that he was registering a simple plea of possession of heroin against Keith and that "count two," for cocaine possession, was "discharged." Attorney Cooper rose to his feet to move that the outstanding bench warrant for Keith's arrest for nonappearance at previous trials be canceled. "Granted," said the judge.

Cooper read lengthy reports from New York's Stevens Psychiatric Center as to how well Keith was doing. Witness after witness testified that Keith had truly donned a hair shirt and kicked drugs. Cooper took a ten-minute recess to bring in fresh witnesses. "I can't believe it," a veteran Toronto court reporter told me. "The fix is in. This is incredible. I just don't know how they did it."

I went up to the gate to ask prosecutor Paul Kennedy what the hell was happening. He acted as if he had been poleaxed. He grinned sheepishly and said: "I agreed to drop the cocaine charge because it's a lesser drug. And for the trafficking thing, Austin could establish a defense against trafficking. I'm sure you noticed that they built a very nice case for Keith's personal habit. I'm going to ask for a six- to twelve-month sentence."

At 11:15, trial resumed with a Toronto *Star* reporter as witness, babbling away about how wonderful and unique and totally unmatchable in any universe were the Stones. Lorne Michaels took the stand—the Stones had just played his "Saturday Night Live Show"—and said that he had picked the Stones over Muhammad Ali as guest hosts for the first show of the season because they were the "number-one rock and roll band in the world" and that Keith "is the group." Cooper got up and said that Keith had started using heroin in 1969 because he was "exhausted" and soon was ingesting at least two and a half grams a day "just to keep normal." He listed Keith's six cures and said he was a very creative person wracked with emotional pain. I believe he said that Keith's everyday life could be hell and that art was often created from pieces of the shattered self. He cited as shattered selves: Sylvia Plath, Vincent van Gogh, Aldous Huxley, Judy Garland, and F. Scott Fitzgerald. Cooper turned up his emotional appeal. "Keith Richards, by pressure of his emotional makeup and pressures on him, has become so wracked he turned to heroin to help him.

Today you are judging him and sentencing him for his habit. I ask you to assess him not only for his weakness, but for the tortured but creative spirit within him." He was moved to tears.

Prosecutor Kennedy's closing for the crown's case was hugely ineffectual. He argued that Keith had been caught with a lot of heroin, that he had been arrested before, and that he was a mature man. And that some of the Stones' songs—although he was vague as to just which ones—were pro-drugs. Had I not known better, I might have thought that someone had a very tight leash on Kennedy. And a muzzle.

Cooper came back to dream-weave Keith as Peter Pan. I am as much a Stones fan as an impartial journalist can be, but I can also smell a setup from a quarter of a mile away. And this one stunk.

I also noticed for the first time that Keith was wearing white socks with his tan suit and that Dan Aykroyd kept winking at Keith and giving him the thumbs-up signal. Lorne Michaels and Dan Aykroyd are Canadian stars.

Cooper, in what was patently bullshit, said that Keith was working on a plan to donate one million dollars to a drug rehabilitation program. (Where is it today?)

Even before I knew of the backroom deals under way, I smelled a bad tuna fish, even though my editor didn't.

Cooper, in his summation, basically said at great length that heroin was not all that bad, so why should Keith go to jail?

Judge Graburn pondered for all of seventeen seconds, before announcing, "I'll give my judgment on this matter at 10:00 tomorrow morning. This is a matter of great importance to Keith Richards and to Canada."

Keith marched out as a hero.

I cornered prosecutor Kennedy, who would not look me in the eye. I asked him some basic questions that even first-week law school students would pose. Why was the trafficking charge reduced to mere possession? Why was the cocaine possession charge eliminated? Was there a deal made? He made lame excuses. The search warrant might have been bad (though the RCMP don't even need a search warrant). The officers may not have questioned Keith closely enough when he was arrested. Keith's plea bargaining to simple possession of heroin (as opposed to intent to traffic) was a real surprise to the crown (which was obvious bullshit).

Even so, the odds in the press section were still sixty to forty that Keith would draw some time.

From what I could gather from governmental sources, Julian Issac of the Department of Justice, who had on June 27, 1977, strongly persuaded the RCMP to drop its trafficking charges against Keith, had been responsible for replacing prosecutor Scott with prosecutor Kennedy, whom no one in that courtroom could accuse of being anything other than a piece of furniture.

After court, to escape the press of English reporters in the lobby of the Four Seasons, I went out for a stroll with Paul Wasserman. "I can't tell you anything," he said.

"After today, that's just what I want to hear," I said.

Wasso was on a shopping trip for Keith and his current girlfriend. When Wasso bought a tube of K-Y Jelly, he said, "Ah, isn't it great that Keith's off smack?"

Tuesday, October 24, 1978

Betting on what Judge Graburn's sentence might be went completely off the board this morning, as the press corps and assorted Stones fanatics sat around Courtroom 5 speculating about the consequences of the previous day's startling turn of events. There was a brief flurry when a wild-eyed young woman, who had been ejected from the Four Seasons Hotel the night before for trying too desperately to get to Keith, climbed over the rail to deposit some drawings (of Keith) in the defendant's box, which Keith would shortly occupy.

At 10:00, Keith arrived, on time for once, wearing yesterday's tan suit again. Judge Graburn lectured the courtroom sternly on behaving properly —or else—and began by reviewing the heroin charge. He noted that Keith had been arrested with 440 caps of 32 percent pure heroin which, the judge admitted, was a lot of pretty strong stuff. But he said that apparently Keith was shooting 10 caps of it a day. He said Keith was a heavy user. But, he said, it seemed that Keith had detoxed and was continuing his therapy, that more therapy was needed, that Keith's only motivation was his desire to create music, and that his treatment should not be interrupted. "The crown seeks a jail term," the judge intoned, "but I will not incarcerate him for addiction and wealth." Gasps from the press section. Keith had won.

The judge continued, "Maybe the Rolling Stones have encouraged drug use in their songs. Still, his efforts have been to move himself away from the drug culture and can only encourage those who emulate him." Keith did not crack a smile.

The judge droned on and on, citing court precedents that led up to his sentence: "No jail or fine is appropriate. The long-term benefit to the community, a large community, entails the continuing treatment for your addiction. I have some concern about a suspended sentence for you, extra-territorial concern, but you are a citizen of the Commonwealth. Judgment is suspended for one year." The terms of probation were these: to keep the peace, to report to his probation officer within twenty-four hours, to continue treatment at the Stevens Center in New York City, to return to Toronto to report to his probation officer on May 7 and September 24, 1979, and to give a benefit performance within the next six months for the Canadian National Institute for the Blind (the latter apparently being a favorite charity of Judge Graburn). Applause rocked the courtroom at 10:55 A.M. Even as Keith walked out smiling, the first "blind justice" jokes started.

I caught up with prosecutor Paul Kennedy outside and asked him if the crown would appeal the sentence. "It's too early to think about an appeal," he said. "I have no objection to the sentence. The crown has not thought about appeal. If you get a member of the Rolling Stones off heroin, you've done some good. If the man *does* do a bona fide cure." He walked hurriedly away, after what seemed to be rather a strange statement from the man Canada picked to prosecute Keith.

Keith went off to get his visa renewed and then to nap back at the hotel. Wasserman scheduled a press conference for 5:30 P.M. in the Four Seasons Windsor Room, by which time most of the fifty or so members of the international press corps were well on their way to getting quite drunk. The Brits were making much light of a visually handicapped girl who had been in the front row for each of Keith's court appearances and hung around the hotel. "A hawlf-blind bird in pursuit of the Stones?" roared one Brit. "Might as well be. All their fans are deaf and dumb anyway!" Great laughter.

Keith's appearance at the press conference was brief. He just said that he was happy that things had gone according to plan and that "at least they got me bail money back so I can get the band up here for the benefit show." After he admitted he did not know the name of his probation officer, the questioning turned a bit rough and Wasserman shut the press conference down. Obviously, the issue of preferential treatment for a Rolling Stone would continue to be a sensitive topic.

There was, predictably, a press outcry. Typical was Toronto *Sun* columnist Paul Rimstead's reaction, which read, in part: "If you, as a taxpaying Canadian, had been apprehended with twenty-two grams of 34 percent heroin and cocaine, what would have happened to you? Would Judge Graburn have let you off . . . ? There are Canadians sitting in jail for lesser drug offenses . . . Let's all send Judge Lloyd Graburn a Rolling Stones record for Christmas. Just to remind him of his finest day in court, upholding the law, Canadian style . . ."

Public reaction was not favorable to Keith, judging from letters to newspapers. Eighty-three-year-old former Prime Minister John G. Diefenbaker was so enraged that he addressed the House of Commons thusly: "In view of the fact that the drug problem is increasing, particularly in this nation, the appropriate ministers of the government should give immediate consideration to appealing the preposterous and more than lenient suspended sentence imposed yesterday in Toronto on Keith Richards of the Rolling Stones . . . which sentence . . . provides that he and his associates should undertake to give a musical concert; a sentence which will be an encouragement to potential wrongdoers all over this nation." Canadian Attorney General Otto Lang said—wrongly—that it was not up to his department to appeal. Ontario Attorney General Roy McMurtry wrote to Lang: "With all due respect to the learned trial Judge, it is my respectful submission that he erred in principle in failing to impose a sentence of incarceration in this case and I am writing to strongly urge that you cause officials of your Department to launch an appeal with respect to the sentence imposed. It is my view that His Honour failed to give sufficient consideration to the aspect of general deterrence in this case and that accordingly the public's perception of a fair and impartial system of justice will diminish substantially should the sentence in question go unchallenged. Mr. Richards may well be described as a teen idol whose mores and values are trendsetters amongst our younger generation. For that reason, I am of the view that a term of imprisonment is crucial to deter like-minded individuals who may see fit to emulate Mr. Richards's attitude to the use of drugs." Attorney General Lang finally directed his department to file an appeal and to seek a jail term for Keith.

Nothing happened.

More than one Canadian official I talked to said that, well, there might have been strong intervention from Pierre Trudeau or from officials wishing to protect Pierre from further embarrassment or there might have been intervention from somewhere else, but definite as hell there had been some intervention somewhere. Because now there seemed to be an urgent governmental wish to forget L'affaire Richards and sweep it under the rug and open no more cans of worms and to get Keith the hell out of the country and pretend it never happened. And that's exactly what happened.

9 Mick

September ??, 1977

Had dinner with Mick Jagger on this date. The occasion was the imminent release of the double album *Love You Live* and the Stones' desire for publicity regarding same.

At Mick's request, we met at David K's, a trendy Chinese restaurant set on the high-rent end of Third Avenue on Manhattan's Upper East Side. Mick was on time and quite charming. We talked about the album during dinner and then ordered beers and sat around talking about this and that.

When I asked the obligatory question about was this the last Stones album because of Keith's bust and all, Mick laughed with relief. "Oh bullshit," he said, "I can say, you know, 'Yeah, it's the last one, you better buy it. There ain't gonna be any more.' I remember telling my father exactly that when Little Richard retired. I tried to get money out of my old man for the record—I said, 'Richard's retired. This is the last record. I got to get this record. Gimme seven and six 'cause he's not gonna make any more records.' And my father said, 'I'm glad he's retired anyway. I ain't giving you the money to buy that trash!'" Mick laughed fondly at the memory. "Do you remember when Richard threw his rings into the river? That time, that was when I was trying to get the money to get his last single."

"Well," I said, "as far as the Stones' such status goes, it seems as though you reached a plateau, way up on the mountain and you can look off into the distance and decide what to do next. There's no pressure and—"

Mick interrupted me. "No no, there's lots of pressure."

"From within or without?"

"Both," he said, signaling our waiter for more beer. "As you know, that's a provocative question. There's a pressure from the band 'cause they want to work and make the best music that they can. Then there's pressure from without 'cause we promised we would make certain albums—

four new albums—and so we will. I'll do it, you know. English people are very funny like that. An Englishman's word and all that. And it really works. It's not a joke. None of it's got anything to do with money. I mean, it translates itself into money, but none of us are greatly concerned with making money."

"So you won't starve tomorrow if it doesn't sell?"

Mick shook his head impatiently. "No, you don't understand what I mean. None of the pressures are concerned with money."

"With image, then?"

He was more impatient, "No, I'm not interested in that. I'm not interested in the public's image of me. I don't know what they expect of me. How can I possibly know? I just try and make the best music I can. Without being rude to any member of the record-buying public, that's not what pushes me to write songs. I do my best, but I don't do it while consciously thinking, 'Wow, I'm doing this for my public.' I know some people do. That's really an old-fashioned show-business concept, you know. 'I'm on the boards. I'm doing the best for my public.' I don't think, rightly or wrongly, without being rude, that I have any obligation to the public to do my best. The first obligation is obviously to myself or my own integrity and it must be 'cause how can I gauge what the public really wants? Any more than that waiter up there can know about those stupid Americans who keep yelling for spoons. Spoons!"

He sipped his beer and glowered at the Americans. "No," he continued, "your first obligation is to your own self, to your conscience or whatever you call it. Don't let yourself down. You may be letting yourself down in the eyes of other people, you know, your peer group, your friends, musicians, and stuff like that and you can make it wider. But you don't know what they want. And they change all the time, anyway. It's an ever-changing fuck, people, isn't it?"

"Do you care at all," I asked, "about what the punk groups are saying about you?"

Mick was delighted. "I've got my punk answers. I've got hundreds of them."

"Well, Johnny Rotten says you should have retired in 1965."

"Well, then he should definitely retire next year. He was on 'Top of the Pops' in England and that was a cop-out for the Sex Pistols. It's difficult for Americans to know what 'Top of the Pops' means, but it's the only pop music show on television—and I do mean pop—and the only place for Top Twenty records and it's the most banal—it's aimed at a real teeny market, people with clean hair and all that."

"People who buy records," I said.

"Yeah, who buy singles. And when the Sex Pistols went on 'Top of the Pops,' they copped out. Now they're on the front of the *Rolling Stone*. That's a real cop-out. If I was Johnny Rotten, I wouldn't do either. I wouldn't do 'Top of the Pops' and I'd tell *Rolling Stone* to go fuck themselves . . . I don't care what Johnny Rotten says. Everything Johnny Rotten says about me is only 'cause he loves me 'cause I'm so good. It's true."

Mick smirked as only an egocentric five-feet-eight Limey rock star with five-inch rubber lips can do.

"Well," I said, "the odd thing is that these groups disown guys like you and the Who while copping all your notes—and attitudes."

Mick smiled gratefully at the acknowledgment. "But they won't ad mit it," he said. "But they're just bands, Jesus Christ! But I'm very pleased about it—well, I'm not pleased at Johnny Rotten, who says all nasty things about me. I know that he feels he has to because I'm, along with the Queen, you know, one of the best things England's got. Me and the Queen." Then he really smirked and glowed and looked around for appreciation. Unfortunately, Mick's audience consisted of me and a hovering Chinese waiter who wanted to know if we wanted more beer. "Anyway," Mick continued, "I wouldn't do those things he's doing 'cause in a year the Sex Pistols are gonna be *phffft!* 'Cause things happen much quicker these days."

"No more playing four years in clubs to get a record deal," I said.

"That's right," Mick said. "Now it takes six months—if that. No Rolling Stones in these days."

"But the punk bands," I said, "sound a lot like the Stones and the Who."

"Yeah," Mick said, nodding, "but they've got something different in a way. And they've got lots of energy. And that's what rock and roll needs. I prefer to hear those bands than a lot of shit that goes on the 'Hollywood Rock Awards' on TV."

"Did you see that?" I asked. "Pretty bad."

"Oh yeah," Mick said, "it was the night I arrived from England, where I'd been very peaceful and happy. You know, England—even with punk rock, which is really only a sort of Saturday afternoon phenomenon —is very quiet. And I got in here and there was this awards show. I love Peter Frampton, but the idea of him as an all-around entertainer to me is a joke. I think it's stupid for Peter Frampton to do comedy sketches with robots in Hollywood. And that silly Olivia Newton-John with that daft Australian accent, what do they think they are, film stars or something?"

"They seem to want to be," I said.

Mick was fuming. "What a dumb—you don't have to do that dumb shit. Or at least do it with class. I mean, Warren Beatty does it better, doesn't he? I mean, Jack Nicholson's funnier at it."

"Frampton is still young and unformed," I said.

"Shit," Mick almost spat, "what's he want to do that shit for? What a bunch of bullshit. This is rock and roll, that's what I'm saying. I feel more in sympathy with Johnny Rotten, I'm sorry. I would never do that shit. Ever. I mean, people call me jet set and all that shit, but I would never do that shit. You know what I mean?"

The nervous hovering waiter was fiercely directed to fetch more beers.

I said, "At least, Stevie Wonder brought on the great songwriter Otis Blackwell."

"Yeah," Mick admitted, "he was the only moment of fun and reality. But what I'm saying is that after being in England and then coming here the first day and seeing that, then I know which side I'm on. I'm not saying that to be fashionable, either. I've never liked that stuff. To see people that I know and really like doing it makes me feel even worse. All their fucking bow ties. Who in the fuck do they think they are? Stupid. I mean, the rock awards should be playing rock and roll, not all this pouncing around with script cards and bow ties. Huh? There's nothing wrong with Hollywood, but, Jesus, that was bullshit."

He mentioned a couple of popular women singers and suggested that rock music specials on TV could be improved if these particular women got awards for "Best Fuck of the Year." "Something different," he said with a straight face.

We studied our beers for a moment. The hovering waiter had no idea what he had on his hands. Mick's real or projected indignation level and his quite distinct pronunciation of the "f—— word" had cleared out a number of tables in our area of David K's. And we showed no inclination of leaving.

"Where was it," I asked, "that I saw this quote of yours about rock and roll being adolescent—"

Mick cut me off. "I object to journalists regurgitating my last week's answers to the gutter press and using them instead of trying to get new ones. I said that rock and roll is basically adolescent music, I believe." He sounded quite prim.

"Well, then," I had to ask, "why are you guys who are anything but adolescent still so good at rock and roll?"

"I don't know," Mick said seriously. "We may be the exceptions. But what I was saying, primarily, I didn't mean you had to be adolescent to play it, I mean mentally. I meant that energy level, that sexual level, all sins, you know. All I was saying was that rock and roll still is adolescent, whether physically or mentally. It's unformed, you know; it's not very sophisticated. There are great singers around, you know, that can sing anything but not rock and roll, as a form, as a feeling, okay? Wanta call Ray Charles a rock artist? Go ahead. Stevie Wonder's a rock and roll artist . . . is he, really? He is, kind of, but, you know what I mean, he's not a rock and roll artist like the Clash are. No, he's not."

"Because he's not young and pissed off?"

"No," Mick said, "he encompasses all the forms and he has an incredible technical virtuosity and he can sing, I mean he can sing anything, jazz, gospel. I'm just saying that rock and roll in its raw form is . . . is—"

"Adolescent," I offered.

"That's what I meant," Mick said. "And I also said it was a dead end. A dead end in music."

"Meaning that after rock and roll you have no place to go?"

"There's no way for it to go except back to the beginning and it's a circle 'cause there ain't nothing, really."

"Well," I said, "if that's true, then you should complete the cycle by playing the El Mocambo, then playing smaller clubs, then playing school dances, and then playing in a garage or basement, and then disbanding altogether."

"Yeah," Mick said, amused, "maybe that's what we'll do."

"I'm serious," I said. "If you're true to the rock theory, you have to do the A to Z, Z to A circuit."

Mick laughed aloud and signaled for more beer. "That's a real sort of Yankee logic there," he said. "Maybe that's what we'll do. I'll suggest it to Keith tonight, see what he thinks of it. No, what I mean, just around me, when you see all these bands springing up, they're all doing these things that have already been done. Nothing new is coming out of it. There ain't nothing new in it, but I'm not complaining that there's nothing new. If it was something I couldn't understand, I'd be more worried. Someone comes out with a new style of writing, you know—when James Joyce came out, all the writers must have started worrying. 'Gee, how can he write like that?' Well, rock and roll hasn't done that, you understand? Not really, not now."

"Who's doing anything new?" I asked. "Andy Gibb? Barry Manilow?"

Mick was furious or seeming to be. "Go fuck all that lot. Silly. I hate their music. I much prefer classical music to some of that shit. Barry Manilow, Andy Gibb. I'm not interested in that. I mean, I don't even really like white music anyway, you know what I mean, I don't want to split hairs. But I've never listened to a lot of white music, never been an aficionado of white bands. Never been my inspiration. Not even Elvis, you know, was particularly inspirational. I know he wasn't really white, but even Elvis was not an inspiration to me."

"Well," I argued, "Buddy Holly was white and he sure as hell influenced you."

Mick backed down. "Buddy was, he was, yes indeed, and that's a great exception. To English people Buddy Holly was an enormous inspiration. Therein lies the difference because he was a songwriter, which Elvis wasn't. And he wrote very simple songs—sort of lesson one in songwriting. Great songs, which had simple changes and nice melodies and changes of tempo and all that. You could learn from Buddy Holly how to write songs, the way he put them together. He was a beautiful writer. He's proven 'cause he keeps having hit after hit. Linda [Ronstadt] keeps doing his songs. She just thinks she's got a good thing going." Smirk.

"Have you," I asked, "heard Linda's version of your 'Tumbling Dice'?"

Mick appeared unsettled briefly but recovered. "Oh yeah. Linda and I were just talking about it. I hope everyone else likes it and buys lots and lots of copies, so then I can take Linda out to dinner." Smirk.

"You are a sly devil, Mick," I said.

He shrugged, the devil given his due. "Well, after two weeks of press interviews, what do you expect? I usually have to talk about which girls I'm sleeping with. In England I did a week of interviews. 'What do you think of punk rock?' 'Who are you fucking?' Da-da-da-da. I did that for six people a day for five days. They all ask the same thing in different languages. The Japanese said, 'What do you think of love?' I said, 'Oh, you mean who am I going to bed with? My wife, of course.' "

We nursed our beers a bit. "You know," I said, "Johnny Rotten announced that when he hits America the first place he will go to is—not CBGB—but Harlem, because 'they will understand' him there."

"Good luck!" Mick laughed sardonically. "Really naïve English idiot. I used to go to Harlem, though, in 1964 because Keith and I used to live with the Ronettes . . . Well, not live with them, but you know what I mean. Their mother was so nice and cooked dinners for us. Keith went out with one Ronette and I went out with another and very nice they were. Used to go wandering around Harlem all the time. Did Rotten really say that?"

As conversation wound down, I found myself stuck with the check. "But only if," Mick said, "you're really sure that asshole Jann Wenner will ultimately pay for this." Mick was convinced enough to let me pick up the tab. Out on Third Avenue, we bid cordial farewells and Mick borrowed $2 for taxi fare. Good-bye, $2.

10 "Cocksucker Blues"

Keith comments on the movie *Cocksucker Blues:* "I just saw it I'm just amazed that Robert Frank hasn't got something better to get on with than touting some five-year-old movie. I wanted it to come out five years ago because I'd rather have it out there than people speculating what scenes there are in it and coloring it whichever way they want to. For me, the movie is actually a lot more hilarious because it puts some of everybody's ideas of what a documentary movie is. Because it's in black and white and because the camera wobbles, everybody thinks, 'Wow, this is for real, man,' and all the time it was obviously set up. It is so obvious a movie is being made. It's so far removed from what actually goes on. It is all set up and still people walk out going, 'Wow, is that how it is on the road?' "

Mick Jagger comments on *Cocksucker Blues:* "Robert Frank seems a very sort of silly, sick person to me and he seems to be trying to ruin Keith's life."

"Frank seemed to say he was showing Keith shooting up in the movie," I said.

"That's not true," Mick said. "Keith is not shooting up in the movie and why in the world should Frank say a thing like that? Why doesn't he go and make another movie and shut his face? That's been five years. Why can't he go and do something else? It was my idea to make that movie. He was just paid to film what I told him to do . . . Maybe he's such a great artist, why doesn't he show us the great art he's made? In the last five years? Instead of being so uptight about this movie? It's our movie. And if I want to go and shred it in the shredder, or if I want to show it to my friends, or if I want to put it in general release, it's up to me. It's not up to him. I'm sorry. That's the way we run this country."

"The Rolling Stones country?"

"Well," Mick said, "that's the way America is, you know. You pay for what you get."

11 Stones Go Country

So there I was on a blistering Texas afternoon, cruising in an overheated, wheezing taxicab that was struggling—at no small expense, mind you—to transport me to Dallas' luxurious Fairmont Hotel from Dallas' perhaps less luxurious Sheraton-Dallas.

Why? Well, the posh Fairmont seemed to be full to overflowing with Rolling Stones and Stones' entourage. Non-entourage personnel were encouraged to commute from the less posh Sheraton. The Fairmont's front desk majordomo informed me imperially that I was on a wild goose chase: "Ain't no rock and rollers here, let alone any Rolling Stones"—not in this bastion of red velvet and Sistine Chapel-esque murals and pristine marble columns. I sighed and went off to wander around the hotel for a bit and to talk to bellboys and maids and so on. In a few minutes, they had provided me with the Stones' rooming list, so I headed for the house phones and started calling. Mick Jagger, registered as "Sam Spade," was not answering in Suite 1900. Keith Richards, registered as "Dr. M. Bush," did not answer in 1200. (Odd that Mick and Keith were seven floors apart. That was not usual.) Charlie Watts, listed as "B. Edwards," did not answer in 2308. Bill Wyman, registered as "W. Stephens," was not answering in 1800. Ron Wood, known to the Fairmont as "R. Biggs," was not picking up in 2100. My next call was answered. It was Tour Commander Peter Rudge, registered as "Big Quid" in Suite 2000. But, as he quickly told me in his clipped tones, he "should be in 2001. What are you doing here anyway, Flippo? No one invited you. We don't need skeptical, cynical writers hanging about. By the by, have you a ticket for the show tomorrow? No? Wal, I'll see what I can do. We must have a drink. Meet me in the lobby." Click.

Ah, what fun. The Rolling Stones were on the road again! I had held out for several weeks, vowing "Never again." But the siren song was too seductive, the call of the road too persistent to resist.

This seemed a tour off-center somehow, a bit out-of-kilter. It had been announced suddenly and only twelve tour dates were definite by the first date, June 10 at the Civic Center in Lakeland, Florida. And even that concert was star-crossed. A longtime, nameless Stones' "friend" was busted by Lakeland police in the Stones' dressing room. He had a large quantity of cocaine in his possession. The Stones' lawyers put in a long night of arguing and pleading and string-pulling and who knows what else to keep the heat off the Stones themselves. The "friend" was escorted to the airport and effectively deported forever from Florida. There was no publicity about the matter. But it set a certain tone for the tour.

As usual, the press greeted this as the "final, final Stones tour" and the band's initial performances did nothing to argue otherwise. Mick and Keith had clearly not been getting on since Keith's heroin bust in Toronto and it was evident in the shows. Oddly, though, the Stones had just released their best album in years. *Some Girls*, a raunchy, biting look inside the shallowness of rock superstardom, actually dethroned the BeeGees' *Saturday Night Fever* from the top of the record charts. Even so, phantoms attended the album. Atlantic Records had reportedly heavily pressured the Stones to tone down the lyrics of the title song, which was fairly explicit about what Mick thought were the sexual tastes of the girls of the world. The Rev. Jesse Jackson was breathing hard down Atlantic's neck to censor the title song because of its suggestion of the sexual tastes of black women. Also because of the cover of the record album, which was a takeoff on trashy wig ads (with famous faces thrown in). A couple of those famous faces threatened litigation and the album cover was subsequently changed. The first shows of the tour were awful. It seemed as if the Stones On the Road were becoming a bad one-note samba. As if to fend off the demons, the Stones played an unscheduled date on June 14 at the 3,265-seat Capitol Theater in Passaic, New Jersey, in which they rose to the occasion and performed heroically. Three days later, I went to their dismal, hollow, empty charade of a show before about eighteen million Stones fanatics in Philadelphia's JFK Stadium. (Which, I feel obliged to point out, is and always has been a football stadium, despite Philip Norman's assertion in *Symphony for the Devil: The Rolling Stones Story* that backstage access to the stadium is via a "tunnel by which, ordinarily, baseball teams come out to play." What was, ordinarily, the last baseball team to come out to play in JFK Stadium, eh, Philip? Ordinarily, no baseball team came out to play by that tunnel. Ever.)

The next day, I called Mick up. "I have the flu," he gasped. "I feel terrible. I'll be all right tomorrow."

I asked him why they had finished the JFK show with "Satisfaction," which he had once vowed to never do again.

"Well," he rasped, "we did 'Satisfaction' at Knebworth [on August

21, 1976, as the lead song], so we can do it. It seemed to be nice to throw it in. Yesterday was the first big gig and, yeah, you're right, the new songs slowed the crowd a bit. But if you just play old numbers, you don't get anywhere. You can't stand still. 'Respectable' and 'Whip' are going over okay. You can't expect us to be a dinosaur and just play old numbers. We won't compromise. You gotta play new ones. Like when Pete Townshend said they [the Who] hadn't done a new song in eight years. We don't want to get to that. Yeah, obviously, the tour was put together quickly. We will add smaller dates to get out of the big halls. Yes, Atlantic did try to get us to drop [the song] 'Some Girls,' but I refused. I've always been opposed to censorship, especially by conglomerates. I've always said, 'If you can't take a joke, it's too fucking bad.' "

What I wondered was whether or not these old geezers were still capable of generating the old road show madness, the wet panty hysteria of their glory days in this era of disco blandness? Were the Stones, once a major social force, still important to loyalists who thought rock's message went beyond a disco bass beat? Did the sixties actually happen? These were just idle thoughts that seemed appropriate to affluent Dallas, which pulled up the drawbridge when it saw social change racing down the LBJ Freeway into the very heart of Big D. Were the Stones still a sort of barometer of what was happening on America's cutting edge?

I got a sort of answer from a Channel 4 news report in my Sheraton cell. Said Channel 4 about tomorrow's Stones show at Will Rogers Auditorium in nearby Fort Worth: The National Guard had been called out after chaos reigned when the 2,300 tickets (for a show by the "London Green-Shoed Cowboys") went on sale and sold out in thirty-two minutes and unhappy people suddenly plunged through plate-glass windows and generally were unhappy.

(A young woman who was convinced that I was well-connected with the Stones asked me for tickets to the show. "None available," I said. "You don't understand," she said, "I am a model and I am very good-looking and I will do anything to get those tickets. Anything." I began to understand. No soap, though. These were tough tickets.)

I sat in the Fairmont lobby, roughly the size of two football fields, draped in red velvet and lit by crystal chandeliers and listened to the good ole boys talk. "Why, hell yes, it was murder," one good ole boy said to another, "I mean, when you walk in and the body's still warm and the coffee's still perkin' and the chicken's still fryin' . . ." The good ole boys started noticing a mountain of red-lip-adorned luggage piling up in the lobby: invasion of the Rolling Stones. Charlie Watts drew double takes when he sashayed in, sporting a white linen suit and a white fedora. He and his wife Shirley and their daughter Seraphina came over to say hello.

(Meanwhile, Rudge and Mick sneaked out to go see Texas soul legend Bobby "Blue" Bland sing at the Longhorn Ballroom, the classic country joint that western swing king Bob Wills built over at the corner of Corinth and Industrial.)

The Watts family sat down with me. Shirley tried a screwdriver for the first time. Seraphina was reading a paperback of *Jaws 2*. "I was against it," said Shirley, "but you have to let them do these things."

I mentioned to Charlie one of the day's news clips about the Stones being in Dallas and what a big deal it was. "You think so?" he asked. "You really think we're that big?"

"Sure, Charlie," I said. "This is bigger than a presidential tour."

"Really?"

"Hell yes. You can't give away tickets to a Jimmy Carter appearance and right now the scalpers are getting $300 for your tickets."

Watts was pleased.

July 18, 1978

Finally moved into the Fairmont, no thanks to the Stones. Went out for a swim in the morning and had a wonderful time talking to Seraphina Watts in the pool. Her dad Charlie, the best drummer in rock and roll history, came up to say hello. We swapped shop talk for a while and got on the subject of "progressive rock."

"I don't think it's possible," Charlie said. "Rock swings with a heavy backbeat and it's done that for twenty-five years. It's supposed to be fun and that's why I like it. It's dance music. But it hasn't really progressed musically. Progression was Miles Davis playing modals. You can't do that in rock. Progression was Coltrane, but you can't do that in rock. McLaughlin is close, but he can't really stretch out. If he tries, it really isn't rock. Chicago didn't influence the orchestra sound the way the Ellington band did, now did they? None of this New Wave is new. Elvis Costello is no different than anything else. No one's really done anything new in rock, now have they?"

I said, "I don't know of a case at hand."

Charlie nodded triumphantly. "Heavy backbeat, that's what it is. That's what the Beatles did and that's what we did." We soaked in the sun—I told Charlie this was Dallas' seventeenth day in a row of 105 degrees-plus temperatures, which amazed him—and we lazily shot the shit for a while. At one point, Charlie asked me, "How can you write about rock and roll? It's silly. It's supposed to be fun. How can you do that?"

"Well," I said, "the only alternatives are politics or gossip."

Charlie nodded sagely. "I see what you mean."

Peter Rudge was looking for a coronary by trying—extremely aggressively—to break the Rolling Stones on American country radio as a country and western group with their single of "Far Away Eyes," in which Mick sounded about as country as you do. He even persuaded Mick to go out to a local Western wear store for a TV interview. The redneck audiences were tolerant: They, like reeds, will bend but they will not break.

As it happened, Peter and I were the last two Stones-others to leave the Fairmont for Fort Worth, so he asked me to share a cab. We dashed out into the Fairmont's courtyard and Peter, in his best Oxford accent, asked a redneck cabbie, "See here, would you like to drive us to Fort Worth?" I (as a Fort Worth native) cringed, but the cabbie was delighted. "I'd love to drive you, buddy," he said, almost cackling with glee.

He lived to rue the moment. There is no equal to Rudge as a talker. He started in on me. "Your last story in *Rolling Stone* was all fucked up. This tour was well planned, by Mick and me in Barbados. Let me tell you about the details." Blah, blah, blah.

When we got to Will Rogers Coliseum, Rudge borrowed $10 from me to pay the cab fare. Good-bye, $10.

A Fort Worth cop stopped Rudge and me at the backstage door and asked, in what I have to admit was an aggressive, redneck manner, "Do yew thank that accent's gonna get yew in, boy?" Rudge did not miss a beat. "No, officer," he said smoothly, "but this backstage pass outranks your badge." Touché.

Rudge went off to harangue the backstage crew to paint the stage lip and bring up the monitors and everything else he could possibly think of. Bill Carter grabbed me by the arm. "Godamn it, Flippo," he growled, "put that damn beer down and come here and do some reporting!" He took me to the front gate, where a little girl stood, demurely, alone. "This is Rita," Carter said, almost tenderly, as he gave her a backstage pass and a ticket. He ignored several almond-eyed honeys in scanty satin pant outfits that would scandalize Vanessa Williams. Rita, it developed, was almost totally blind and had been following the Stones tour by bus. She had saved up her money for three years just for this Stones tour and, naturally, had been robbed of $200 in the Philly bus station and almost raped. She was down to $12. Carter took her backstage to meet the Stones. Bill Wyman's wife Astrid gave her $100.

She sat, beaming, in the Stones' hospitality suite, which looked like every fern bar hospitality suite on the tour, since that's what it was: same blue Oriental Kirstan carpet, overstuffed tan modular couches, oak coffee tables, and semicomatose rock and rollers scattered here and there, in various stages of repose.

The Fort Worth show was good, the Stones beginning to gain musical cohesiveness and momentum. I spent part of the show with tour head of security Jim Callaghan at the backstage door, witnessing the elaborate, ridiculous, and often touching methods fans will use to try to get backstage. "There's no scam I haven't seen at least once," Callaghan said wryly. Meticulously done counterfeit backstage passes were common. "Throw him out," Callaghan ordered a Fort Worth cop. There was an endless series of doe-eyed girls who claimed their boyfriends were Stones roadies or sound engineers. "Throw 'em out," Callaghan directed. A phony doctor. "Out!" Attempted deliveries of unordered flowers, food, guitars, sound equipment, clothes, and even drugs. "Out!" Suspiciously healthy-looking "terminally ill" people whose last wish was to meet the Stones. "Out!" A phony cop. "Out! And lock him up!" A phony cleanup crew. "Out!" Phony security guards. "Out! Out! Out!" It restored my faith in good old American ingenuity. Phony heads of local musicians' unions, phony governor's sons and daughters, phony fire department inspectors, phony limo drivers, phony network TV representatives, phony health department inspectors. And, of course, the old blatant, straight-ahead sex approach. What fun.

What was even more fun was the getaway after the show. Five siren-screaming, red-light-flashing police motorcycle escorts headed up a procession of five black Cadillac limos and one white one (guess who rode in the white one), as we raced the thirty or so miles back to the sanctuary of Dallas' Fairmont. The procession reminded me of Elvis Presley's funeral.

Back at the hotel, there was an all-night birthday party in the Far East Room for Stones pianist Ian Stewart. Jim Callaghan was throwing out some ingenious girls who were wearing phony Fairmont maids' uniforms. "Cocksucker Blues" was blasting out of the speakers. "Remember this?" Keith yelled, as he took his knife to crack a half-gallon bottle of Rebel Yell sour mash. Mick stuck his head in for a minute, looking gaunt and drained, and left. I noticed that he had started wearing glasses. Ron Wood led the singing of "Happy Birthday" and the revelry continued. Someone had rounded up a bunch of incredibly glossy, high-tech, sex-drenched, friendly Dallas female Stones fans. "We are the encore," one of them told me. She said she was there because "The Stones are the only ones that still make me quiver and shake." Well.

Off to Houston later in the day. The Stones had banned writers from traveling on their chartered Convair 580 turbo-prop and it was overcrowded anyway, so Stones attorney Bill Carter and tour accountant Bill Zysblat and I chartered a light plane for the trip, since we were returning to the Fairmont after the show. "Oh," Peter Rudge said to me, rather sarcastically, out at Cooper Aviation, as he waited to board the Convair and my little plane came taxiing up, "so you're traveling by private plane now, eh? You and the lawyer and the accountant, eh? How convenient. You got your limo lined up in Houston? You got any open seats on the plane?"

On the quick flight down, Zysblat told me that, after all expenses were paid, the Stones would make less than $1,000, total, from the Fort Worth show. Such small dates were clearly a luxury for the Stones. For the tour, though, Zysblat said that for every $1 that came through the gate, the Stones tour was generating $3 for the GNP. "I did a workup," he said. "If this tour grosses $10 million, it will generate $30 million to the GNP. That's bigger than a lot of corporations."

Backstage at Sam Houston Coliseum in Houston, we could hear the distant report of large firecrackers detonating outside, as the Stones army worked itself into a frenzy. Amid the familiar ferns and furniture, Charlie Watts did stretching exercises, Mick was silent on one of the couches. Bill Wyman was flexing his left hand (he had fallen off the stage July 10 in St. Paul and was still recovering from that). "I'm okay now," he said, "just a little swelling in the hand." Ron Wood was nowhere to be seen. Vitamin B_{12} ampoules from the tour doctor's earlier visit littered the floor. Whether their effect is actually physical or psychological, Vitamin B_{12} shots remain a rock tour necessity. Keith was over in a corner, slicing the top off a fifth of Jack Daniel's with his ever-present blade. He offered me a swig and chided, "You can't handle your Jack Daniel's like you used to. I noticed you faded out and left Stu's party at 5:00 this morning." I could only laugh. Keith, of course, had closed down the party.

Over in another corner, Peter Rudge was berating photographer Peter Beard for not sending him pictures fast enough. Or something.

Peter Tosh, the opening act (who was then signed to Rolling Stones Records), was onstage. Mick stirred and said, "Wal, I'm going onstage. I'll be back in five minutes." He went out for a duet with Tosh on "Don't Look Back."

No one paid much attention. Prince Rupert Lowenstein, the Stones' silver-haired, portly British financial adviser, was talking with some prominent Houston socialites and passing around a matted Stones group photograph for the band to autograph for him. "Might as well use all available resources, eh," he said, winking.

"So how are things with this crew, Prince Rupert?" I asked.

He positively beamed. "The Rolling Stones ship of state is on a very even keel. Tip-top. Yes, indeed. I've been popping in on a few shows."

"Well," I said, "will there be a Rolling Stones in 1981 or even 1984?"

"Oh yes," he said, "indeed onto 1987 and 1991 and on and on."

The Houston show was disappointing. Mick was forgetting the words to some songs and Keith was laying out frequently, letting Wood pick up the guitar load. Nothing worked right. And then, irony of ironies, during "Shattered," a young man fell out of the balcony and landed on his head, injuring himself badly. Another young man lay convulsing on the filthy red tile floor backstage, victim of who knew what. Firecrackers still resounded from out on the streets where the non-ticket-holders were raising hell. It was time to get out of Houston. One Houston newspaper claimed that Charlie and Shirley Watts got into an argument as the Stones were boarding the Convair and that Mick kicked them both off the plane and that they had then taken a limo all the way from Houston back to Dallas.

Back at the Fairmont, I stopped in at Keith's suite at 2:45 in the morning. He was fast asleep, dead tired, one arm held grotesquely up in the air. A lot of hard-eyed people I didn't know were drinking his liquor and milling around and waiting for something to happen. Very edgy.

Mick was watching videotapes in Jane Rose's room and taking notes on a legal pad. On the screen, a man was asking people standing on line to view Elvis Presley lying in state at Graceland if they were going to scream when Mick Jagger came onstage. The people were not amused, but Mick was. "I'm just doing my editing notes," he told me. "I'll meet you in Woody's room."

Ron Wood was on the phone to room service in Suite 2100 and waved me in. "And six tonics and two Cokes and four glasses and some milk if you have any," he finished up his order. "Milk?" I asked. "Isn't that out of character?"

He laughed and pointed at a glamorous, slinky, sequined bimbo arranged sensuously on his couch. "It's for the chick," he said. "How about some brandy?" He cracked a bottle—one of many handy—and slipped a Jimmy Reed tape into his cassette player and sat me down and poured me a drink, his dark eyes twinkling. The "chick" gave me a languid smile. Ron Wood is undoubtedly the most charming, most gregarious, most cocker-spanielish rock and roller ever. No one does not like him (although Rod Stewart will never forgive Mick Jagger for stealing Wood from his band). Already on this tour, Woody had offered me his "chick," to take along and do with as I wanted. The chick was agreeable. He was puzzled when I turned down his offer. He was only trying to be friendly and to mainly share the spoils of rock and roll. The very soul of generosity.

He lifted his glass in a toast. "So, Woody," I said, "compared to the '75 tour, you are a Rolling Stone now."

He beamed. "Oh yeah, I know exactly what you mean. Looking back on '75, I had an awful big gap to fill and no one gave me any clues, you know." We talked a while about how he had adjusted to becoming a Stone and the Stones' lead guitarist. Keyboard player Ian McLagen, a mate of Wood's from the Faces (who had been added to the Stones tour), came in for a drink. In the background, Jimmy Reed was singing "I'm Going to New York."

Mick walked in and poured himself a brandy. " 'Cocksucker Blues,' " he said. "Did you see the sign for that tonight in the audience?" He laughed.

Woody turned up Jimmy Reed. "Mick," he said, "you remember that stack of Jimmy Reed records that Pete Townshend bought you for your birthday? If there was any one person more influential than Muddy [Waters], it's Jimmy Reed."

Mick sat down and motioned for me to turn on my tape recorder: interview time. He waited for a question.

"Is rock progressing at all or is it static?" I finally ventured.

"I can only answer that question as I experience it," Woody began.

Mick cut him off with a long, involved history of how jazz developed into rhythm and blues and how it took a long time for white people to learn how to play the "colored people's music" and that that was where rock and roll came from. "But," he said, "the Stones are not creating anything new, personally, that I can see. But we don't know for sure. That's the adventure."

We talked for a couple of hours about the state of rock and roll, a typical *Rolling Stone* magazine interview, and drank a lot of brandy and reached no great conclusions. Mick said he knew more about the decline of the West than Solzhenitsyn did, that he believed in the Lord, that he actually thought he could be a C&W singer, that rock and roll critics were beneath contempt, that he was a dedicated "show-business person," that he thought the Stones were actually a punk band, and that pushy women bothered him and he wanted a traditional family. It was obvious that there were plenty of burrs under his saddle.

Mick started singing "Do You Think I Really Care?"—an unreleased Stones song cut in their last Paris sessions. McLagen went out and got an electric piano, Woody got his acoustic guitar, Mick found a harmonica, and all we lacked was a drummer.

Mick enlisted me. "Now, this song is called 'High and Lonesome,' " he instructed me, as we sloshed more glasses full of brandy. "You take this telephone book and slap it with your hand, like this. You'll be percussion. This is a blues." He started singing: "High and lonesome, that's what I am today/High and lonesome, that's what I am today/I'm gonna break up with ya baby/It's the very last thing I say."

I found that drumming for the Rolling Stones was not as easy as I thought. We ran through three takes of "High and Lonesome" before

Mick was content enough with my percussion to move on to Jimmy Reed's "Little Rain Falling." Then Mick stopped Chuck Berry's "Back in the U.S.A." to give me another drum lesson. "You got to get the backbeat," he said. We moved on to "Blue Moon of Kentucky" and "Mystery Train," Mick eerily aping Elvis's versions of both.

(I have to tell you now that I taped all of this, with Mick's approval. Shortly after I got back to New York, my apartment was burglarized. Jewelry, cameras, tape recorders, stereos were taken. The only tapes out of the several hundred that I have that were stolen were my tapes of this eight-hour session with Mick. They have never surfaced. I wonder if the burglar knew what he was getting. The contents of the tapes were price-less. If you ever run across them, let me know. By the by, Mick's personal bodyguard on this tour, James Harrington, was later arrested for allegedly burgling Mick. I'm sure there is no connection, although Harrington asked me for my address, which I foolishly gave him.)

We did Buddy Holly's "Maybe Baby" pretty well and Jimmy Reed's "Oh Baby, You Don't Have to Go" and "Big Boss Man." Mick was still not entirely happy with my drumming, but he didn't have much choice, did he?

We took a break and Mick borrowed a cigarette from me. "You know," he said in that solemn but quavery tone peculiar to drunken phi-losophy delivered in the middle of the night, "Solzhenitsyn's right in a lot of ways. About America. When we were in France, we were cut off from the media and no one wrote about us and that's civilized and calm. Solzhenitsyn said everyone in the U.S. is subject to this terrible TV and radio. I agree. When we toured here three years ago, it was all flim-flam, right? This time, I'll fuckin' do anything. I'll crawl on people, I'll play out of tune and as loud as possible, I'll tear me T-shirt up, I'll throw the microphone down. Punk, punk, punk."

He jumped into a C&W number he had been working on, called "Got No Spare Parts, Got No Oil to Change": "If I want something bad enough, I always find a way to get through/I tell you lonely hearts ain't made to break/I got no spare parts, I got no oil to change."

Woody closed the curtains against dawn's harsh light and fetched another bottle of brandy. Mick improvised lyrics for Jimmy Reed's "Bright Lights, Big City": "We got a tape machine and liquor/We got no womens/We don't need no womens/Go fuck my wife and don't come back."

We all sat and drank quietly for a while. Mick brooded. Then he launched into "Cocksucker Blues," the notorious Stones underground leg-end (which the band submitted to Decca in 1970 to fulfill a contractual agreement. The song was of course never released, although bootleg copies of it do circulate). Mick was practically howling: "Wait'll I get my cock sucked/Wait'll I get my ass fucked/Well, I don't have much money/But I know where to put it every time."

We were staggering by that point. "This's 'Do You Think I Really Care,' " Mick said and sang, "Do you think I could ever care about a girl whose name ain't there/I saw her on the subway/I saw her on the D train/I saw her eatin' pizza on 42nd and Broadway/I saw her on the E train/I saw her on the highway/Oh, Ronnie, I want a Yellow Cab to help me get out of this rain."

It was noon and Mick went to sleep. His bodyguard, Harrington, came to help us carry him to bed. "Oh, this happens all the time," he said.

While I slept, a viper crawled into the nest. Someone made a special point of bringing to Dallas and placing into Rudge's hands an advance copy of the next issue of *Rolling Stone* magazine. In which issue reviewer Dave Marsh savaged the Stones' performance at JFK Stadium and generally kicked them all around the block, for being the Stones. The *Some Girls* album fared no better in *Rolling Stone*. I didn't realize how tender were the Stones' egos.

Thursday night I went with Keith and his entourage out to Showco in Dallas to watch rough film footage shot of the Fort Worth show. Keith passed me his half-gallon bottle of Rebel Yell and apologized for having gone to sleep the night before. "I really conked out." "That's okay," I said, "Mick filled in for you and he kept me up drumming all night."

"Yeah, he told me," Keith said.

"But I think I failed the audition for the band," I said.

Keith laughed and slapped me on the back. "That's okay. Everybody does!"

I ran into him a few hours later, when we had an interview scheduled. "Well, Flet Chippo, you're off," he said. "I don't understand," I said. "You're off the tour. Good-bye. That's it," he said. "Bullshit," I said.

I was mystified, but not for long. Rudge came calling, eager to blame me for *Rolling Stone's* shortcomings and to tell me how hurt and angry everyone in the band and, indeed, the entire Stones organization was by this flagrant betrayal of trust. Apparently, the band had had a meeting and was divided about whether or not to kick me off the tour immediately. The entire level of paranoia had been so great on tour that I was not really surprised, but I was angry and decided to see just how long I could ride this out.

While the Stones played Tucson, I flew ahead to Los Angeles and settled into the Westwood Marquis, a nice little hideaway in a residential area hard by the UCLA campus. All of the L.A. rock community was abuzz about the Stones' Anaheim Stadium show, set for July 23.

The band got into the Marquis in the middle of the night to learn that a woman named Marsha Hunt had gotten an injunction against the Stones and might well succeed in freezing all proceeds from the Anaheim concert. Why? She had a child that she said Mick had fathered and she wanted her child support raised from $17 a week to $2,000 a week. Talk about "Some Girls." Model Jerry Hall was traveling with Mick and his wife Bianca was reportedly headed for L.A. Late in the night, police arrived at the Marquis to remove a hysterical woman from the Stones' floor

I ran into Jerry Hall and she told me that Mick had not slept in two days. FBI agents arrived at the Marquis because of some serious death threats the Stones had been receiving. The agents circulated mug shots of a suspect to hotel employees. The hysterical woman reappeared at the hotel. One of Keith's teeth had fallen out and he needed an immediate replacement. Things were tough all around.

Wasserman called to tell me that "Mick and Keith are so pissed off by the reviews that they won't talk. I have never seen Mick so livid. I tried to explain it to Mick, but they think it's a grand plot on *Rolling Stone's* part. The theory of the carrot and the stick. You have no ticket or pass for the show. That was a collective decision."

I had a long, strange meeting with Rudge in the hotel bar, during the course of which I was accused of spearheading a *Rolling Stone* vendetta against the Rolling Stones. I picked up the check for our drinks.

I decided to go ahead and go to the Anaheim show, only because the band had forbidden me to. It was not a terribly good show. Back at the hotel, I had drinks with Wasserman (guess who picked up the check) and he said Mick had decided to kick me off the tour. "He won't listen to me. You can try to talk to him."

I went to a house phone and called Mick. He was spitting mad. "I'm not pissed at you," he shouted, "I'm fucking pissed off at *Rolling Stone*. I got real mad at this vicious shit. Jann Wenner writes or directs all this shit. I've given all this great access. This is the end. No more interviews. I don't mind criticism—real criticism—but I don't expect the kind of bitchiness in these two reviews. I can smell it. It stinks. *Rolling Stone* will always set you up and then knock you down. That cunt Jann Wenner. I've known *Rolling Stone* a long time. I don't trust many people, you know, and I trusted *Rolling Stone* and they let me down. I like you and I'm sorry it was you that was here and not them. I'm sorry it's you that has to suffer for it. Good-bye."

So that was that. Without telling me, Dave Marsh and Paul Nelson (who had written the *Some Girls* review) sent a telegram to Mick, which read as follows:

DEAR MICK: DIDN'T MEAN TO SPOIL YOUR BIRTHDAY.
PLEASE ACCEPT OUR SINCEREST APOLOGIES. WE WERE ONLY
TRYING TO FOLLOW YOUR LONG-STANDING INSTRUCTIONS NOT
TO TAKE YOU SERIOUSLY. JANN WENNER ASSURES US THAT IT
CANNOT HAPPEN AGAIN. DAVE MARSH, PAUL NELSON.

Jann later wrote a peculiar sort of rebuttal of his own writers' views on the Stones.

And, later, when Paul Gambaccini interviewed Mick on his show on BBC Radio 1, the subject came up:

BBC: That brings us to another thing: *Rolling Stone* magazine.

Mick: This is very popular here, though. Wasn't it a popular story here?

BBC: Yes, a big article in one of the music papers about how after some adverse reviews in *Rolling Stone* some facilities were denied.

Mick: Not toilets!

BBC: And they were thrown off the tour to the extent that Jann Wenner, the editor, had to write a piece himself about the Stones and Bob Dylan. What was the story from your point of view?

Mick: Well, I just think it was an example of the manipulation of the media.

BBC: From your point of view.

Mick: Yes, from our point of view. It is also an example of just fun. You know, there is a certain fun in just smashing up hotel rooms and, you know what I mean, panty parties. We won't mention the more violent pursuits of rock bands on the road. It was a joke because we were at the end of the tour. We just turned around and said, "This is the end of the tour and not the beginning. This coverage, this is it—we have had enough of your criticism. Get off the tour." And they all took it seriously! We were only just acting out a fantasy. It wasn't power. Say the guy said, "Well, I am not going, Mick." But he actually believed we wanted him off the tour to the extent that the editor had to write—we didn't ask him to write— rebuttal speeches. We just kicked him off the tour because we were bored with them. They were around all the time, you know, in the bathroom every time we went there.

BBC: Is it tempting at times to pull stunts like that? Often you are in a position now, in terms of other people's lives, say in terms of the life of Chet Flippo, who was the reporter.

Mick: Chet Flippo—it wasn't anything in Chet Flippo's life. Anyway, it is only a one-day thing. It was not that we kicked Chet Flippo off the tour and put him out of a job for six weeks. We put him out of a job for one day. And I told Chet Flippo that it was hurting more because he was my friend, that it had to be him rather than some of the other people that work there. Radio is a different medium than touring or being covered. It is still to me like a fireside chat. It is a different medium, especially in this country and especially on the BBC. But that whole thing in America with radio and *Rolling Stone.* It's crazy.

BBC: It makes everything count.

Mick: Count, yes. They made rock and roll count and I never imagined that it would count. It would only count as person to person. It would never count as something to be discussed. I never thought . . . believed that anyone would discuss rock and roll as they do now. And here we are, discussing it!

BBC: Do you feel that you can cut gossips who are after you out of your life?

Mick: You cannot really ever cut it out. But with *Rolling Stone* I was saying, "Yes, I can cut it out of my life. This is how you deal with it." That wasn't the gossip part of it, but that was one way to say it. Actually, you have to accept it as certain and deal with it. People sometimes say to me, "Mick, all this gossip that people talk about you, you don't like it but why don't you use it, manipulate it, have fun with it." Accept it's got to be, which is an attitude. I guess that's better than being antagonistic. You gotta put up with it. A lot of the reason I don't like living in England is that there is too much of that part in England.

12 Oshawa

April 21, 1979

They say that rock and roll never forgets, but all was sweetness and light when I went up to Canada to witness the Rolling Stones fulfill Keith's "sentence" for his conviction for drug possession by performing for the blind. Had it been any other band, all of the combined circumstances would have amazed me, but for the Stones this was normal. The Toronto airport was jammed with young backpacking Stones fans headed for Oshawa, a General Motors town of about 100,000, some thirty-two miles east of Toronto, where Keith's "sentence" was to be executed on Sunday, April 22. At the airport's phone banks, once I'd cleared customs, I could hear enterprising young Stones fans calling all the major hotels in Toronto and shrewdly asking for some of the lesser-known Stones employees, who might actually be registered under their own names. I checked into the Four Seasons Hotel and found only a dozen or so Stones fans lounging outside.

As usual, the Toronto newspapers trumpeted the Stones' arrival on their front pages. You'd think nothing else ever happened in Canada. I called up Richard van Abbe and he just groaned. "This is the trendiest affair to hit Canada in years. I wish I were somewhere else. I hear ticket prices are as high as $700 for a pair."

The whole affair, as usual, was a last-minute, patched-together, slightly hysterical Stones Major Event. And since it would be the only Stones concert anywhere in the world this year, an added note of hysteria nudged along the craziness. Stones crazies just had to go to this show: It might be the final, final, absolutely final one forever.

Apart from the fan and press uproar, there was a new furor over Judge Lloyd Graburn, who, just six months earlier, had had the power to sentence Keith Richards to life in prison for his drug convictions and had instead sentenced him to play a benefit concert for the blind, which had made even Keith Richards laugh. Judge Graburn had maintained a stoic silence since then, but an incredible front-page story in the Toronto *Star*

suggested that he had not had the slightest idea of just who in the world
the Rolling Stones or Keith Richards were when he passed sentence. And
that, just before passing sentence, he had called the CNIB (Canadian
Institute for the Blind) and asked them if they would mind if he sentenced a "young musician" to play a benefit there. "No problem," they
said. When they heard who it was later, there was consternation at the
CNIB.

(Anyone who bothered to read the court transcript, of course, would
note that Judge Graburn knew exactly who the Rolling Stones and Keith
Richards were. What was going on here with the Toronto *Star* and Judge
Graburn?)

After the crown appealed Judge Graburn's sentence, it appeared the
concert might never happen—to the CNIB's great relief. But Judge
Graburn on April 6 had turned down the crown's claim that Keith had
turned Canada's courts into "a laughingstock." Judge Graburn upheld his
own sentence, with no questions asked. On with the show. Apparently, no
Toronto venues were available and so Oshawa's tiny (4,500-seat) Civic
Auditorium was a strange compromise reached when Jagger met with the
CNIB and a Toronto promoter. What others had forgotten and what
Jagger reminded them of was that Judge Graburn's sentence was for Keith
to perform for the blind, not necessarily to raise a lot of money for them.

The whole massive Stones tour apparatus came to town: tractor
trailer trucks full of sound equipment up from Dallas, technicians, roadies,
bodyguards, accountants, lawyers (Keith was due in court again on April
23). Even though the Oshawa show was ostensibly being put on by the
New Barbarians—a pickup group of Keith, Ron Wood, Ian McLagen,
bassist Stanley Clarke, Meters drummer Ziggy Modeliste, and longtime
Stones ally Bobby Keys on sax—all the Stones were summoned by Mick
for this occasion. The whole thing was obviously going to cost a hell of a
lot.

That night I went out to Studio Centre, on West Lakeshore outside
Toronto, for the rehearsal. Perhaps two dozen employees and friends
watched in a gymnasium-sized space as all the Stones (with Ian Stewart
and Ian McLagen added on keyboards) worked through an all-night rehearsal.

Back to the sweetness and light: During the first break, I felt someone grab me from behind. It was Mick, who shook my hand and then
wheeled me around to face Keith. "This is Mr. Flippo, Keith," Mick said
dryly. "He wrote—" "—our obituary!" Keith laughed as he finished
Mick's sentence. Keith shook my hand. "Come and get a beer." The story
I had done on the '78 tour had been frank and honest, maybe tough. At
least we understood each other. We drank together. Keith was practically

ecstatic—for him—with enthusiasm about doing the shows later in the day. "It'll be a good show, I promise," Keith said. Keith, the irrepressible rock and roll optimist. Mick, the realist, the cynical side of the Glimmer Twins, was already bitching. "Some people already objected to us printing up programs in braille because it was supposedly patronizing the blind," he told me. "That's like illiterate people complaining about programs with printing on them because they can't read them."

They went back up onstage and started "Shattered." John Belushi, who had come in to emcee the shows, did a convincing act of hawking Blues Brothers T-shirts for $5 each to the miniscule crowd. I said hello and bought him a free beer. He wanted to know why *Rolling Stone* magazine was so down on the Blues Brothers. I told him why. He said, "Oh, I see. Now I know who's responsible and why." He was relieved.

He pointed toward the Stones onstage and said, "Man, I'm not just here on an ego trip or because I'm a groupie. I love these guys. They believe in what they're doing. And I want to be with 'em because of that. I love them because they're a lousy rock and roll band. Who the hell wants to listen to ELP [Emerson, Lake, and Palmer]?"

Rehearsal wound down at about 5:00 in the morning. "Actually," Mick said, "these shows may be better than the first show of a tour because we're just loose. Keith said, 'We'll just go ahead and do *Some Girls* and see how it works.' "

Back at the Four Seasons Hotel, the Toronto Sunday *Star* already proclaimed from the lobby newsstand in bold letters: STONES CONCERT MAY LOSE MONEY.

There was a mob scene outside the low gray Civic Auditorium that afternoon. Scalpers were still asking up to $325 a pair of tickets. Terrified neighbors had barricaded their driveways and front yards with cars and wheelbarrows and lawn mowers and anything else they could find to fend off the huns. The backpacking hordes were camped out everywhere. Some of the "blindies" (as Mick called them) who supposedly held 1,300 of the 4,500 seats available for each of the two performances told me, as they came in, that they hadn't the faintest idea of who the New Barbarians or even the Rolling Stones were(!), but that it was nice to go to a free concert. Culture, you know.

Belushi came out onstage at about 4:45 P.M. and screamed, "I'm a sleazy actor on a late-night TV show, but I'm going to present some real musicians!"

It was quite a day musically. Two New Barbarians sets, two full-blown Rolling Stones concerts with all the stops pulled out. (For Stones' historians, I think this was the first and only time that Mick and Keith did "Prodigal Son" together onstage, which was a very moving moment.)

After the show, I suddenly remembered how easy it is to become accustomed to having a police escort guide your limo through the rabble back to your four-star hotel, where guards escort you up from the garage on the freight elevator—to avoid the crush of fans—to your suite, where the champagne has been properly chilled and the oysters and shrimp wait patiently on their beds of cracked ice and the roast beef is groaning in its own ripe juices. Because that's exactly what happened.

This calls for a brief but essential digression on two rock and roll subjects: the public and sex. The former is supposed to be all that a rock and roll band cares about and the latter is all that the former thinks the rock and roll band cares about. The truth is that, on any rock tour, the public does not really exist for the performers. The audience is an abstract, picked up and packed into the tractor-trailer trucks, along with the lights and amps and backstage ferns, and unpacked in the next hall. There is always another audience. Just ask the Who, who were amazingly callous about the eleven Who fans who died at their Cincinnati show, while the band dallied backstage and ignored the welfare of their fans. Watch the movie *Gimme Shelter*, in which Mick Jagger indifferently looks at film footage that shows a member of his audience at Altamont being savagely stabbed to death, stabbed by Hell's Angels that he had approved as security guards for the concert. The audience exists only as box office receipts, only as dollars passing through the gates. It does not bother me so much that no rock and roll performer I have ever known or interviewed had even the slightest idea of who his or her audience actually was, as it bothers me that none of them really cared a damn to find out. Well, so much for that spleen-venting. Now, on to sex. Supposed to be the whole reason for rock and roll, right? Maybe not. After years of studying and traveling with the Rolling Stones, I finally concluded that they didn't know anything about either the public or sex. That's right. They didn't have time for either. Just being a Rolling Stone was a twenty-four hour a day gig and it was hard, at that. What actually do you do, after being a Rolling Stone all day? You got up and did it all night, that's what. Precious little time left for anything else. The whole sex thing was a touchy subject on Stones tours, just as it was on every major rock tour, for several reasons: legal reasons (minors), medical reasons (every disease under the sun came parading into every rock and roll hotel), pain-in-the-ass reasons (someone who will follow you for the rest of your life), child-support suits, law firms' sudden decision to use good-looking "chicks" to slap subpoenas on rock and rollers for any and every lawsuit. And just plain road fatigue: "I'm too tired tonight, darling."

Up in Suite 2907 of the Four Seasons in Toronto, Mick sank down into the plush depths of his beige velvet couch and invited me to do the same. Jerry Hall opened up us both frosty bottles of Heineken and rolled us a nice homemade Bull Durham cigarette and we fired it up and passed it around. Jerry, in her skin-tight jeans and tighter-than-skin green sweater, sat down and started tickling Mick with her bare feet. Jee-zus. Wouldn't it be nice to be a rock and roll star.

Mick ignored her and put on a tape from the Oshawa show. It takes him hours to wind down after a show. "If it'd just been a matter of charity, you know," he said to no one in particular, "of providing money, we'd just have written them a check. But the judge just told Keith to play for disabled people. We put on a show." He was obviously very proud of that show.

We listened to the tape of that show. "We wanted to do it as uncommercially as possible," Mick said. "We refused these bullshit four-page newspaper ads of 'so-and-so congratulates the Rolling Stones.' This was fun . . . fun," Mick said, as he got up to turn the volume up.

We were surrounded and assaulted and caressed by the Rolling Stones. I can never forget watching him standing there, reflected in three mirrors in the living room, Jerry Hall and I each reflected, watching Mick as he stood with his hands on the controls of his Aiwa cassette deck. He withdrew deeper and deeper into himself as he listened to himself and his band. Intently listening, laughing at a mistake, punching triumphantly with his fist into the air when he heard himself hitting the note, smiling and nodding when Keith was hitting his notes. He turned once, to acknowledge us briefly, as he started dancing to the Rolling Stones. Dancing first to his lover and his guest. Then to himself. And then just to the Rolling Stones. Just to the Rolling Stones.

APPENDIX I
The Rolling Stones Tour History

1962: July 12, London (Marquee Club); December 26, London (Picadilly Club).

1963: May 4, Battersea; August 11, Richmond; September 29, London; October 1, Streatham; October 2, Edmonton; October 3, Southend; October 4, Guildford; October 5, Watford; October 6, Cardiff; October 8, Cheltenham; October 9, Worcester; October 10, Wolverhampton; October 11, Derby; October 12, Doncaster; October 13, Liverpool; October 16, Manchester; October 17, Glasgow; October 18, Newcastle; October 19, Bradford; October 20, Hanley; October 22, Sheffield; October 23, Nottingham; October 24, Birmingham; October 25, Taunton; October 26, Bournemouth; October 27, Salisbury; October 29, Southampton; October 30, St. Albans; October 31, Lewisham; November 1, Rochester; November 2, Ipswich; November 3, Hammersmith.

1964: January 6, Harrow; January 7, Slough; January 8, Maidstone; January 9, Kettering; January 10, Walthamstow; January 12, Tooting; January 14, Mansfield, January 15, Bedford, January 20, Woolwich, January 22, Shrewsbury, January 26, Leicester; January 27, Bristol; February 8, Edmonton; February 8, Tottenham; February 9, Leicester; February 10, Cheltenham; February 11, Rugby; February 12, Guildford; February 13, Kingston; February 14, Watford; February 15, Rochester; February 16, Portsmouth; February 17, Greenford; February 18, Colchester; February 19, Stockton; February 20, Sunderland; February 21, Hanley; February 22, Bournemouth; February 23, Birmingham; February 24, Southend; February 25, Romford; February 26, York; February 27, Sheffield; February 28, Cardiff; February 29, Brighton; March 1, Liverpool; March 2, Nottingham; March 3, Blackpool; March 5, Blackburn; March 6, Wolverhampton; March 7, Morecambe; May 19, Hamilton; June 5, San Bernardino (California: first U.S. tour starts here); June 6, San Antonio; June 7, San Antonio; June 12, Minneapolis; June 13, Omaha; June 14, Detroit; June 16, Oxford (England); June 17, Pittsburgh (Pennsylvania); June 19, Harrisburg; June 20, New York City (Carnegie Hall); June 26, London; July 24, Blackpool; July 31, Belfast; August 3, Wiltshire; August 7, Richmond; August 8, The Hague; September 5, Finsbury Park; September 6, Leicester; September 8, Colchester; September 9, Luton; September 10, Cheltenham; September 11, Cardiff; September 13, Liverpool; September 14, Chester; September 15, Manchester; September 16, Wigan; September 17, Carlisle; September 18, Newcastle; September 19, Edinburgh; September 20, Stockton; September 21,

Hull; September 22, Lincoln; September 24, Doncaster; September 25, Hanley; September 26, Bradford; September 27, Birmingham; September 28, Romford; September 29, Guildford; October 1, Bristol; October 2, Exeter; October 3, Edmonton; October 4, Streatham; October 5, Wolverhampton; October 6, Watford; October 8, Lewisham; October 9, Ipswich; October 10, Southend; October 11, Brighton; October 20, Paris; October 24, New York City; October 25, New York City ("Ed Sullivan Show"); October 26, Sacramento; October 31, Long Beach; November 1, San Diego; November 3, Cleveland; November 4, Providence; November 11, Minneapolis; November 12, Fort Wayne; November 13, Dayton; November 14, Louisville; November 15, Chicago.

1965: January 6, Belfast; January 7, Dublin; January 8, Cork; January 10, Hammersmith; January 22, Sydney (Australia); January 23, Sydney; January 25, Brisbane; January 27, Sydney; January 28, Melbourne; January 29, Melbourne; January 30, Melbourne; February 1, Christchurch; February 2, Invercargill; February 3, Dunedin; February 4, Auckland; February 5, Auckland; February 6, Auckland; February 8, Wellington; February 10, Melbourne; February 11, Adelaide; February 13, Perth; February 16, Singapore; March 5, Edmonton (Great Britain); March 6, Liverpool; March 7, Manchester; March 8, Scarborough; March 9, Sutherland; March 10, Huddersfield; March 11, Sheffield; March 12, Leicester; March 13, Rugby; March 14, Rochester; March 15, Guildford; March 16, Greenford; March 17, Southend; March 18, Romford; April 17, Paris; April 18, Paris; April 23, Montreal; April 24, Ottawa; April 25, Toronto; April 26, London (Ontario); April 29, Albany; April 30, Worcester (Massachusetts); May 1, New York City; May 1, Philadelphia; May 2, New York City ("Ed Sullivan Show"); May 4, Statesboro; May 5, Atlanta; May 6, Tampa; May 7, Birmingham; May 8, Jacksonville; May 9, Chicago; May 14, San Francisco; May 15, San Bernardino; May 16, Long Beach; May 20, San Diego; May 21, San Jose; May 22, Fresno; May 23, Sacramento; May 29, New York City; May 30, New York City; June 15, Glasgow; June 16, Edinburgh; June 17, Dundee; June 18, Aberdeen; June 24, Oslo; June 25, Pori (Finland); June 26, Copenhagen; June 29, Malmo (Sweden); July 16, Exeter; July 17, Portsmouth; July 18, Brighton; July 25, Great Yarmouth; August 1, London; September 3, Belfast; September 4, Dublin; September 11, Munster (Germany); September 12, Essen; September 13, Hamburg; September 14, Munich; September 15, Berlin; September 17, Vienna; September 24, Finsbury Park; September 25, Southampton; September 26, Bristol; September 27, Cheltenham; September 28, Cardiff; September 29, Shrewsbury; September 30, Hanley; October 1, Chester; October 2, Wigan; October 3, Manchester; October 4, Bradford; October 5, Carlisle; October 6, Glasgow; October 7, Newcastle; October 8, Stockton; October 9, Leeds; October 10, Liverpool; October 11, Sheffield; October 12, Doncaster; October 13, Leicester; October 14, Birmingham; October 15, Cambridge; October 16, Southend; October 17, Tooting; October 29, Montreal; October 30, Ithaca (New York); October 30, Syracuse; October 31, Toronto; November 1, Rochester; November 3, Providence; November 4, New Haven; November 5, Boston; November 6, New York City; November 6, Philadelphia; November 7, Newark; November 10, Raleigh; November 12, Greensboro; November 13, Washington, D.C.; November 13, Baltimore; November 14, Knoxville; November 15, Charlotte; November 16, Nashville; November 17, Memphis; November 19, Jackson; November 20, Houston; November 21, Fort Worth; November 21, Dallas; November 23, Tulsa; November 24, Pittsburgh; November 25, Milwaukee; November 25, Columbus; November 26, Detroit; November 27, Cincinnati; November 27, Dayton; November 28, Chicago; November 29, Denver; November 30, Phoenix; December 1, Vancouver; December 2, Seattle; December 3, Sacramento; December 4, San Jose; December 5, San Diego.

1966: February 13, New York City ("Ed Sullivan Show"); February 18, Sydney; February 19, Sydney; February 21, Brisbane; February 22, Adelaide; February 25, Melbourne; February 25, Melbourne; February 26, Melbourne; February 28, Wellington; March 1, Auckland; March 2, Perth; March 26, Amsterdam; March 27, Brussels; March 28, Paris; March 29, Paris; June 24, Lynn (Massachusetts); June 25, Cleveland; June 25, Pittsburgh; June 26, Washington, D.C.; June 26, Baltimore; June 27, Hartford; June 28, Buffalo; June 29, Toronto; June 30, Montreal; July 1, Atlantic City; July 2, Forest Hills; July 3, Asbury Park; July 4, Virginia Beach; July 6, Syracuse; July 8, Detroit; July 9, Indianapolis; July 10, Chicago; July 11, Houston; July 12, St. Louis; July 14, Winnipeg; July 15, Omaha; July 19, Vancouver; July 20, Seattle; July 21, Portland; July 22, Sacramento; July 23, Salt Lake City; July 24, Bakersfield; July 25, Los Angeles; July 26, San Francisco; July 28, Honolulu; August 10, New York City ("Ed Sullivan Show"); September 23, London; September 24, Leeds; September 25, Liverpool; September 28, Manchester; September 29, Stockton; September 30, Glasgow; October 1, Newcastle; October 2, Ipswich; October 6, Birmingham; October 7, Bristol; October 8, Cardiff; October 9, Southampton.

1967: January 13, New York City ("Ed Sullivan Show"); March 25, Orebro (Sweden); March 26, Halsingborg (Sweden); March 29, Bremen (Germany); March 30, Cologne; March 31, Dortmund; April 1, Hamburg; April 2, Vienna; April 5, Bologna; April 6, Rome; April 8, Milan; April 9, Genoa; April 11, Paris; April 13, Warsaw; April 14, Zurich; April 15, The Hague; April 17, Athens.

1968: There were no public concerts by the Rolling Stones in 1968.

1969: July 5, London (Brian Jones memorial concert in Hyde Park); November 7, Fort Collins (Colorado); November 8, Los Angeles; November 9, Oakland; November 10, San Diego; November 11, Phoenix; November 13, Dallas; November 14, Auburn; November 15, Champaign; November 16, Chicago; November 20, Los Angeles; November 21, Los Angeles; November 23, New York City ("Ed Sullivan Show"); November 24, Detroit; November 25, Philadelphia; November 26, Baltimore; November 27, New York City; November 28, New York City; November 29, Boston; November 30, Palm Beach; December 6, Altamont; December 14, London; December 21, London.

1970: September 2, Helsinki; September 3, Malmo; September 4, Stockholm; September 6, Goteborg; September 9, Arhus; September 12, Copenhagen; September 14, Hamburg; September 16, Berlin; September 18, Cologne; September 20, Stuttgart; September 23, Paris; September 24, Paris; September 27, Vienna; September 29, Rome; October 1, Milan; October 3, Lyon; October 5, Frankfurt; October 7, Essen; October 9, Amsterdam.

1971: March 4, Newcastle; March 5, Manchester; March 6, Coventry; March 8, Glasgow; March 9, Bristol; March 10, Brighton; March 12, Liverpool; March 13, Leeds; March 14, London; March 26, London.

1972: June 3, Vancouver; June 4, Seattle; June 6, San Francisco; June 8, San Francisco; June 9, Los Angeles; June 10, Long Beach; June 11, Los Angeles; June 13, San Diego; June 14, Tucson; June 15, Albuquerque; June 16, Denver; June 18, St. Paul; June 19, Chicago; June 20, Chicago; June 22, Kansas City; June 24, Fort Worth; June 25, Houston; June 27, Mobile; June 28, Tuscaloosa; June 29, Nashville; July 4, Washington D.C.; July 5, Norfolk; July 6, Charlotte; July 7, Knoxville; July 9, St. Louis; July 11, Akron; July 12, Indianapolis; July 13, Detroit; July 14, Detroit; July 15, Toronto; July 17, Montreal; July 18, Boston; July 19, Boston; July 20, Philadelphia; July 21, Philadelphia; July 22, Pittsburgh; July 24, New York City; July 25, New York City; July 26, New York City.

1973: January 18, Los Angeles (Nicaragua benefit); January 22, Honolulu; February 5, Hong Kong; February 11, Auckland; February 13, Brisbane; February 14, Brisbane; February 17, Melbourne; February 18, Melbourne; February 20, Adelaide; February 21, Adelaide; February 24, Perth; February 26, Sydney; February 27, Sydney; September 1, Vienna; September 3, Mannheim; September 4, Cologne; September 7, London; September 8, London; September 9, London; September 11, Manchester; September 12, Manchester; September 13, Newcastle; September 16, Glasgow; September 17, Glasgow; September 19, Birmingham; September 25, Bern; September 26, Bern; September 28, Munich; September 30, Frankfurt; October 2, Hamburg; October 4, Arhus; October 6, Goteborg; October 7, Copenhagen; October 9, Essen; October 10, Essen; October 11, Essen; October 13, Rotterdam; October 14, Rotterdam; October 15, Antwerp; October 17, Brussels; October 19, Berlin.

1974: There were no public concerts by the Rolling Stones in 1974.

1975: May 1, New York City (Fifth Avenue flatbed truck concert); June 1, Baton Rouge; June 3, San Antonio; June 4, San Antonio; June 6, Kansas City; June 8, Milwaukee; June 9, St. Paul; June 11, Boston; June 12, Boston; June 14, Cleveland; June 15, Buffalo; June 17, Toronto; June 18, Toronto; June 22, New York City; June 23, New York City; June 24, New York City; June 25, New York City; June 26, New York City; June 27, New York City; June 29, Philadelphia; June 30, Philadelphia; July 1, Washington, D.C.; July 2, Washington, D.C.; July 4, Memphis; July 6, Dallas; July 9, Los Angeles; July 10, Los Angeles; July 11, Los Angeles; July 12, Los Angeles; July 13, Los Angeles; July 15, San Francisco; July 16, San Francisco; July 18, Seattle; July 19, Denver; July 23, Chicago; July 24, Chicago; July 26, Bloomington; July 27, Detroit; July 28, Detroit; July 30, Atlanta; July 31, Greensboro; August 2, Jacksonville; August 4, Louisville; August 6, Hampton; August 8, Buffalo.

1976: April 28, Frankfurt; April 29, Frankfurt; April 30, Munster; May 2, Kiel; May 3, Berlin; May 4, Bremen; May 6, Brussels; May 7, Brussels; May 10, Glasgow; May 11, Glasgow; May 12, Glasgow; May 17, Stafford; May 18, Stafford; May 21, London; May 22, London; May 23, London; May 25, London; May 26, London; May 27, London; May 29, The Hague; May 30, The Hague; June 1, Dortmund; June 2, Cologne; June 4, Paris; June 5, Paris; June 6, Paris; June 7, Paris; June 9, Lyon; June 11, Barcelona; June 13, Nice; June 15, Zurich; June 16, Munich; June 17, Munich; June 19, Stuttgart; June 21, Zagreb; June 23, Vienna; August 21, Knebworth.

1977: March 4, Toronto (El Mocambo Tavern); March 5, Toronto (El Mocambo Tavern).

1978: June 10, Lakeland (Florida); June 12, Atlanta; June 14, Passaic; June 15, Washington, D.C.; June 17, Philadelphia; June 19, New York City; June 21, Hampton; June 22, Myrtle Beach; June 26, Greensboro; June 28, Memphis; June 29, Lexington; July 1, Cleveland; July 4, Buffalo; July 6, Detroit; July 8, Chicago; July 10, St. Paul; July 11, St. Louis; July 13, New Orleans; July 16, Boulder; July 18, Fort Worth; July 19, Houston; July 21, Tucson; July 23, Anaheim; July 24, Anaheim; July 26, Oakland; October 7, New York City ("Saturday Night Live").

1979: April 22, Oshawa (Canada).

1980: There were no public concerts by the Rolling Stones in 1980.

1981: September 14, Worcester (Massachusetts, at Sir Morgan's Cove); September 25, Philadelphia; September 26, Philadelphia; September 27, Buffalo; October 1, Rockford (Illinois); October 3, Boulder; October 4, Boulder; October 7, San Diego; October 9, Los Angeles; October 11, Los Angeles; October 14, Seattle; October 15, Seattle; October 17, San Francisco; October 18, San Francisco; October 24, Orlando; October 25, Orlando; October 26, Atlanta; October 28, Houston; October 29, Houston; October 31, Dallas; November 1, Dallas; November 3, Louisville; November 5, East Rutherford (New Jersey); November 6, East Rutherford; November 7, East Rutherford; November 9, Hartford; November 10, Hartford; November 12, New York City; November 13, New York City; November 16, Cleveland; November 17, Cleveland; November 19, St. Louis; November 20, Cedar Falls (Iowa); November 21, St. Paul; November 22, Chicago (Checkerboard Lounge jam); November 23, Chicago; November 24, Chicago; November 25, Chicago; November 27, Syracuse; November 28, Syracuse; November 30, Pontiac; December 1, Pontiac; December 5, New Orleans; December 7, Washington, D.C.; December 8, Washington, D.C.; December 9, Washington, D.C.; December 11, Lexington; December 13, Phoenix; December 14, Kansas City; December 15, Kansas City; December 18, Hampton; December 19, Hampton.

1982: May 26, Aberdeen; May 27, Glasgow; May 28, Edinburgh; May 30, London; June 2, Rotterdam; June 4, Rotterdam; June 5, Rotterdam; June 6, Hannover; June 7, Hannover; June 8, Berlin; June 10, Munich; June 11, Munich; June 13, Paris; June 14, Paris; June 16, Lyon; June 19, Goteborg; June 20, Goteborg; June 23, Newcastle; June 25, London; June 26, London; June 27, Bristol; June 29,

Frankfurt; June 30, Frankfurt; July 1, Frankfurt; July 3, Vienna; July 4, Cologne; July 5, Cologne; July 8, Madrid; July 9, Madrid; July 11, Turin; July 12, Turin; July 15, Basel; July 17, Naples; July 24, Dublin; July 25, Leeds.

APPENDIX II

Royal Canadian
Mounted Police Report

The following is the Royal Canadian Mounted Police (RCMP) internal report regarding the arrest of Keith Richards in Toronto in 1977.

"RE: Keith RICHARDS
Alias: K. REDBLAND [sic]
Charged: Section 4(2) and 3(1)
Narcotic Control Act

"This report is submitted in response to a request from Superintendent W. R. BENNETT. The facts of the case and my involvement in the matter are set as follows in chronological order.

"Thursday, February 24, 1977

"On Thursday, February 24, 1977, I was on duty at the Toronto International Airport Drug Section. At approximately 7:25 P.M., arrived at Terminal #2. Upon arrival I was advised by Canada Customs they had in custody a lady with a small quantity of hashish and other drug-related paraphernalia, namely spoon [and] hypodermic needle. The lady identified herself as Anita PALLENBERG, common-law wife of Rolling Stones guitarist Keith RICHARDS. She was subsequently arrested and taken to the office at Terminal #1 and charged with Possession of Hashish (10 grams), and released on a appearance notice.
"The spoon and hypodermic needle was taken to the Dominion Analyst and the hypodermic needle was found to contain traces of heroin. Subsequently a warrant was obtained for the arrest of Anita PALLENBERG and a warrant to search her residence was obtained.

"Charges against Anita PALLENBERG:

—Possession of Hashish. Section 3(1) N.C.A.

—Possession of Heroin. Section 3(1) N.C.A."

"Sunday, February 27, 1977

"Accompanied by four members of the RCMP (Peter HADLEY, Bill SEWARD, Bernie BARBE, and Beverly PURCELLS), I attended at the temporary residence of Anita PALLENBERG at the Harbour Castle Hotel and after approximately two hours of attempting to locate her room, a search warrant was executed at room 3223-24-25, which was registered under the name of K. REDBLAND[sic] and is an alias used by Keith RICHARDS.

"The following exhibits were seized.

—One passport in the name of Keith RICHARDS

—Minister's Permit to enter Canada

—Hypodermic needle cover

—Plastic bag with traces of white powder

—Three red-coloured pills

—Harbour Castle sugar bag containing 2 grams of resin material (believed to be Hashish)

—Gold foil paper with traces of white powder

—Plastic bag containing 5 grams of Cocaine

—Razor blade with white traces of white powder

—Switchblade knife with traces of white powder

—Hypodermic needle with liquid in the base

—Brass lighter with traces of white powder

—Silver bowl with traces of white powder

—Teaspoon with traces of white powder

—Purple pouch with traces of white powder

—Plastic bag containing 22 grams of Heroin

"These exhibits were turned over to Constable SEWARD, RCMP, who acted as exhibit officer. RICHARDS admitted ownership of the exhibits and was arrested on the charge of 'Possession for the Purpose of Trafficking.' Mr. RICHARDS was released later the same evening after a mini-bail hearing before a Justice of the Peace in the presence of Mr. Clay POWELL, who was RICHARDS' Attorney at the time.

"Charges against Mr. Keith RICHARDS:

—Possession of Heroin for the Purpose of Trafficking. Section 4(2) N.C.A.

—Possession of Cocaine. Section 3(1) N.C.A."

"Friday, March 4, 1977

"Anita PALLENBERG appeared in Brampton Provincial Court and pleaded Guilty to Possession of Heroin and Hashish. She was fined $200.00 on each count."

"Tuesday, March 8, 1977

"Mr. RICHARDS appeared in Old City Hall Court and it was at this time that the charge of Possession of Cocaine was laid. Another bail hearing was held and Mr. RICHARDS was released on $25,000 cash bail. The case was remanded to March 14, 1977."

"Monday, March 14, 1977

"Mr. RICHARDS appeared Courtroom #26, Old City Hall, and a trial date of June 27, 1977 was set."

"Monday, June 6, 1977

"On June 6, 1977, Mr. Mike STEINBERG, Federal Crown Prosecutor, advised that Mr. Clayton POWELL was taking the warrant to the Supreme Court of Ontario. Mr. STEINBERG requested that I bring the warrant and certificate that would establish that the Justice of the Peace is a Justice for the Province of Ontario. Both items were taken to Mr. STEINBERG."

"Wednesday, June 8, 1977

"The validity of the search warrant was challenged at the Supreme Court of Ontario. The Justice ruled that the warrant was defective due to the fact that a specific peace officer was not named on the face of the warrant."

"Monday, June 27, 1977

"Mr. RICHARDS failed to appear in Court at Old City Hall, but was represented by his lawyer, Mr. Austin COOPER. A bench warrant was issued for the arrest of Mr. RICHARDS with instructions that it was not to be executed until Tuesday, July 19, 1977, at which time a new trial date was to be set. Mr. David SCOTT, Federal Crown Prosecutor, requested a meeting with myself at the Department of Justice at 5:00 P.M. Staff Superintendent L. W. SPRY, Ontario Provincial Police was advised. Superintendent D. HEATON, RCMP, was also advised and he requested to attend the meeting. A meeting was held at the Department of Justice with the Director, Mr. OLSON, Mr. ISSAC, and Mr. SCOTT for the Department of Justice, also Superintendent HEATON and Corporal HOLLIS of the RCMP and myself. It was suggested by Mr. ISSAC of the Department of Justice that a plea to simple possession of heroin be taken. Superintendent HEA-

TON objected and, after lengthy discussion, it was decided that we would proceed with the possession for the purpose charge."

"Tuesday, July 19, 1977

"Mr. RICHARDS failed to appear in Court, but was represented by his lawyer, Mr. Austin COOPER. A new trial was set for Friday, December 2, 1977. No motion was made by the Federal Prosecutor to have RICHARDS' bail forfeited for his not having appeared on this date or the following dates of nonappearance:

Monday, June 27, 1977
Tuesday, July 19, 1977
Monday, February 6, 1978
Monday, March 6, 1978."

"Monday, October 31, 1977

"On Monday, October 31, 1977, a letter was forwarded to Federal Department of Justice requesting guidance in order to be able to enter RICHARDS' criminal record at the preliminary hearing, in the event that he elected to proceed with the trial before a Provincial Court Judge. A meeting was held with Mr. Paul KENNEDY, Department Justice, who was the Federal Prosecutor in charge of the RICHARDS case, and he advised that we would not require anyone from England in order to enter his record. We would proceed without it."

"Friday, December 2, 1977

"Mr. RICHARDS appeared in Old City Hall, Courtroom #27, and a Preliminary Hearing was conducted. Mr. RICHARDS was committed for Trial, and was remanded to February 6, 1978, assignment Court to set a trial date (Bench warrant rescinded, no action taken on bail)."

"Friday, February 3, 1978

"Mrs. Gerda SHLATTNER, from the Department of Justice contacted me and and [sic] she advised that Mr. RICHARDS would not appear in Court on Monday, February 6, 1978, but that he would appear on Monday, March 6, 1978 in assignment Court."

"Wednesday, February 15, 1978

"Constable William SEWARD, RCMP, who was the exhibit officer in the case, was killed in a vehicle accident."

"Monday, February 27, 1978

"The transcript from Preliminary Hearing was reviewed by myself and there appeared to be no problems [with] Constable SEWARD's evidence [sic]. Mr. Paul KENNEDY, Federal Prosecutor in charge of the case was contacted and he advised that he would come to the office and review the evidence."

"Monday, March 6, 1978

"Mr. RICHARDS again failed to appear in Court. Mr. Austin COOPER, representing Mr. RICHARDS, appeared and a trial date of October 23, 1978, was set."

"Tuesday, March 7, 1978

"Mr. Paul KENNEDY reviewed the evidence and asked that new analysis of heroin be taken."

"Monday, October 16, 1978

"Mr. Paul KENNEDY, Federal Prosecutor, contacted me and advised that Mr. COOPER had instructed him that a plea to possession would be made on Monday, October 23, 1978. Mr. KENNEDY also advised that the plea had been authorized by Mr. OLSON, Department of Justice and Staff Superintendent HEATON, RCMP."

"Monday, October 23, 1978

"Mr. RICHARDS appeared in Court and pleaded Guilty to Possession of Heroin. No evidence was offered on the charge of Possession of Cocaine. For his sentencing, only one previous conviction for a criminal offence was introduced to the court. Mr. RICHARDS was remanded to October 24, 1978, at 10:00 A.M. for sentencing. RICHARDS' criminal record as advised by Detective Sergeant MULHOLLAND, New Scotland Yard via telephone is as follows:

"24/10/73 Marboror [sic] Mag. Court (London)

1) Possession of Firearm	Fined 75 pounds
2) Possession of ammuniation [sic]	Fined 25 pounds
3) Possession of cannabis (marihuana)	Fined 10 pounds
4) Possession of cannabis (resin)	Fined 10 pounds
5) Possession of Firearm	Fined 25 pounds
6) Possession of Mandrax	Fined 10 pounds
7) Possession of Methadone	Fined 10 pounds
8) Possession of Methidine [sic]	Fined 10 pounds

9) Possession of Heroin   Fined 50 pounds
10) Possession of Chinese Heroin [!] Fined 50 pounds

"15/10/73 Nice, FRANCE Court of Grand Inctance

Use, supply, traffic in Cannabis (resin) Sentence 1 yr. S.S.
Use, supply, traffic in Heroin   Fined 5,000 francs

"12/01/77 Albury Crown Court

1) Possession of LSD-25   Fined 750 pounds
2) Possession of Cocaine   Fined 250 pounds"

"Tuesday, October 24, 1978

"Mr. RICHARDS was given a suspended sentence and placed on probation for one year.
"Conditions of Probation
No fine, no jail.
To be of good behaviour.
Report to probation officer within 24 hours.
Return on May 7, 1979, and report to probation officer.
Return on September 24, 1979, and report to probation officer.
To continue treatment for heroin addiction at The Stevens Institute in New York, U.S.A.
To give a benefit performance for the Canadian Institute for the Blind within the next six months, either by himself or with a group of his choice."

A. J. HACHINSKI,
Provincial Constable,
Drug Enforcement Section, T.I.A. Unit,
Special Investigations Branch
/kr

APPENDIX III

Emotional Rescue

June 23, 1980

This is Keith's idea of touring this year: On a June night in 1980 (to promote the *Emotional Rescue* album) he marched into the Rockefeller Center offices of Rolling Stones Records at six P.M., loudly announcing, "I'm ready for my bacon and eggs!" He was waving a fifth of Jack Daniel's. He had just awakened and wanted breakfast—the sour-mash bourbon kind. He seated himself with a flourish at Earl McGrath's desk and tried to crack the seal on the Black Jack bottle, without success. "I've got a key we could try," I ventured, but Keith cut me off by whipping out an enormous gravity knife and—*kachunk!*—snapping it open. He winked at me and held up the knife: "This is the key to the highway!" He poured us both hefty tumblers of Jack and toasted me.

We did all the requisite talk about the new album. He said that he was the only one of the group eager to get out and tour again: "My idea is to get out another album this year and then we can get these motherfuckers out on the *road!* Instead of the same old treadmill of road, studio, road, studio, road, studio, we can take extended road trips or do anything we want to do; be movie stars or make solo albums." Keith, who had finally gotten off heroin after the Canadian unpleasantness, produced a Vicks inhaler that was dribbling grains of a shiny white powder.

June 25, 1980

Had tea with Bill Wyman in his suite at the Plaza Hotel. A very pleasant afternoon. He said that he plans to pack it in soon. "I *am* going to retire from the Rolling Stones. I really do want to do other things, you know. I don't want to wait till I'm sixty; that'd be too late. So, at the end of 1982, I'll go for something else. When I got into rock and roll, I thought it'd last two or three years, maybe five, and I was just after some extra cash. I never saw it being anymore than three years, a bit of cash, a bit of fun, and getting around town. *Suddenly*—here I am eighteen years later and it's become the most dominant part of my life, and I didn't really want it to go like that, you know. Here I am, just turned forty as it were, and I'm *still* playing rock and roll."

June 30, 1980

"I'm 'fraid rock and roll has *no* future," Mick Jagger said. His famous lips formed a perfect *moue* of distaste, as if they hated to utter such words of treason.

Jagger was curled up on the chocolate-brown sofa in the airy living room of his second-floor Manhattan apartment. Golden sunbeams and raucous street sounds flooded through his open windows and he welcomed both, jumping up to lean out the window when a reggae beat wafted in from a passing radio.

"Why doesn't it?" I asked him while opening two bottles of Löwenbräu.

He turned back from the window and laughed. The flashing diamond set in his left incisor was a mark of his long years of service to rock and roll. The age lines around his eyes were as distinct as the weariness and cynicism in his voice.

" 'Cause it *doesn't*," he said flatly. "There is no future in rock and roll. It's only recycled past." He sounded genuinely sad. We both fell silent and stared into our beers.

After a suitably brief period of mourning, Jagger laughed cynically. I had been invited to his place because the Stones had a new album (*Emotional Rescue*) and needed to publicize it, since they couldn't quite get it together enough to lash a tour together. For once all of the Stones were in New York City at the same time to—in their own peculiar fashion—flog and hype a Stones album. Only four days before, they had held a suitably perverse Stones album party. Several hundred select personages were herded through the three dank floors of a poorly air-conditioned club called Danceteria in the garment district's Shampan Building. The place was decorated oddly: There were hundreds of copies of *Emotional Rescue* taped to the walls, to be sure, but the other decor consisted of dozens of surgical gloves plastered up everywhere. There were hospital beds here and there, along with many wheelchairs and numerous IV bottles full of whiskey and vodka. The waiters were wearing green surgical gowns and the waitresses were dressed as nurses. There were two dozen X-rays of the various Stones hanging above the buffet table. On the top floor, eight giant screen TVs showed an extremely graphic video of an ovarian cyst operation. "Let Me Go" from the new album was on the sound system. TV monitors were showing the gory bits from such cult film classics as *Death Race 2000, Piranha,* and *Summer School Teachers.*

Suddenly there was a flurry of activity: the people who were acting bored while watching the ovarian cyst being painstakingly removed now turned their heads ever so slightly to act even more bored while watching Mick sweep by in his new outfit, which consisted of a shiny gray gabardine suit, a skinny maroon tie, and boxy sunglasses. A stampede of photographers followed in his wake. Rolling Stones Records president Earl McGrath—dressed up in a white lab coat for the occasion—ruefully brought up the tail of the procession.

For a little while, the various Stones made perfunctory appearances for the photo op and then disappeared. Then a man and a woman got into a hospital bed that was on the bandstand, under a hot pink spotlight. Down on the dance floor, wheelchair races were commencing. Stones official Peter Rudge stood by the dance floor, sipping some IV vodka and mopping his wet brow. He looked around at the pallid attempts at hospital humor and laughed. "We tried to have this at Bellevue," he said, "but they wouldn't let us."

Marybeth Medley, a tour publicist from various Stones tours, walked up to Paul Wasserman and handed him a copy of *Geriatrics* magazine. "Well, Paul," she said, "did you get the Stones a spread in *Geriatrics* yet?"

"No," he played along. "These Stones tend to die under the hot lights."
She and Rudge laughed knowingly. What the hell had he meant by that?

Several days later, as Mick smiled his cynical smile at me in his apartment and waited for me to perform whatever it was I was there to perform, I began to get a glimmer of understanding. Wasso was undoubtedly referring to the tendency of delicate hothouse orchids not to bear up under too detailed a scrutiny. Or maybe he simply meant that the Stones—their pallid complexions a uniform graveyard gray from prolonged lack of exposure to either sunlight or fresh air—genuinely were old geezers who wouldn't hold up well under the operating lamp.

Back in his sunny living room, Mick was spreading and cleaning some special tobacco leaves on the cover of Lynyrd Skynyrd's *Street Survivors* album. As he concentrated on rolling some of the tobacco into a cigarette, he told me, as patiently as any teacher would instruct a slightly backward but interested student, why rock and roll is really not worth talking about.

"Rock and roll is a funny thing," he said. "There are two different attitudes, right? One is the English attitude, like when Pete Townshend talks about rock and roll like a religion. And then there are the others, like me, who think it's really a lot of overblown nonsense. *Why bother?* I mean, it's not worth bothering about. As a form of art *or* of music."

"But Mick, is it a form of art?" I asked. "I mean, England's got all these art students forming bands now, and they talk about it as art and about 'distancing themselves from rock and roll's traditions.' "

"*Well,*" he fired up his cigarette and took a long drag. As he lazily exhaled a long plume of smoke, he continued, "I *do* kind of see it as a form of art, but what I'm saying is that there's no point in me trying to start some spiritual or cultural organization to *distance* myself from the traditions of rock and roll. It doesn't seem important enough. In other words, it's not like a great movement in *painting*. I just think...I don't know. I'm not going to take sides, really. I think the music seems to be in a pretty healthy state because there are so many things going on."

Warming to his subject, he got up and began to pace the room. "And then you've got all these idiots who review rock and roll—I can't read them. All these people who try to read so much into the music, read things into it that aren't there. It's totally phony, isn't it, because I know that the things they read into it *aren't* there."

"Is it, then," I asked, "like these theoretical bands that say they're reinventing rock and roll?"

"Oh, *yeah.* I mean, for anyone who is in some sort of business or art or whatever you want to call it, and who actually makes larger claims for himself—I don't know what that is. Let's take Rough Trade [a British militantly independent record label], right? To my mind, it *is* connected to the rock establishment because it's gonna make a journalistic impression. They have a great line, don't they? Journalists will hook stories on that and they'll be noticed no matter how anonymous they say they want to be. Does that make sense?" He offered me a communal drag off his cigarette.

"Yeah," I said, after choking and wheezing. "They can be noble and still be in the rock press. When you talk about there being two attitudes to rock and roll, would that mean that there are two ways to play 'Louie, Louie' and one of them is to claim that it's art?"

Jagger laughed. "Yeah, *yeah*. I think so. That is Frank Zappa's thing. He bases his musical teachings on that and it is one of his ways of saying rock and roll is all trash. And it *is* trash. This very irate disc jockey said to me, 'I was having this interview with Johnny Rotten, a.k.a. John Lydon, and he said that rock and roll is a lot of rubbish, trashy music, and I was shocked!' And I said, 'Well, that's one of the few things I am able to agree with him on. 'It *is* all trash.' "

"Have you ever talked to Lydon? That might be funny."

Mick got up and headed for the kitchen: "No, I haven't talked to him and, no, it might not be very much *fun* at all."

He smiled archly and fetched two more bottles of Löwenbräu. We watched the teenagers, walking by on Central Park South, blasting disco sounds from their enormous boom boxes.

"Mick, is *Emotional Rescue* a New York City album, now that you and Keith live here?"

He answered seriously: "I don't think so. To me, New York is like Lou Reed and all those other bands."

"But the rhythms in 'Dance' and 'Emotional Rescue' sound like the city, don't they?"

"That *is* New York, yeah. English people hate it, 'cause they say it's all disco."

"But it's *not*."

"I know, but that's what *they* think it is, you see. It's just black music."

"What about the title song? How did you work that up, all that falsetto stuff?"

"I wrote that on a electric piano in the studio, then Charlie [Watts] and Woody [Ron Wood] and I cut it immediately, live. It was all done very quickly. I think the vocals could've been better. It's just one of those recording-studio things. You would *never* really write a song like that in *real life*. Comes out in the studio, 'cause it's all ad-libbed, the end part. It was never planned like that."

"But that part's really funny, the speech."

"Yeah, it's all a joke, really. There's a lot of pastiche all over the album. It's all our piss-taking, in other words. Pastiche is just a big word for it."

"How did you go about recording the album?"

He threw up his hands in mock despair. "It took *forever*. I started writing a ton of songs last summer, then Charlie and I did a few demos. Some of them came out of that. Some had been written before. Then we recorded a whole lot of newer things, which weren't really complete. *Then* we went back and more or less chose the ones we started with. I mean, it was just so haphazard and slapdash. Too much work was made out of it. I think Parkinson's disease or whatever sets in if you've got no real cutoff date, 'cause you just keep going until you've done *everything* you can possibly think of. And then you say well, great, but now we've got forty songs, some of which are good and some of which *could* be good if only they were, you know, *different*. At the end, you think, Jesus, *where* am I? It's *stupid*. That's a *dumb* way of doing it. We *do* have a lot of material, admittedly, but that's *not* the point. The point is that it took two years to get it. You could've easily made it in nine months. Nobody had any proper vision of it.

Nobody fucking knew where they were going. That includes me. You get bored with things very quickly. My attention span is so limited. You know, I just love to make up songs and I don't even like to finish the words. I just like to sing 'oooh' all the way through. And then I'm happy after that. I don't want to do anymore. That's *it*. I don't even want to hear it again."

"Can you stand to do the mixing, or does Keith do it?"

Jagger shot me a scornful look and curled his lip: "You've *got* to be kidding. Keith gets into remixing in phases, sometimes."

"What's the story on this song 'Claudine' which was supposedly dropped from the album for legal reasons?"

"Well, it was *never* gonna be on the album." He winked. "That's *legal* talk. It's not really about Claudine Longet. It's beyond that. I just liked the name, to be honest, and then I made a song around it. It's not her. Unfortunately, this being such a litigious country...."

"Well, you've already got a full quote of misogyny on the album."

He smiled and poured us more beer. "Yeah, I've got a lot of... well, it's not too misogynous. But there is a bit of a one-track mind in there. Everybody's been reminding me that the album has only got one subject, which is *girls*. Obviously, that's got to change."

"Obviously, that's all you think about."

"Yeah. Maybe I'll become a Marxist rock and roller and make a Marxist album. Fuck all this girl stuff. Make an album with anonymous musicians—apart from *myself*—who won't get paid."

"Do women slag you about your girl songs?"

He grew serious: "Never, actually. I think they take it with a pinch of salt, to be honest. Well, the other day in the lift, some woman came up to me and said, 'You're the one who wrote that song about the Puerto Rican girls.' I said, 'Uhm, well, I *have* written songs.' The weirdest things do come out. There are a lot of cover versions lately of 'Under My Thumb.' Carly Simon recorded it, but she didn't put it out."

We heard a sudden series of explosions down the street and Mick seemed alarmed. "Is that a *gun?*" he asked, peering down CPW.

"I don't think so," I said. "Guns aren't that loud."

We looked up and down: There didn't seem to be any shooting victims. Mick relit his special cigarette, which he had allowed to go out in an ashtray.

"Mick," I asked, "did it ever seem to you that ten or twelve years ago rock and roll was a powerful social force and that since then it's been slowly defanged or co-opted?"

He shook his head. "No. That was obviously a false vision."

"But, for example, 'Street Fighting Man' was a rallying point, politically."

Jagger shrugged. "Yeah, but that was during that radical Vietnam time. It was merely *then*. You've always got to have good tunes if you're marching. But the tunes *don't make the march*. Basically, rock and roll isn't protest, and never was. It's *not* political. It's only—it promotes interfamilial tension. It *used* to. Now it can't even do that, because fathers don't ever get outraged with the music. Either they like it or it sounds similar to what they liked as kids. So, rock and roll's *gone* that's all gone. You see, that was very important. The whole rebellion in rock and roll was about not being able to make noise at night and not being able to play that rock and roll so loud and boogie-woogie and not being able to use the car and all that."

So you think Johnny Rotten is trying to rebel against *you* because he's got nothing else to rebel against?"

Jagger laughed. "*Yeah.* But that doesn't work either. Can't possibly work. It'd be like me rebelling against Eddie Cochran. Pointless. Everyone knows that those people were very good at what they did, so you can't rebel against the Rolling Stones or the Beatles. By the way, 'Is John Lennon ever gonna make another record?' is a question I'm asked over and over. Do you know?"

"I have no idea."

"He lives next door. Why don't we just go by and see him? I never see him."

"I heard that Lennon once said you'd never retire because you couldn't stand not being king."

Jagger smiled enormously. "Ha! I bet he was thinking about himself. Don't you?"

September 12, 1981

One of the Stones' bodyguards had told me what to expect but I had only half-believed him. When I finally saw it happen, the hair on the back of my neck actually stood on end.

It was about three in the morning and the Stones had been rehearsing for an hour or so in a barn at Long View Farm, a live-in recording and rehearsal facility near North Brookfield, Massachusetts. The red barn itself is perched atop a hill with a commanding view of the surrounding lowlands. Stanley Stellemokus, a dairy farmer whose spread is downwind from Long View's 145 acres, said that his cows started giving more milk after the Stones started their all-night rehearsals. Stanley himself said that he had begun to stay up past his usual bedtime to listen to the Stones' music roll down at him like distant thunder.

The Stones were grinding into "Under My Thumb" and I had just stepped outside the barn for some air. The music was just as loud outside.

Soft moonlight illuminated the valley below. Jagger's vocal boomed down the hill. I suddenly noticed tiny figures moving in the fields below. They slowly came into focus, moving almost in slow motion. They were humans, wandering in over the hills, drawn by the Stones' music. They were determined to get into that rehearsal barn at any cost. All that mattered to them was the sound. The Stones' bodyguards and the local cops had gotten used to these nightly visits by the Stones Zomboids, these flapping apparitions who came from God knows where and all said that they just "had to see the Stones." It was a new wrinkle for me: all these rock and roll Rip van Winkles shaking a decade's sleep from out of their eyes.

The Stones themselves were surprised to find that they were such a big deal again. Their hastily-thrown-together tour would draw almost 300,000 paying customers in the first three days of a three-month-long tour. Greed was not a factor, they said.

Mick said, when I asked him about the tour after that morning's rehearsal, that none of them thought the tour would be a big deal. "It started off as a twenty-gig tour," he said, "the same as the '78 one, and then it got bigger, as they do. And I just let it get bigger. I don't know what happened, but there was much more of a demand than there was in 1978. We were quite a big band then, we had a number one album, everything, right? It still took us like five or six days to sell out these places. This time, they nearly all went in one day. That's why it got longer. It got twenty gigs longer. But that's very financially lucrative. We're still going to play the theaters and the clubs. When you came in just now, I was setting up a club date in Chicago. It's so weird going from those huge shows to playin' little bitty clubs but it's very good for us. We can rehearse new numbers and just goof off as well."

Was it becoming, I asked, an esthetic mistake for an aging band such as the Stones to play the huge stadiums?

Jagger reached for a Marlboro and shook his head impatently. "It's good money, first of all," he said emphatically. "It's *fantastic* money and it gives us the money and it also generates the tour and it lets me pay for a lot of stage effects and expensive scenery and things which otherwise would be prohibitively expensive. Like on the '75 tour; I didn't make any money. Well, I made *some*. But I played to three-quarters of a million people and I made around a hundred thousand dollars."

He smiled. "I mean, mate, that's *money* but people expected it to be more. But anyway, the thing is, if the demand is there, if people sold out a show in Philadelphia, Buffalo, Boulder—you know how laid back Boulder is and if that sold out in a day and there's a demand to do a second show, you might as well do it, because what else are you gonna do?"